AMERICAN ORIENTAL SERIES
VOLUME 52

MADURESE PHONOLOGY AND MORPHOLOGY

AMERICAN ORIENTAL SERIES

VOLUME 52

EDITOR

ERNEST BENDER

ASSOCIATE EDITORS

WILLIAM W. HALLO   GEORGE F. HOURANI

CHAUNCEY S. GOODRICH

AMERICAN ORIENTAL SOCIETY

NEW HAVEN, CONNECTICUT

1968

MADURESE PHONOLOGY
AND
MORPHOLOGY

BY

ALAN M. STEVENS

AMERICAN ORIENTAL SOCIETY
NEW HAVEN, CONNECTICUT

1968

For

MY PARENTS AND JACKIE

PRINTED IN THE UNITED STATES OF AMERICA

CUSHING-MALLOY, INC., ANN ARBOR, MICHIGAN

TABLE OF CONTENTS

ACKNOWLEDGMENTS

This book is a revised and corrected version of my Ph.D. dissertation (Yale University, 1964). I would like to thank the American Oriental Society and especially Dr. Ernest Bender and Dr. Ferris J. Stephens for their support and advice in preparing this manuscript for publication.

The topic of the dissertation was suggested to me by Professor Isidore Dyen. I want to thank him and the other members of the faculty of the Department of Linguistics at Yale University who provided me with my linguistic training and Yale University itself for its continued support.

Research was carried out in Indonesia from 1960 to 1962. A National Science Foundation Cooperative Fellowship enabled me to do preliminary research at Yale during the 1959-1960 academic year, and the field work itself was generously supported by a Ford Foundation Foreign Area Training Fellowship. I wish to thank the staff of the Ford Foundation who were so helpful to me both in New York and in Djakarta.

The list of Indonesians, besides informants, who aided and encouraged me is too long to mention here. The patience, interest, and insights of my principal informant, Mohammad Saleh Troenodjojo, can never be forgotten. Other Madurese who gave of their time and knowledge are R. P. Surjomataram, Taha Prawirokoesoemo, Oemar Sastrodiwirjo, Maalim Maapi, Bakri, and A. Moethallib. Many others helped by their hospitality and generosity.

CHAPTER I

INTRODUCTION

Madurese[1] is a Malayo-Polynesian language spoken by about six million[2]
people in parts of East Java, the adjacent island of Madura, and on a large number of smaller islands in the vicinity, all in the Republic of Indonesia. This
grammar will be of the standard dialect, i.e. the dialect considered "best" and
now being taught in Madurese schools.[3] It is spoken in Eastern Madura which has
the city of Sumenep [Madurese: sɑmənəp or suŋənəp] as its administrative and
cultural capital.

Madurese forms part of the sub-family of Malayo-Polynesian which includes
the languages of western Indonesia and of the Philippines. More narrowly, it is
closely allied to Javanese, Sundanese, Balinese, and Malay. It has generally
been considered most closely related to Javanese.[4] Much of the apparent close-
ness to Javanese in the lexicon is in the so-called high vocabulary (Madurese:
alus; Jav. krama),[5] and this is highly suspect of having been borrowed. The low
vocabulary (Madurese: kasar; Jav. ngoko), however, shows greater affinity to
Malay. Grammatically, however, there seem to be more similarities between
Madurese and Javanese than between Madurese and Malay.[6]

In a recent paper by I. Dyen[7] the question of Madurese relationships arose
(42):

> Madurese, which Esser[8] placed in the same Java-group, shows a
> percentage with Malay (51.2 o/o) that is significantly higher
> than its percentage with Javanese (38.6 o/o). ... These critical
> percentages with Malay are suspect because of the position of
> Malay in the Indonesian archipelago. ... If Madurese is not more
> closely related to Malay than it is to Javanese or to Sundanese,

1

it has certainly a large number of Malay loans in its vocabulary list. It would, however, be surprising if the number were so great that its relationship with Javanese or Sundanese were closer than with Malay. This suggests that if Madurese is not more closely related with Malay than with Javanese or Sundanese, then all four are about equally related.

In a later paper[9] and in personal communications, Dyen suggests that Javanese has lost some of the frequent vocabulary which would have been cognate with these items in Madurese, and that Madurese, at the same time, has borrowed heavily from Malay (at least in the low vocabulary) thus explaining the apparent discrepancy between being lexically closer to Malay and grammatically closer to Javanese. The entire question, however, has still not been satisfactorily solved.

Madura, with a present population of 2,147,741[10] of which 99 o/o are ethnically Madurese, now accounts for less than half of the total number of Madurese speakers. The inhospitable soil of Madura has forced many people to settle in East Java[11] where they now number about four million. Further west in Java there are very few Madurese. In all of Central Java in 1930 there were only some two thousand Madurese out of a total population of fifteen million.[12] Lekkerkerker[13] states there were 16,003 Madurese living in the rest of Indonesia (outside of Java and Madura) in that year.[14]

Madurese is also the main language of the island of Bawean[15] (population: 31,150), located to the north of Surabaja, and of the Sapudi islands[16] (population: 63,534), to the east of Madura. There are also some Madurese speakers in the Masalembu islands,[17] to the north and east of Bawean.

A rather divergent dialect of Madurese is spoken on some of the islands in the Kangean Archipelago (population: 40,743). These lie to the east of the Sapudi group. According to one informant, the division between Madurese and non-Madurese speaking islands in this group is as follows; alternate names of islands are in parentheses:[18]

Madurese	Non-Madurese
Kangean	Saobi (Saubi)
Paliat	Sabunten (Sabuntan, Sabunting, Masabunten)
Sapandjang (Pandjang)	Sapangkor (Sapangkur)
	Saebus
	Sadulang Besar
	Sadulang Ketjil
	Pagerungan Besar
	Pagerungan Ketjil
	Sakala
	Saséél
	Sapeken (Sapekkang, Masapekang)
	All smaller islands

Kiliaan[19] (1:5-12) divides Madurese dialects into two main groups: West Madurese and East Madurese. He puts the language of Pamekasan and of Bangkalan in West Madurese and places Sumenep and Kangean in East Madurese. He does not discuss the Madurese spoken on Java.

My impression is that the following would seem more accurate:

    A. Maduran

        1. West Madurese

            a. Bawean

            b. Bangkalan

        2. Central Madurese

            a. Pamekesan

            b. Sampang

        3. East Madurese

            a. Sumenep

            b. Sapudi

    B. Kangean

The language of central Madura is intermediate between East and West, having some features of one and some features of the other. On Madura itself, extending through Sapudi, there is apparently a chain of dialects with no appreciable break at any point. There is no difficulty in mutual comprehension among them. The language of Kangean is quite separate. Although it does share some features with East Madurese, a 200-word Swadesh list shows only 75 o/o cognates with the latter. People who speak East Madurese claim that Kangean speech is barely understandable.

Dialects spoken on Java vary according to the place of origin of the inhabitants.[20] Particular sections and even particular villages are said to be East, Central, or West in origin. As is to be expected, these dialects have more Javanese loan words than the island dialects.

Kiliaan (1:5-12) discusses some of the outstanding differences between the dialects. These as well as those discovered in my own research will be mentioned in the appropriate sections of the grammar. This dialect discussion is not meant to be exhaustive.

East Madurese, particularly the dialect of Sumenep, is now considered standard Madurese. Educated people from all over the Madurese-speaking area now use this dialect or an approximation to it when speaking to people from other parts of the area, and it is becoming more and more common in their daily speech.

There has been little previous work on Madurese.[21] Earlier grammars are:

> Elzevier Stokmans, W. J. and Marinissen, J. C. P., _Handleiding met woordenboek tot de beoefening der Madoereesche taal_ (Soerabaja, 1930).
>
> Hendriks, H., _Madoereesch, beknopte opgave van de gronden der Madoereesche taal met beschrijving van klankleer en uitspraak_ (Hilversum, 1913).
>
> Kiliaan, H. N., _Madoereesche Spraakkunst_ (Batavia, 1897). (two volumes)
>
> > I. Inleiding en Klankleer.
> >
> > II. Woordleer en Syntaxis.

Penninga, P. en Hendriks, H., *Practische handleiding voor het aanleeren der Madoereesche taal* (Semarang, 1930, 2nd ed. 1942).

Penninga, P. en Hendriks, H., *Madurees in één maand* (Semarang, 1937).

Sosrodanoekoesoemo, R., *De Madoereesche taal- en letterkunde* (Weltevreden, 1921).

Vreede, A., *Handleiding tot de beoefening der Madoereesche taal* (Leiden, 1882-90).

Wirjoasmoro, M., *Paramasastra Madura* (Madurese Grammar) (Jogjakarta, 1950).

Wirjowidjojo, M. S., *Spraakkunst en taaleigen van het Madoereesch* (Semarang, 1939).

The majority of these were practical grammars designed for Dutch administrators or planters. The only book on this list published since Indonesian independence - that by Wirjoasmoro - is in Madurese, and is intended for school children. The only attempt at a full-scale scientific grammar was by Kiliaan.

The only significant article I have found contains a long section on Madurese phonemics.

Berg, C. C., Beschouwingen over de grondslagen der spelling, *Tijdscrift voor Indische Taal-, Land- en Volkenkunde* 81.96-180 (1941).

Only two full-scale dictionaries exist:

Kiliaan, H. N., *Madoereesch-Nederlandsch Woordenboek* (Leiden, 1904).

Penninga, P., en Hendriks, H., *Practisch Madurees-Nederlands Woordenboek and Practisch Nederlands-Madurees Woordenboek* (two volumes) (Semarang, 1913).

The first of these is by far the better. The second ignores many phonemic distinctions, lacks dialect information, and to a great extent is just a simplified copy of Kiliaan's work.

Many readers and other school books, in both Latin and Madurese script, were published during Dutch times by the Balai Poestaka (Batavia, Weltevreden). The present Balai Pustaka (Djakarta) has also published a few readers. The one now mostly used in schools is:

Wirjoasmoro, M., and Troenodjojo, M. S., Basa Madura Umum (Common Madurese Language) (Jogjakarta, 1952).

The largest collections of books in and on Madurese are in the Lembaga Bahasa dan Budaja (Society of Language and Culture) at the Museum in Djakarta and in the library of the Urusan Adat-Istiadat dan Tjeritera Rakjat (Custom and Folk Stories Section of the Department of Education) in Djokjakarta. There is also a sizable collection at the library of Leiden University in Holland. As far as I know, the only public collection of any kind located on Madura itself is in the Jajasan Perpustakaan Madura (Madurese Library Foundation) in Pamekesan.

Madurese was formerly written with a syllabary derived from Javanese script.[22] This is still taught in schools, but for practical purposes Latin script is mainly used today. The present spelling using Latin script is based on the recommendations of M. A. ten Kate, c.s. (Inspecteur, Hoofd van de Dienst der Provinciale Onderwijsaangelegenheden) in his circular of 16 January 1940.[23] This spelling will be discussed below.

FOOTNOTES

1. Many English speakers say _Maduranese_ based on the parallels: Java:
   Javanese, Sunda: Sundanese, Bali: Balinese. To my knowledge, however,
   Madurese is the form that has been used in all previous English language
   sources, e.g. Dyen (op. cit. in fn. 7 below); C. F. and F. M. Voegelin,
   Languages Now Spoken by over a Million Speakers, _Anthropological Linguis-
   tics_ 3.8.13-22 (November, 1961). It is also parallel to the Dutch form:
   Madoerees(ch).

2. This figure is an extrapolation from the 1930 census. Unless otherwise
   noted, all population figures given in this Introduction are from that
   census: _Volkstelling_ 1930 (Batavia, 1934). _Deel II: Inheemsche Bevolking_
   van Midden-Java en de Vorstenlanden and _Deel III: Inheemsche Bevolking van_
   Oost-Java.

   At that time the Madurese formed 28.95 o/o of the population of East
   Java. The present population of East Java (1961 census) is 21,792,000. If
   the percentage of Madurese has remained the same, there would be about six
   million today. This result was checked, by the same method, against the
   Madurese population per "residency" (an administrative division) in East
   Java.

3. In Madurese speaking areas, Madurese is used as the language of instruction
   for the first three grades. After that, Indonesian is the language of instruction, Madurese being taught as a subject to youngsters until they are
   in the lower grades of high school and to prospective teachers throughout
   high school. See _Konperensi bahasa2 daerah di Djakarta pada tanggal 28-30_
   Agustus 1961 (mimeographed) (Conference on regional languages (held) in

Djakarta 28-30 August 1961).

4. E.g. see a recent book, apparently based only on previous sources: R. Salzner, <u>Sprachenatlas des Indopazifischen Raumes</u> (Wiesbaden, 1960), Volume 1, page 11, in which Madurese is placed in a Java-group along with Javanese and Sundanese.

> Kiliaan, for reference see fn. 19 below, is unsure of this: (1:1)
>
> Doch het getal Javaansche woorden vooral, die in het Madoereesch teruggevonden worden, is groot zonder dat van verreweg de meeste bewezen kan worden dat ze overgenomen zijn; terwijl een nauwere verwantschap tusschen het Javaansch en Madoereesch dan die tusschen zustertalen onderling pleegt te bestaan ook niet aangetoond kan worden. ... en dan zouden het Javaansch en Madoereesch één taal hebben uitgemakt, lang nadat zij zich van de grondtaal hadden afgescheiden. Er is evenwel geen reden om het laatste te beweren.

5. See A. Stevens, Language levels in Madurese, <u>Language</u> 41.294-302 (1965).

6. Those similarities not shared with Malay are:

> Mad. -a Jav. -o   'future, irrealis'
>
> Mad. a- Jav. a-   'intransitive verbal prefix'
>
> Mad. -an Jav. -an 'frequentative, comparative'

But these are not common Madurese-Javanese innovations, for Malagasy also has -a 'imperative', and a- 'instrumental passive' (see O. Dahl, <u>Malgache et Maanyan</u> (Oslo, 1951). Cognates of -a also occur in Bisayan, Buginese, and Sundanese (see R. A. Kern, De Conjunctief in het Boeginees, 162-69 in <u>Bingkisan Budi</u>, <u>een bundel opstellen aan Dr. R. S. van Ronkel</u> (Leyde, 1950).

7. The Lexicostatistic Classification of the Malayo-polynesian Languages, <u>Language</u> 38.38-46 (1962).

8. <u>Atlas van Tropisch Nederland</u> Map 9 (The Hague, 1938).

9. Lexicostatistically Determined Borrowing and Taboo, <u>Language</u> 39.60-66 (1963).

10. 1961 census results for East Java as reported in the newspaper <u>Surabaja</u>

Post, 12 January 1962.

11. It is difficult to say for how long large numbers of Madurese have been living in East Java. The earliest reference I have been able to find indicates that a large number of Madurese were brought to East Java in the 13th century to help with the harvest (Veth, *Java*, 1:59 (Haarlem, 1896). There were dynastic connections between East Java and Madura up until the Dutch conquest. Reports from the early 19th century (e.g. H. L. Domis, *De Residentie Passoeroeang op het eiland Java* ('s Gravenhage, 1836) and W. R. van Hoevell, *Reis over Java, Madura, en Bali* (Amsterdam, 1849) show that the percentages in at least Pasuruan and Besuki (East Java) were as great then as they are today. During Dutch times the Madurese were often used as government soldiers, and many probably settled on Java. Since the nineteenth century Madurese have come to East Java to work on the plantations. At the end of the season they would return to Madura. Thus connections have never been broken between mainland and island Madurese.

For a description of Madurese living in East Java see: R. S. P. Atmosoedirdjo, *Vergelijkende adatrechtlijke studie van Oostjavase Madoereezen en Oesingers* (Amsterdam, 1952).

12. That this was only a temporary working population for the most part can be seen from the sex ratio (*Volkstelling* II:18), only 370.1 women to 1000 men, and from the abnormal age distributions (loc. cit.).

13. *Land en Volk van Java* 505 (Groningen, 1938).

14. Mostly in West Borneo, Bali, and Lombok. See Lekkerkerker, op. cit. 211.

15. Also called *Lobok* or *Lubuk* in the older literature. In present day Madurese called *Babian* '(island) of pigs'. See J. Vredenbregt, Bawean migrations, *Bijdragen tot de Taal-, Land-, en Volkenkunde van Nederlandsch-Indïe* 120.109-39 (1964) where the 1958 population is given as 47,662.

16. Sapudi consists of sixteen islands. The main ones are: Sapudi (Madurese: Poḍaj), Raas, Sarok, Sotjè, Gili Anjar, Tunduk, Kamudi, Telangutimur,

Telangutengah, Telanguajer, Bulumanuk, Padjangan, Guagua. Some of these are not permanently inhabited. See F. J. Jochin, Beschrijving van den Sapoedi-Archipel, <u>Tijdschrift voor Indische Taal-, Land- en Volkenkunde</u> 36.343-93 (1893) and C. Lekkerkerker, Sapoedi en Bawean, overbevolking en ontvolking, <u>Koloniale Tijdschrift</u> 24.459-76 (1935).

17. The main islands are (alternate names in parentheses): Masalèmbu Besar (Salèmbu), Masalèmbu Ketjil (Sakambing), and Karamian. See C. Lekkerkerker, De Salèmboe-eilanden, Java's verste Oosthoek, <u>Indische Gids</u> 52.540-50 (1930).

18. Kangean consists of about thirty islands, some uninhabited. See J. L. van Gennep, Bijdrage tot de kennis van den Kangean-Archipel, <u>Bijdragen tot de Taal-, Land-, en Volkenkunde van Nederlandsch-Indië</u> 46.89-108 (1896).

   The non-Madurese population consists of Makassarese, Buginese, and Kambangese. The latter are also called Badjo and their language was referred to by my informants as Badjo or Baunsamabadjo.

19. All references to Kiliaan, unless otherwise stated, will be to <u>Madoereesche Spraakkunst</u>. For reference see page 4.

20. Madurese immigrants to Java tend to go to areas already inhabited by people from their own part of Madura. In 1930 (<u>Volkstelling</u> III:31f) more than a quarter of a million people in East Java were classified as Madurese immigrants. The following table shows their place of origin and their most usual places of settlement.

Origin	Settlement
Bangkalan	Surabaja, Malang, Kediri, Bodjonegoro, Madiun
Sampang	Djember, Lumadjang, Malang
Pamekasan	Djember, Banjuwangi, Lumadjang, Panarukan
Sumenep	Banjuwangi, Djember, Bondowoso

Some residencies along the north coast of Java (Pasuruan, Besuki, Kraksaan, etc.) which are no longer places of immigration for Madurese, apparently because of overcrowding, must have been settled along the same lines in the past.

21. For a general bibliography of Madurese see E. M. Uhlenbeck, <u>A Critical Survey of Studies on the Languages of Java and Madura</u> 174-197 (= Bibliographical Series 7) ('s-Gravenhage, 1964) and my review of this in <u>Journal of the American Oriental Society</u> 85.607-8 (1965).

22. For many centuries Javanese was the court and literary language of Madura. Written literature consisted of reworked Javanese stories or of Madurese stories written in Javanese or Kawi-miring (a form of Old Javanese). See R. Sosrodanoekoesoemo, Literatuur en kunst in Madoera, <u>Djawa</u> 7.163-71 (1927).

23. Entitled (in Madurese): <u>Poko': Oba'anna ger-oger nolès otja' Madoera ngganggoej aksara Latèn</u>. (Subject: Changes in the rules for writing Madurese using Latin letters).

CHAPTER II

PHONOLOGY

Introduction

The method used here in describing the phonology of Madurese is that which
has been called generative.[1] However, certain aspects of some previous generative work will not be used for Madurese. In particular the analysis by
distinctive features[2] seems to offer in this case no advantages over the
traditional articulation-based classification. The former method, in any case,
is difficult to apply to Madurese since explanations of how to use it in new
cases have never been clearly presented in print.[3]

The patternings of Madurese phones have been analyzed and are here presented as (a) a set of symbols (juncture symbols and segmental symbols for
words, stress and pitch symbols for sentences) and (b) a set of partially
ordered rules of the form AX → BX, to be read: A immediately preceding X becomes
B, or rewrite A immediately preceding X as B. "Partially ordered" means that
some of these rules must be carried out in the right order, i.e. before certain
other rules.

The phonologic transcription (consisting of symbols in the set just
mentioned plus certain morphophonemic symbols) represents the greatest amount of
abstraction and generalizing from the known data, taking into account: phonetics;
phonetic, morphologic, and syntactic distribution; and morphophonemics. The
implications and therefore results of this approach differ from those of traditional phonemic analysis in several ways:

(1) There is no sharp division between levels (morphophonemic, phonemic,
allophonic) and therefore no place in the sequence of rules that exhibits the

"phonemic" level.[4]

(2) Ary transcription leads to one and only one phonetic reading (allowing, of course, for individual variations, and for optional rules), but the reverse is not true. The so-called bi-uniqueness requirement is therefore not present.[5]

(3) As a result of the above two differences, so-called coexistent phonemic systems[6] and overlapping[7] become possible.

(4) No rule need be absolute, i.e. a limited number of "exceptions" are permitted for each rule. Only the greatest amount of generality is aimed at.

The following problems in Madurese, among others, are treated more simply here than by the traditional contrastive approach:

(1) Higher and lower schwa qualities are non-contrastive. However, this pair acts in many ways like other, contrastive pairs (e.g. i, ε; u, ɔ). The parallelism of these pairs and the rules predicting the location of their members are clearly formulated by the method used here.

(2) Vowel nasalization is contrastive. By the method used here its location is predictable.

(3) Certain chameleon morphemes such as the reduplications exhibit phenomena otherwise unknown in Madurese: for example, contrastive nasalization of vowels, contrastive syllabification, and otherwise non-occurring consonant clusters. Rules governing the form of these morphemes predict the correct results and bring them into line with the rest of the language.

Ordering

The importance of partial ordering can be seen from the following example (slightly simplified):

As a result of nasalization rules (following certain vowel rules which change i to e) we have:

> niat 'intention' → nẽãt

As a result of a later rule a glide is placed between the vowels as follows:

13

n$\tilde{\text{e}}$$\tilde{\text{a}}$t → n$\tilde{\text{e}}j\tilde{\text{a}}$t

If the second rule had preceded the first, we would have:

niat → nejat   (glide rule)

nejat → n$\tilde{\text{e}}$jat   (nasalization rule)

Nasalization would incorrectly be absent from the second vowel.

Form of symbols

The following conventions hold for all class symbols, i.e. symbols under which are subsumed more than one member:

(1) Any same symbol (e.g. C) is the same member of the class over any rule. Thus in CC, $C_x C_x$, C → C, and $C_x → C_x$ the same member of C or C_x respectively is meant.

(2) When sub-numbered (e.g. $C_1 C_2$) the symbols in a rule are the same or different members of the class. Thus in $C_1 C_2$, or $C_{x_1} C_{x_2}$, C_1 equals C_2 and C_{x_1} equals C_{x_2}, or C_1 is a different member of the class C from C_2 and C_{x_1} is similarly different from C_{x_2}.

(3) When sub-numbered with a dash (e.g. $C_1 C_{-1}$) the symbols in a rule are different members of the class. Thus C_1 and C_{-1} are different members of the class C; similarly for C_{x_1} and $C_{x_{-1}}$.

(4) When sub-lettered with a dash (e.g. C_{-s}) all members of the class except those after the dash are meant, i.e. C_{-s} means any consonant except stops.

Form of rules

The following conventions and definitions concern the form of rules:

(1) AX → BX means rewrite A in the environment _X [i.e. AX] as B in the environment _X [i.e. BX].

(2) AX → AX means that no change takes place. Such a rule will be referred to as "no change."

(3) (A)BX → (A)CX means that B in the environment _X [i.e. BX] is to be

14

rewritten as C in the environment _X [i.e. CX] and that B in the environment A_X
[i.e. ABX] is to be rewritten as C in the environment A_X [i.e. ACX]. In other
words (A) is optionally present; if it is present, it must appear on both sides
of the arrow.

(4) cyclic rule: a certain rule or set of rules is to be applied again and
again, each being applied to the product of the previous rule, until the rule or
rules no longer can be applied.

(5) eliminate: a symbol X is said to have been eliminated when it no longer
appears on the left-hand side of any subsequent rule, i.e. all X have been rewritten as some other symbol or have become zero.

All forms enter the phonology from the morphology (Chapter IV below). The
transcription of these forms is in the 'initial' or 'S_1' stage. Non-automatic
morphophonemic rules are applied (Chapter III); then after passing through the
partially ordered juncture rules (J-Rules) and phonologic rules (P-Rules) they
are in the 'final' or 'S_2' stage. On reaching the final stage they are then
passed through the phonetic rules. Forms which result from J-Rules or P-Rules
but are not final stage forms (because all such rules have not been applied to
them yet) are in the 'intermediate' stage. Schematically the system looks like
the following:

Morphology → S_1 → (by morphophonemic rules, by J-Rules, and P-Rules)
intermediate stages → S_2 → (by phonetic rules) phonetic reality.

Symbols

Juncture Symbols

The junctures of Madurese have been devised with a view to finding the
smallest number of symbols (and rules) covering all morpheme[8] boundary phenomena.

Junctures differ from other phonologic symbols in two ways: they only occur
at morpheme boundaries; and they are all eliminated by the end of the phonologic
rules, i.e. they have no phonetic existence themselves, but do have various

effects on adjacent symbols.

There are five junctures in Madurese. The first four junctures given below are in order of increasingly closer ties between the adjacent morphemes:

> Word juncture is symbolized by a space between words, or by #
> when a space would be unclear.

> Plus juncture is symbolized by + (plus sign).

> Dot juncture is symbolized by . (period).

> Close juncture is symbolized by - (hyphen).

> Combination juncture is symbolized by $\cdot$ (hyphen over period).

> The symbol | (vertical) will be used as a cover notation for
> the junctures listed above.

Segmental symbols

Cover terms are given for all classes (e.g. consonant, labial, spirant). Cover notations for all classes containing more than one member (e.g. C, V) are given in parentheses after the cover terms. Thus the class of consonants is preceded by Consonants (C).

Consonants (C)

Madurese has 26 native and about five[9] foreign consonant symbols.

Native consonants

Stops (C_s)

	Labial (C_b)	Dental (C_d)	Alveolar (C_{av})	Palatal (C_p)	Velar (C_k)
Voiceless (C_{vl})	p	t	ṭ	c	k
Voiced (C_v)	b	d	ḍ	z	g
Aspirated (C_a)	bh	dh	ḍh	zh	gh

The symbols for the aspirated stops (bh, dh, ḍh, zh, gh) are unitary symbols; they are not clusters of voiced stop plus h.[10]

Nasals (C_n)

Labial	Apical	Palatal	Velar
m	n	ñ	ŋ

16

Note that there are only four nasal positions as opposed to five stop positions.

The term homorganic (C^h) means the member of the class in the same position as another consonant of a different class (e.g. labial nasal is homorganic to labial stop). Note that the apical nasal (n) is homorganic to both dental and alveolar stops.

<u>Liquids</u> (C_r)

Trill	Lateral
r	l

<u>Glides</u> (C_g)

Labial	**Palatal**
w	j

<u>Spirant</u>

s

<u>Glottal</u>

q

<u>Breath</u>

h

The symbols w and h only occur in loan words,[11] and j appears in native words only in morpheme final position. However w, h, and j occur rather consistently in loan words; i.e. most speakers do not substitute native sounds for them. Among them h is least often replaced. The symbols j and w also occur rather consistently today, but the existence of competing forms suggests that substitutions were more frequently made for them in past times. Words with j often have competing forms with z, and similarly words with w often have competing forms with b. It is interesting to note that Madurese has z in inherited words where some related languages have j, e.g. Malay raja 'great, main'; Madurese raza 'big'. Similarly Madurese has b where some related languages have w, e.g. Javanese watu 'stone'; Madurese batu 'stone'.

Examples of competing forms in Madurese with j-z and w-b are as follows:

jakin	zakin	'convinced'
jatim	zatim	'orphan'
hiwan	kiban	'animal'
wakkil	bakkil	'representative'

In recent years large numbers of loan words from Indonesian containing j, w, and h have entered Madurese, and these sounds cannot be considered foreign in the same way that the following are.

Foreign consonants

Foreign consonants are used consistently by only some speakers. Other speakers use competing forms in which a native consonant or cluster of consonants substitute for the foreign consonant. Examples of such competing forms are to be found in Appendix 1 below.

The foreign consonants which occurred in the corpus were the following:

voiced apical spirant	ƶ
voiceless velar spirant	X
voiced velar spirant	ǧ
labial spirant	f
palatal spirant	š

Vowels (V)

From a strictly contrastive point of view there are nine different vowels in Madurese:

	front	central	back
high	/i/	/ə/	/u/
mid	/e/	/N/	/o/
low	/ɛ/	/a/	/ɔ/

Well over 95 percent of the corpus requires only four vowels.[12] It is simpler to construct a vowel system which applies to this part of the corpus and to append two vowel collections to account for the remainder of the corpus

than to deal with the alternations separately under a rubric such as morphophonemics. The three vowel collections are called respectively (1) alternating vowels,
(2) non-alternating vowels, and (3) special vowels. At stage S_1 alternating
vowels are represented as vowel symbols without diacritics; non-alternating
vowels and special vowels are written as vowel symbols with diacritics.[13]

Only three of the four alternating vowels actually consist of alternating
contrastive vowel pairs. The fourth, ə, consists of only a single contrastive
vowel, but, parallel to the others, of a pair of non-contrastive vowels. The
distribution of the member vowels of an alternating vowel is according to certain
rules to be given below (pages 24-27).

The alternating vowels and their member pairs are:

front (V_f)	central (V_c)	low (V_w)	back (V_b)
i (í, è)	ə (ś, ə̀)	a (á, à)	u (ú, ò)

There are seven non-alternating vowels, each consisting of a single contrastive vowel. Six of them are however arranged in pairs of vowels, one higher
and one lower. The seventh vowel is regarded as a higher vowel.

	front (V_f)	central (V_c)[14]	low (V_w)	back (V_b)
higher (V_H)	í	ś	á	ú
lower (V_L)	è	(ə̀)	à	ò

Non-alternating vowels are the unexpected member of the pair of alternating
vowels according to the rules to be given below. Thus à appears in the word bàŋ
'bank' because according to the rules, báŋ would be expected. If the latter word
occurred, it would be written with an alternating vowel, *baŋ. Similarly for the
word gárpú 'fork'; the expected gárpò, which would be written *garpu, does not
occur.

A few minimal pairs containing alternating and non-alternating vowels
occur. They are listed in Appendix 2 below.

Non-alternating vowels occur only in loan words and in some reduced forms
of native words where the loss of a consonant has produced the wrong member of

the alternating pair as in bàŋ 'bank' (loan word), and in kaq-ímma 'where' (re-duced form). For a discussion of reduced forms see pages 187-188.

All words in the corpus containing non-alternating vowels are listed in Appendix 2. Competing forms containing alternating and non-alternating vowels are also listed in Appendix 2.

There are two special vowels. They only occur in loan words.

<u>front</u> (V_f)   <u>back</u> (V_b)

ɛ́   ó

All words in the corpus containing special vowels are listed in Appendix 2. Competing forms containing special and alternating vowels are also given in Appendix 2.

<u>Intonational Symbols</u>[15]

<u>Terminals</u>.

These occur in sentence final position.

<u>Fall</u> symbolized by . (period).

<u>Rise</u> symbolized by ? (question mark).

<u>Sustain</u> symbolized by ! (exclamation mark).

<u>Internals</u>.

These occur in sentence medial position.

<u>Lift</u> symbolized by / (slash).

<u>Rise</u> symbolized by , (comma).

<u>Sustain</u> symbolized by + (plus between spaces).

<u>Clusters</u>

The following clusters cannot occur:

1. $\quad \partial \begin{bmatrix} V \\ | \\ C_g \\ q \\ hC \end{bmatrix}$

2. $|VV$

i.e. a sequence of same vowels without intervening juncture does
not occur after a juncture.

3. h|

4. |q

5. ij

6. uw

7. C_{av} C_r [16]

8. rd[17]

9. Syllable final C_p, C_{av}, C_v, and w except in a geminate cluster.

Rules for the location of syllable division will be given below.

Occurring clusters and canonical forms of morphemes are given in Appendix 3
below. A table of root initial and root final list frequencies for the segmental symbols is also given below in Appendix 3.

Restriction 3 above is only true of East and Central Madurese. In West
Madurese, Vh# occurs in contrast with V# when the word is followed by pause.
Where there is no following pause, this h disappears (see Kiliaan 1:5, 51).

RULES

The words in stage S_1, which come from the morphology (Chapter IV), are
first passed through the morphophonemic rules (Chapter III below). The rules to
be given here then convert the results into the S_2 stage. These rules are divided into juncture rules (J-Rules) and phonologic rules (P-Rules).

All words containing the symbols (morphemes) R, Rf, Rt, Rtw, Rtm, and S are
to be set aside and not passed through the rules at this point. The rules covering them will be given at a later point in the sequence of phonologic rules.

Juncture rules (J-Rules)

Juncture rules are those with the same non-word-junctural symbol on both
sides of the arrow. Only the adjacent segmental symbols change: e.g. C. → CC.

Each juncture is associated with a set of rules. Each of the sets of rules associated with a juncture is symbolized by J followed by a number.

Each of the rules of a set is presented in outline form after a letter of the alphabet; each rule is thereafter referred to by its set number and letter (e.g. J-1b, J-3a, etc.). Unless otherwise noted the rules of a set are not ordered.

J-1. Rules implied by dot juncture (.).

   a. $C_{-q} \cdot V \rightarrow C_{-q} C_{-q} \cdot V$

   saŋ.aliq → saŋŋ.aliq   'my ygr. sibling'

   lincak.ipun → lincakk.ipun   'his couch'

   kabhar.aghi → kabharr.aghi   'report'

   b. $VC_{-q} \cdot n \rightarrow VC_{-q} \cdot C_{-q}$

   surat.na → surat.ta   'his letter' (obsolescent)

   c. $\left| C \begin{bmatrix} V \\ a \end{bmatrix} \cdot CV \rightarrow \left| C \begin{bmatrix} V \\ a \end{bmatrix} \cdot CCV \right.$

   gha.ghaman → gha.gghaman   'weapon'

Elsewhere there is 'no change'.

J-2. Rules implied by any juncture (|).

J-2 rules generate nasalization of certain vowels. The rules are optional, i.e. the results of applying the rules are in free variation with the results obtained when these rules are omitted.

The symbol for vowel nasalization is tilde over the vowel, e.g. ã.

   a. $\left| VV \begin{bmatrix} | \\ C \end{bmatrix} \rightarrow \left| \tilde{V}\tilde{V} \begin{bmatrix} | \\ C \end{bmatrix} \right.$

   aiŋ → ãĩŋ 'water'

   ka-aup-an → ka-ãũp-an 'shaded'

   b. (optional)

   $\left| VV \begin{bmatrix} | \\ C \end{bmatrix} \rightarrow \left| \tilde{V}V \begin{bmatrix} | \\ C \end{bmatrix} \right.$

   aiŋ → ãiŋ 'water'

   c. $\left| V \right| VV \begin{bmatrix} | \\ V \end{bmatrix} \rightarrow \left| \tilde{V} \right| \tilde{V}\tilde{V} \begin{bmatrix} | \\ C \end{bmatrix}$

   a-ias → ã-ĩãs 'to decorate oneself'

i. aiŋ → ĩ.ãĩŋ 'in the water'

All words beginning with VV are listed in Appendix 4 below. Note that the cooccurrence restrictions already given will prevent a sequence of same vowels without intervening juncture from appearing in this position. For this reason V_1V_{-1} has not been written in the rules.

One word, isa or ésa 'evening prayer', occurs with irregular initial nasalization, i.e. isa → ĩsa; ésa → ḗsa.

The nasalization symbol x̃ is not to be taken into consideration for the rest of the J- and P-Rules.

J-3.   Rules implied by close juncture (-).

a. $C_s\text{-}V \rightarrow C_a^h\text{-}V$

uruk-a → urugh-a 'will add'

ka-aup-an → (by J-2) ka-ãũp-an → ka-ãũbh-an 'shade'

b. $C_s\text{-}\begin{bmatrix} n \\ C_s \end{bmatrix} \rightarrow C_a^h\text{-}C_a^h$

Note that these are written in the following way (cf. fn. 10):

$C_a C_a \rightarrow C_v^h C_a$

e.g. bhbh → bbh

ghgh → ggh

bhuṭuk-na → bhuṭug-gha 'his fertilizer'

puqlut-na → puqlud-dha 'his pencil'

səbhut-taghi → səbhud-dhaghi 'mention'

c. $C\begin{bmatrix} -s \\ -q \end{bmatrix}\text{-}n \rightarrow C\begin{bmatrix} -s \\ -q \end{bmatrix}\text{-}C\begin{bmatrix} -s \\ -q \end{bmatrix}$

sunar-na → sunar-ra 'its rays'

kərbhuj-na → kərbhuj-ja 'his water buffalo'

Elsewhere there is 'no change'.

J-4.   Rules implied by combination juncture (-̣).

First apply rules for dot juncture (J-1) and then rules for close juncture (J-3).

23

kabhar-̣aghi → kabhar-raghi → kabhar-raghi 'report'

səbhut-̣aghi → səbhut-taghi → səbhud-dhaghi 'mention'

Phonologic rules (P-Rules)

The symbols which precede an alternating vowel determine its quality. Each alternating vowel consists of a pair of intermediate stage vowels. The rules by which the intermediate stage vowels are generated are given in Rule P-1.

Three classes of determinants must first be defined: neutral determinant (D_N), higher determinant (D_H), and lower determinant (D_L):

The members of D_N are: s-, j-, -s, -j, C_r(-), q(-)

The members of D_H are: C_v, C_a, C_g other than those already mentioned, i.e. j not followed or preceded by close juncture, all w.

The members of D_L are: all other consonants, i.e. C_{vs}, s not followed or preceded by close juncture, C_n, h, f, ś, X.

In East Madurese, s- and -s are optionally members of D_L for some speakers, i.e. all s are members of D_L for them. In West Madurese, s- and -s are optionally members of D_N or of D_H (cf. Kiliaan 1:7).

The membership of ǧ is unknown since it is so rare.

Alternating vowels are now divided into higher (V_H) and lower (V_L) alternates. Non-alternating vowels have already been divided into higher and lower alternants (page 19 above).

		V_H	V_L
low (V_w)	a	á	à
front (V_f)	i	í	è
back (V_b)	u	ú	ò
central (V_c)	ə	ə́	ə̀

P-1. These rules must be applied in the order given below.

a. $D_H V \rightarrow D_H V_H$

bhabhar → bhábhár 'give birth'

ghighi → ghíghí 'tooth'

babi → bábí 'pig'

buḍi → búḍí 'back'

b. $V_{H_1} (D_{N_1})V_2 [(D_{N_2})(D_{N_3})V_3]\ldots\# \rightarrow$

$\quad V_{H_1}(D_{N_1})V_{H_2}[(D_{N_2})(D_{N_3})V_{H_3}]\ldots\#$

This means that the quality of the higher vowel alternant has effect through any combination of D_N consonants or lack of consonants until the next non-D_N consonant or the end of the word. At the next non-D_N consonant the effect stops.

bila → (by P-1a) bíla → (by P-1b) bílá 'when'

baḍa-a → (by P-1a) báḍá-a → (by P-1b) báḍá-á 'will be'

ka-bhaghus-an → (by P-1a) ka-bhághús-an → (by P-1b) ka-bhághús-án 'goodness'

kərbhuj-na → (by J-3c) kərbhuj-ja → (by P-1a) kərbhúj-ja → (by P-1b) kərbhúj-já 'his water buffalo'

Note that rule P-1b works for non-alternating vowels too.

ía → íá 'yes' $[V_H V \rightarrow V_H V_H]$

kaúla → kaúlá 'I' $[C_L VV_H D_N V \rightarrow C_L VV_H D_N V_H]$

c. All other $V \rightarrow V_L$

pili → pèlè 'choose'

laraŋ → làràŋ 'forbid'

pulu → pòlò 'island'

inghi → (by P-1a) inghí → (by P-1c) ènghí 'yes'

d. Special vowels undergo 'no change'.

There are some conditions which have uncertain outcomes. It is not clear what happens in the case of $V_s D_N V$ (special vowel plus neutral determinant plus vowel). Only two examples occur in the corpus. In these cases the second vowel becomes the same special vowel as the first, i.e. $V_s D_N V \rightarrow V_s D_N V_s$.

ŋósér-i → ŋóséré 'to be a coachman'

ñopér-i → ñópéré 'to be a driver'

<u>Comments</u>:

Since s and j are neutral determinants only when followed or preceded by close juncture (including close juncture resulting from combination juncture) and not in other positions, the following differences result:

bassa → bássa 'wet' [...sV_L]

bhaghus-a → bhághús-á 'will be good' [...s$\bar{V}_H$]

majjit → màjjít 'corpse' [...jV_H]

apuj-na → apuj-ja → apój-jà 'his fire' [...jV_L]

ŋapuj-i → ŋapójě 'to provoke' [...jV_L]

Note also that rule P-1b is effective only through close juncture; for example through dot juncture: ɖu.ari → ɖú.àrě 'two days', and not *ɖú.árí.

Rule P-1b is not effective in the Kangean dialect, e.g. bəraq → bə́rǎq 'heavy' in other dialects, but → bə́rǎq in Kangean.

West Madurese has higher vowel alternants in the case of N-D_HV(D_NV) → $C_n V_H$($D_N V_H$). For example, in West Madurese: N-ghiba → ŋíbá 'to carry'; N-ghuriŋ →ŋúríŋ 'to fry'. The standard East Madurese follows the above rules, i.e. N-ghiba → ŋěbá 'to carry', and N-ghuriŋ → à-ghúríŋ 'to fry' (the rules for N- are given below).

West Madurese also has forms with superlative meaning such as the following (rules for R will be given below): kiniq → kěněq 'small' (all dialects); R+kíníq → níq+kíníq 'very small' (West Madurese).

Madurese can be viewed as being in the process of changing from a four vowel system where the higher-lower alternants of the vowels were completely determined by the above rules to a system in which such determination will cease to exist. In East Madurese the original system is still quite strong. This is witnessed by the frequent substitution of "madurized" forms for foreign words which go against the determinant rules. Those which have not been madurized stand out quite clearly in East Madurese. In West Madurese, which is geographically closer to Javanese and Malay, the process has gone much farther, e.g. there are many more loans, cases of elided consonants resulting in non-alternating vowels, and morphological processes such as those mentioned above.

Examples of all possible combinations of $V_H D_N V$ and $V_L D_N V$ have been listed in Appendix 5 below. Also given in Appendix 5 are examples of $V_1 D_N D_N V_2$ and $D_H V_1 D_{N_1} V_2 D_{N_2} V_3$.

P-2. - → $\emptyset$ Close juncture is eliminated.

> ka-bhaghus-an → (by P-1) kà-bhághùs-àn → (by P-2) kàbhághùsàn 'goodness'

P-3. əCV → əCCV A consonant is geminated after ə and before a vowel.

> pəsən → (by P-1) pə̀sə̀n → pə̀ssə̀n 'order'
>
> bəli → (by P-1) bə̀lí → bə̀llí 'buy'
>
> rəŋiq → (by P-1) rə̀ŋèq → rə̀ŋŋèq 'mosquito'
>
> səhak → (by P-1) sə̀hàk → sə̀hhàk 'chess'
>
> səbhut → (by P-1) sə̀bhùt → sə̀bbhùt 'mention'
>
> bhədhi → (by P-1) bhə̀ḍhí → bhə̀ḍḍhí 'sand'

P-4. Other geminations.

> a. $VC_s C_r$ → $VC_s C_s C_r$ A stop is geminated before a liquid.
>
> sutra → (by P-1) sòtrà → sòttrà 'silk'
>
> taplaq → (by P-1) tàplàq → tàpplàq 'tablecloth'
>
> zhughlaŋ → (by P-1) zhùghláŋ → zhùgghláŋ 'ditch'

An irregularity is the loan word pabrik → pàbrík 'factory'.

> b. Vsr → Vssr The symbol s following a vowel and preceding an r is

geminated.

> asriŋ → (by P-1) àsrèŋ → àssrèŋ 'frequent'
>
> pasra → (by P-1) pàsrà → pàssrà 'hand over'

The loan word asrama → àsràmà 'dormitory' is irregular.

Comments:

Kiliaan (1:40) claims that Vsl → Vssl, but he gives no examples. In my corpus there were two such cases: éslam → éslằm 'Islam' .and aslí → àslí 'original', both loan words, and neither showing geminated s.

Kiliaan (1:40) also claims that $VmC_r → VmmC_r$. He gives as examples: lommra 'usual', ammre 'in order to'. My informants always said lứnbrà → lứnbrà 'usual' and anbri → ànbrí 'in order to'. No examples of geminated m in this position occur in the corpus.

Kiliaan (1:40) also claims that h is geminated between vowel and liquid or between vowel and j, i.e.

$$Vh \begin{bmatrix} C_r \\ j \end{bmatrix} → Vhh \begin{bmatrix} C_r \\ j \end{bmatrix}$$

He gives as example cahhja 'light'. This and similar words were always pronounced with single h by my informants, e.g. cahja → (by P-1) cằhjá 'light'; mahrép → (by P-1) mằhrép 'evening prayer'.

There is one case of $VC_sj → VC_sC_sj$ and no counter cases: pakjaq → pằkkjàq 'kind of sandal'.

P-5.[18]
$$\begin{bmatrix} \# \\ \#C \end{bmatrix} ề.ề → \begin{bmatrix} \# \\ \#C \end{bmatrix} ềjề$$

    i.iluŋ-na → (by J-3c) i.iluŋ-ŋa → (by P-1,2) ề.ềlðŋŋà → ềjềlðŋŋà
      'in his nose'

    i.issi-i (by P-1,2) ề.ềssềề → ềjềssềề 'be filled'

P-6.   . → ∅   Dot juncture is eliminated.

    saŋ.aliq → (by J-2a) saŋŋ.aliq → (by P-1) sằŋŋ.àlềq → sằŋŋàlềq
      'my younger sibling'

P-7. VV → V_qV q is generated between same vowels. For example:

    liir → (by P-1) lềềr → lềqềr 'neck'

    tuut → (by P-1) tð̀ðt → tðqðt 'knee'

    baa → (by P-1) bá́á → báqá 'flood'

    dhuum → (by P-1) dhứứm → dhứqứm 'distribute'

The rather ad hoc nature of P-5 where a glide is generated between certain

28

èĕ sequences in relation to P-7 where q is generated between all other same
vowel sequences is necessary because of another change taking place in Madurese.
Rule P-9 below places a glide between certain vowel sequences. This glide has
now been extended, in fast speech, to between certain èĕ clusters of the type
given in Rule P-5. Other èĕ sequences, for example where the second è is in a
suffix, follow Rule P-7. For a discussion of the spread of intervocalic glides
in Madurese see C. C. Berg, op. cit., pp. 151-8.

 The contrasts produced by Rules P-5 and P-7 can be seen in the following
word:

   i.issi-i → (by P-1) è.èssè-è → (by P-2) è.èssèè → (by P-5)
   èjèssèè → (by P-7) èjèssèqè 'be filled'

P-8. Nasalization of vowels.

  a. $C_n V_1 (V_2) \rightarrow C_n \tilde{V}_1 (\tilde{V}_2)$

   nasiq → (by P-1) nàsèq → nã̀sèq 'rice'

   maus → (by P-1) màðs → mã̀ðs 'to read'

  b. $C_n (V_1) V_2 \begin{bmatrix} h \\ q \end{bmatrix} V_3 \rightarrow C_n (\tilde{V}_1) \tilde{V}_2 \begin{bmatrix} h \\ q \end{bmatrix} \tilde{V}_3$

   i-naiq-i → ènàèqè → ènã̀ẽqè̃ 'be climbed on'

   maha → màhà → mã̀hã̀ 'great'

   ñuun → ñòðn → ñòqðn → ñõ̀qõ̀n 'to request'

 In subsequent rules the nasalization symbol is not to be taken into account
unless specifically mentioned.

P-9. Glide generation rules.

  a. $V_f V \rightarrow V_f j V$

   siaŋ (by P-1) sèàŋ → sèjàŋ 'daylight'

   rubhia → (by P-1) rðbhíá → rðbhíjá 'wife'

  b. $V_b V \rightarrow V_b w V$

   suara → (by P-1) sðàrà → sðwàrà 'voice'

   ghua → (by P-1) ghúá → ghúwá 'cave'

Note that nasalization has already been generated in many cases to which P-9 would apply:

niat → (by P-1) nẽàt → (by P-8) nẽä̀t → (by P-9a) nẽjä̀t 'intention'

mua → (by P-1) mòä → (by P-8) mòä̀ → (by P-9b) mõ̀wä̀ 'face'

P-10. Syllabification rules. Syllable division is indicated by / (slash).

Syllable rules are to be applied in the order given below. Syllable rules are cyclic, i.e. each sub-rule is applied, and then the entire set of sub-rules is reapplied again and again until they no longer can be applied, that is when the end of the word is reached.

a. $\#V_1V_2 \rightarrow \#V_1/V_2$

aup → (by J-2) ãũp → (by P-1) ã̀õp → à̀/õp 'take shelter'

b. $\#(C)Vq \rightarrow \#(C)V/q$

suun → (by P-1) sòòn → (by P-7) sòqòn → sòq/òn 'request'

c. $\#(C_1)V_1C_2V_2\ldots \rightarrow \#(C_1)V_1/C_2V_2\ldots$

cucu → (by P-1) còcò → cò/cò 'stab'

bila → (by P-1) bílá → bí/lá 'when'

d. $\#(C_1)VC_2C_3\ldots \rightarrow \#(C_1)VC_2/C_3\ldots$

tantu → (by P-1) tàntò → tàn/tò 'sure'

putra → (by P-1) pòtrà → (by P-4a) pòttrà → pòt/trà 'son'

e. Cyclic until the end of the word.

f. $\ldots\# \rightarrow \ldots/$

A longer example is the following:

sa-anpun-na 'after' → (by P-1) sà-ànpòn-nà → (by P-2) sàànpònnà →
(by P-7) sàqànpònnà → (by P-8) sàqànpònnà̀ → (by P-10b)
sàq/ànpònnà̀ → (by P-10e, 10c) sàq/àn/pònnà̀ → (by P-10e, 10c)
sàq/àn/pòn/nà̀ → (by P-10e, 10f) sàq/àn/pòn/nà̀/

The syllabification symbol is not to be taken into account in subsequent rules unless specifically mentioned.

P-11. Shortening (S+) rules. These must be carried out in the order given below.

a. Apply all J and P rules in the correct order.
b. Short form equals final syllable of the word.

S+sittuŋ → (by J-1 through P-11a) S+sèt/tòŋ → tòŋ 'one'

S+ḍua-q → (by J-1 through P-11a) S+ḍú/wáq → wáq 'two'

S+inghi → (by J-1 through P-11a) S+èn/ghí → ghí 'yes'

S+uriŋ → (by J-1 through P-11a) S+ò/rèŋ → rèŋ 'person'

For P-Rules 12, 13 and 14 the end point of the root must be known. Since the suffixes and their limitations of cooccurrence are known, the end point of the root can be determined by examination of the S_1 form. What occurs after the root can only be of the following shape:

$$(-n) \ (|\text{suffix}) \begin{pmatrix} -na \\ .ipun \\ -a \end{pmatrix}$$

P-12. Elision.

In certain cases a CV/C which is the third syllable back from the end of the root becomes /CC by elision of the vowel or becomes Cə/C by a change of vowel. This elision is apparently most frequent in West Madurese and quite common in Central Madurese. In the dialect being studied here, East Madurese, elision is an optional possibility, and some speakers consider it substandard. Elision rules follow:

a. Locate root end.

b. Apply all J- and P-Rules.

c. Elide vowel of third syllable from root end in the following cases:

   1. The most usual environment in which elision occurs is $CV/C_r → /CC_r$, for example:

      balandha → blándhá 'Dutch'

      balandha-an → blándháqán 'Dutch'

      baranpa → bránpà 'how much'

      ŋa-baranpa-i → ŋàbránpàè 'do it with how many'

   2. Next most common is $CV/C_n → /CC_n$, for example:

      sanapan → snàpàn 'rifle'

      saŋaza → sŋàzá 'purposely'

31

3. Next most common are cases of $CV_1V_{-1} \rightarrow CV_1/C_gV_{-1} \rightarrow /CC_gV_{-1}$, for example:

biasa → bíjásà → bjásà 'ordinary'

suara → sòwàrà → swàrà 'voice'

su.aliq → sòwàlèq → swàlèq 'with younger sibling'

These occur only with cases of j and w that have been generated by P-9.

4. Least common are cases of $CV/C_s \rightarrow /CC_s$.

The consonant clusters allowed are only those already given in the discussion of permitted consonant clusters (Appendix 3). For example:

sakucí → skòcí 'sloop'

d. Optionally in types 1-4 and elsewhere $CV/C \rightarrow C\partial/C$.

Comments

Elision usually does not carry back across a morpheme boundary (i.e. juncture of any kind), for example ta-mira 'very red' does not become *tmèrà. Certain morpheme boundaries however may be passed over. It should be remembered that in any case the application of elision rules is optional in East Madurese. Examples across morpheme boundaries follow:

ZA-lauq → zha-lauq → zhláúq 'to the south'

ka.luar → klòwàr 'to the outside'

sa-mankin → smànkèn 'now'

However, sa-ñata-na 'in fact' does not become *sñàtànà. More study is needed on this point.

Note that J- and P-Rules are not to be reapplied to the elided form. Thus N-pa-ka.luar 'to extract' becomes màklòwàr and not *màkklòwàr (by P-4a). The syllable division falling between the two consonants is also in contrast to syllable division elsewhere in Madurese, e.g. mà/klò/wàr.

In his grammar, Kiliaan (1:82) has an example of this elision taking place in the third syllable from the end of the word where this is not the third syllable from the end of the root, e.g. ka-tòraŋ-an 'explanation' → kàtràŋàn. Such contractions were said to be impossible by my informants. Kiliaan also claims (loc. cit.) that this could then become kåttrȧŋȧn (by my P-4a). This too is in contradiction to my findings. Perhaps Kiliaan's statements are valid for West Madurese.

The weakening of the third syllable from the end of the root and word is apparently moving from west to east on Madura. In West and to a lesser extent in Central Madurese the various types of elision discussed in this section always occur or V → ə. This is even true across morpheme boundaries never crossed in East Madurese (plus reapplication of P-4 and P-3), e.g. (Kiliaan 1:82) ka.ḍaləm → kəḍḍȧlə́m 'to the inside'; sa.rupia → sərrȯpė̇jȧ 'one rupiah'. West Madurese has gone so far as to drop the entire first syllable of many tri-syllabic or longer roots, e.g. East Madurese kalanbhi; West Madurese lanbhi 'upper garment'. Some of these contractions have spread throughout Madura. A contraction of the city name paməkasan → məkasan is quite common in all of Madura. Other such contracted forms will be discussed in the section dealing with the morphology of substitutes (see pages 187-188).

Another type of weakening which takes place in West Madurese is that any suffix of the form -an → -ən when followed by another suffix (see Kiliaan 1:60):

kun+kun-an-na → kȯn+kȯnȧnnȧ 'his order' → kȯn+kȯnə̇nnȧ

mati-an-a → måtė̇jȧnȧ 'will kill' → måtė̇jə̇nnȧ

A table of examples of elision has been given in Appendix 6.

P-13. Reduplications.

There are three types of reduplication in Madurese: R (end reduplication); Rf (front reduplication); and Rt (total reduplication). Root reduplication (CVC+CVC) will be discussed in the section dealing with morphology.

The rules for the various types of reduplication are as follows:

A.   R (end reduplication)

a.   Locate root end.

b.   Apply all morphophonemic and P-Rules up through the root end and following symbol. Ignore P-6 (. → ∅).

    c. R → last syllable of the root plus an -n|, -q|, or generated q which

        follows the root end.

    d. Apply all J-Rules and P-Rules in sequence to the result.

For ease of reading the R referred to in c above has been underlined in the
following examples:

        R+abit → R+<u>abít</u> → bít+abít 'finally'

        R.abit → R.<u>abít</u> → bít.abít → bíttabít → bíttabít 'finally'

        a-R+taña → à-R+ta<u>ñà</u> → a-ñà+tañà → añà+tañà 'to ask'

        i-R+taña-i → èR+ta<u>ñàè</u> → èñàtañàè 'keep on being asked'

        R+bua-an → R+búw<u>áqá</u>n → wáq+búwáqán 'fruits'

        R+main-an → R+mà<u>è</u>nàn → èn+màènàn 'toys'

        R+N-pa-tau → R+màt<u>aò</u> → ò+màtaò 'to pretend to know'

        R+N-asta-n-i → R+ŋàs<u>tanè</u> → tàn+ŋàstanè 'to hold'

B. Rf (front reduplication)

    a. Apply all J- and P-Rules. Ignore P-6 (. → ∅).

    b. If Rf|C, then Rf → first CV of what follows.

    c. Optionally this CV → Ca.

    d. If Rf|V, then Rf → R (i.e. apply R rules as given above).

    e. Reapply all J-Rules, and then all P-Rules.

The Rf part is underlined in the following examples:

        Rf+N-tulis → Rf+<u>nò</u>lès → nò+nòlès 'keep on writing' optionally →
        nà+nòlès 'id'

        Rf.ghaman → Rf.<u>ghámàn</u> → ghá.ghámàn → ghágghámàn 'weapon'

        Rf.ənəm → Rf.ə<u>nəm</u> → nəm.ənəm → nəmmənəm 'six'

C. Rt (total reduplication)

There are two sub-types of total reduplication. In the first type, to be
symbolized Rtm, morpheme total reduplication, the rules are as follows:

    a. Same as rule P-13 Aa and P-13Ab above, i.e. same as for R.

b. Rtm → everything up to the next non-dot juncture (i.e. dot juncture is passed over).

c. Follow rules P-13Ac and d, substituting Rtm for R in the formulations.

The Rtm part is underlined in the following examples:

Rtm+bua-an → Rtm+búwáqan → búwáq+búwáqán 'fruits'

pa-Rtm+N-cukur-na → pa-Rtm+ñukur-na → paRtm+ñòkòr-nà →
pañòkòr+ñòkòrrà 'his constant shaving'

N-pa-Rtm+ka.buḍi-aghi → màRtm+kàbúḍíjághí → màkàbúḍí+kàbúḍíjághí
'keep on moving (something) back (for someone)'

In the second type of total reduplication, symbolized Rtw, word total reduplication, the following rules apply:

a. Same as Rtm-a.

b. Rtw → everything up to the next -na#, -a#, or #, whichever comes first.

c. Same as Rtm-c.

The Rtw part is underlined in the following examples:

Rtw+paŋ-ladhin → Rtw+pàŋlàdhín → pàŋlàdhín+pàŋlàdhín 'servants'

Rtw+sakula-an → Rtw+sàkòlàqàn → sàkòlàqàn+sàkòlàqàn 'schools'

Rtw+paŋ-cukur-na → Rtw+pàñòkòr-nà → pàñòkòr+pàñòkòrrà 'his razors'

If the next morpheme boundary and following word boundary coincide, there is no difference between Rtm and Rtw. In this case only Rt is written.

P-14. Resyllabification.

a. Reapply Rule P-10 to all results of P-13.

b. + → /.

Comments

The above three rules (P-11, 12, 13) involve the reapplication of certain rules given theretofore plus additional sub-rules. It might have been possible to insert the rules covering these processes into the ordered set of rules already given, but this would have involved fragmenting them. Their natural coherence suggested keeping them together.

One of the reasons for using the present method was the existence of the forms generated by rules P-11, 12, 13. The generated forms contain consonant clusters, consonant plus vowel clusters, nasalized vowels, and syllabic divisions which run completely contrary to what occurs elsewhere in Madurese. Consideration of this material on the same level as the rest of the corpus would have necessitated setting up more vowels, and nasalized as opposed to oral vowels, as well as make it impossible to give any coherent set of syllable division rules. By regarding these contrary forms as the result of a special set of rules it was possible to describe and explain their forms both simply and succinctly.

The following examples illustrate some of the contrary forms resulting from rules P-11, 12, 13:

> S+balluq → lûq 'eight' (lower consonant plus higher vowel)
>
> R+niat → jằt+nềjằt 'intentions' (first syllable nasalized)
>
> a-R+uba → àbáòbá 'keep on changing' (higher vowel followed by
>
> > lower vowel)
>
> R+abit → bɪt/àbɪt 'finally' (contrary syllable division)

S_2 Rules

All forms have now reached the S_2 stage. The following rules convert these forms into their phonetic reality. Examples are in their S_2 form.

<u>Vowel quality rules</u> to be applied in the order 1, 2, 3.

1. Individual qualities

    a. C_aə → C_a[ɨ] (high central unrounded), e.g. bhôndɔ̂r 'true'

    b. other ɔ̂ → [ə̂] (raised schwa), e.g. bɔ̂lɪ 'buy'

    c. ɔ̃̂ → [ə̃̂] (raised nasalized schwa), e.g. mɔ̃̂lɛ̀ 'to buy'

    d. #əC_s → #[ə̌]C_s (lowered schwa), e.g. əpàq 'father'

    e. other ə → [ə] (schwa; mid central unrounded), e.g. sərèŋ 'often'

    f. è → [Ẽ] to [ɛ̃] (mid range front unrounded), e.g. mɛ̀rà 'red'

36

g. èj → [E]j, e.g. sèjàŋ 'daylight'

h. è# → [ɛ̂] (raised ɛ), e.g. màtè 'dead'

i. other è → [ɛ], e.g. sèttòŋ 'one'

j. C$_a$á → C$_a$[Λ̂]^{19} (raised low back unrounded), e.g. bhábhár 'give
    birth'

k. other á → [Λ]^{19} (low to mid back unrounded), e.g. báráq 'west'

l. à → [a] (low central or slightly fronted unrounded), e.g. làràŋ
    'forbid'

m. optional

    a# → [ǎ̂]# (raised and shortened [a]), e.g. bássà 'wet'
    à (third or further syllable back from end of root) → [ǎ̂],^{20} e.g.
       tàrètàn 'sibling'

n. é → [e], e.g. satέ 'shish kabob'

o. ó → [o], e.g. sótó 'kind of soup'

p. íC/ → [I]C/, e.g. ghínzhέl 'kidney'

q. other í → [i], e.g. ghíghí 'tooth'

r. úC/ → [U]C/, e.g. ghúndhúŋ 'bunch'

s. other ú → [u], e.g. ghúrú

t. òw/ → [ɔ̂]w, e.g. sòwàrà 'voice'

u. òr/ → [ɔ]r, e.g. àntòr 'collide'

v. ò/ → [ɔ], e.g. sòsò 'breast'

w. other ò → [ɒ] (low back slightly rounded), e.g. ghúnòŋ 'mountain';
    cànkòk 'cup'

2. General qualities

    a. All ə, e, ɨ qualities produced by la-w are raised and slightly
        fronted following C$_p$ (palatal consonant), e.g. cèlèŋ 'black',
        zhónèŋ 'stand', cèlèŋ 'wild pig', cèjà 'bland'

    b. V/ → [Vˑ]/ (longer vowel), e.g. màtà 'eye', còcò 'stab'
        VC/ → [V̆]C/ (shorter vowel), e.g. màttà 'raw', còccò 'stab again

37

and again'

3. Epenthetic schwa

    a. $rC_{-r} \to r\breve{\mathrm{e}}C_{-r}$ (short ə), e.g. sòrbhàzà → sòrə̆bhàzà 'Surabaja'; mè̃jàrsa → mè̃jàrə̆sà 'to hear'

    b. $1C_{-1} \to 1^{\cdot\mathrm{ə}}C$ (the resulting 1 is half long, i.e. longer than a single 1 but not as long as a geminated 1 and is followed by a slight schwa color), e.g. mòlzà → mòl$^{\cdot\mathrm{ə}}$zà 'noble'; pəlkàq → pəl$^{\cdot\mathrm{ə}}$kàq 'thirsty'

    c. $r\#$ (in very slow, careful speech) $\to r^{\mathrm{ə}}\#$, e.g. bhàbhàr → bhàbhàr^{ə} 'to give birth'

Consonant quality rules

Only those which are not obvious from the categories given above on pages 16-17 will be explained.

    a. $nC_s \to C_n^h C_s$, e.g. np → [mp]; nbh → [mbh]; nḍh → [ṇḍh]; nk → [ŋk]

    b. n elsewhere → [apical nasal in either dental or post-dental position]

    c. $C_v \to$ [voiced, lax stop]

    d. $C_{vs} \to$ [voiceless, tense stop]

    e. $C_{vs}/ \to$ [unreleased stop]/

    f. $C_a \to$ [voiceless stop with indifferent tension followed by strong aspiration]

    g. gh → [velar stop further forward than k or g followed by strong aspiration]

    h. $C_a C_a \to$ [long voiceless stop with indifferent tension followed by strong aspiration]

    i. $C_d \to$ [dental stop]

    j. $C_{av} \to$ [alveolar stop with larger area of tongue contact than dentals.

    k. 1/ → [lateral, sometimes with velar coarticulation]/

    l. other 1 → [lateral]

m. j → [high front glide (no palatal friction)]

n. w → [high back glide (no labial friction)]

o. h → [voiceless breath of same quality as vowel in the same syllable];

e.g. hàl 'matter' has [a] quality h, as does àhmàt 'man's name'.

For some speakers this quality is in free variation with a voiceless velar spirant [X] with only slight velar friction. For other speakers these two qualities contrast in words of different origin: Indonesian, Javanese, Dutch [h] → Madurese h; Dutch, Arabic [X] → Madurese X.

p. r → [apical trill]

q. r# → [apical trill] in free variation with [apical tap].

r. f → [f]

s. ż → [z]

t. ś → [palatal s]

u. ǧ → [voiced velar spirant]

v. X → [voiceless velar spirant]

Intonation

a. . → [rapid drop in pitch on final syllable of the last word in the sentence]

b. ? → [rapid rise in pitch on the final syllable of the last word of the sentence]

c. ! → [sustaining of the pitch of the final syllable of the last word in the sentence]

d. / → [slight pitch rise on the final syllable of the preceding word accompanied by a slight pause before continuing, or by a slight drawling of this final syllable]

e. , → [a greater pitch rise than in d accompanied by a slightly longer pause]

f. + → [the pitch of the preceding syllable is sustained with approximately the same length pause as in e]

APPENDIX 1

Competing forms containing foreign and native consonants.

Foreign	Native	Examples		
f	p	nafas	napas	'breath'
ž	zh	žáman	zhaman	'time'
š	ss	mašarakat	massarakat	'society
ɣ	h	maɣrép	mahrép	'evening prayer'
ɣ	g	aɣèn	agèn	'agent'
X	h	Xàbhar	kabhar	'news'
X	k	Xèwàn	kiban	'animal'

APPENDIX 2

Minimal pairs for alternating and non-alternating vowels.

alternating		non-alternating	
buku	'joint'	bukū	'book'
kupi	'flask'	kupī	'coffee'
ban	'and'	bằn	'(auto) tire'
susu	'breast'	sūsū	'milk'
ia	'scream'	īa	'yes'

Competing forms containing alternating and non-alternating vowels.

alternating	non-alternating	
sapiɗa	sapiɗằ	'bicycle'
ənbha	ənbằ	'grandfather'
ruɗa	ruɗằ	'wheel'
ranzaŋ	ranzằŋ	'bed'
halwa	halwằ	'halvah'
jakin	jằkin	'convinced'
udur	ūdur	'hindrance'
umat	ūmat	'community'
biasa	biằsa	'ordinary'

Competing forms containing different consonants.

	non-alternating	
zita	cīta	'blouse'
⎧ kubhi	kupī	'coffee'
⎩ ghubhi (obsolete)		
sadrika	satrīka	'(to) iron'
zakin	jằkin	'convinced'

Following are all cases in the corpus which exhibit the non-alternating
vowels: ī, ề; ū, ồ; ấ, ằ. The symbols to the left are the consonants preceding the non-alternating vowels which appear at the top of the columns.

41

	á à	í è	ú ò
p		kupí 'coffee' tupí 'hat' pídató 'speech' píŋ+puŋ 'pingpong'	púlísí 'police' púlpin 'fountain pen' gárpú 'fork' púsat 'center'
b	abàt 'century' barlfàn 'jewel' biàsa 'usual' bólà 'thread' ənbà 'grandfather' bàŋ 'bank' kíblàt 'facing Mekka' tabràq 'collide' bàn '(auto) tire'	bènsín 'gasoline' bècaq 'tri-shaw' sərbèt 'napkin' runbèŋ 'old clothes'	runbòŋan 'group'
t		platína 'platinum' satríka '(to) iron' rutí 'bread'	pantún 'Malay song'
d	kuməndàn 'commander'	risídèn 'resident'	dòktər 'doctor'
ḍ	ḍamí 'peace' ḍasí 'necktie' sanḍàl 'sandal' sapiḍà 'bicycle' prupagànḍà 'propaganda' ḍiàlik 'dialect' pídàtó 'speech' bəḍàl 'pedal' ruḍà 'wheel'	muḍèl 'model'	zànḍòn 'speak' ḍònpit 'purse' manḍòr 'foreman'
c		cíta 'blouse' ící 'ten cents'	gincú 'rouge'
z	zànḍòn 'speak' mazàlla 'magazine' zàs 'jacket'		
k	ranzàŋ 'bed'	jàkín 'convinced' kíblàt 'facing Mekka' kíló 'kilometer' kíta 'we'	bukú 'book' kúé 'cake' bànkú 'bench' kaúla 'I'

	á a	í è	ú ò
k		kulí 'coolie' hakím 'judge'	
g	gáŋ 'alley' gárpú 'fork' gəlàs 'glass' prupagánḍa 'propaganda' gàs 'natural gas'	agèn 'agent'	mugòq 'go on strike' gòliq 'kind of puppet'
m		patmí 'first wife' bismílla 'Moslem prayer'	límún 'carbonated drink'
n		sínuním 'synonym' harmuníka 'harmonica'	
r	R+arrán 'spiritless'	ríngit 'two and a half rupiahs' tiurí 'theory'	ka-rúsú-an 'riot'
l	lákka 'just' lá 'exclamation'	alíp 'Alif' úsallí 'pray' límún 'carbonated drink' laí 'slate' lít 'member'	lúsín 'dozen'
s		N-uŋsí 'evacuate' kuŋsí-an 'business group' risídèn 'resident' upsínər 'inspector' pinsíun 'retired' púlísí 'police' kupərasí 'cooperative' taksí 'taxi' sínuním 'synonym' úsúl 'suggestion'	ka-rúsú-an 'riot' súút 'good fortune' kasúsú 'hurried' súsú 'milk' palsú 'counterfeit'
h	háwa 'weather' sahádat 'Moslem confession of faith' R+lahá 'not work hard'		

	á à	í è	ú ò
w	hawà 'weather'		
	halwà 'halvah'		
	hiwàn 'animal'		
j	jàkin 'convinced'		rujòq 'take away'
	rujàl 'generous'		

ini- tial		ía 'yes'	úsallí 'pray'
		ící 'ten cents'	údur 'hindrance'
	bound	íntu	úsúl 'suggestion'
	pronominal	ímma	úmat 'community'
	morphemes	íssa	úmúm 'usual'
		ía	[taq] úsa '(not) necessary'

Following is a complete list of forms containing the special vowels é and
ó which occur in the corpus:

é	ó
antré 'line up'	bólà 'thread'
lutré 'lottery'	sópér 'chauffeur'
gózér 'bicycle tire'	sótó 'kind of soup'
kósér 'coachman'	tókó 'shop'
saté 'shish kabob'	dókar 'horse drawn carriage'
kúé 'cake'	gózér 'bicycle tire'
sópér 'chauffeur'	kósér 'coachman'
ganbér 'kind of snack'	radíó 'radio'
ɖónpét 'purse'	səpór 'railroad'
dhurén 'durian'	ɖónpét 'purse'
kélu 'kilometer'	sətróp 'syrup'
məsén 'machine'	píɖató 'speech'
əpél 'pill'	gincó 'rouge'
mahrép 'evening prayer'	manɖór 'foreman'
éslam 'evening prayer'	biskóp 'movies
ésa 'evening prayer'	sóri 'late afternoon'

Many of those given in the above lists have competing forms with alternating
or non-alternating vowels substituting for the special vowels. The following
list is not meant to be exhaustive:

special vowel	competing form(s)
kúé	kui 'cake'
lutré	lutri 'lottery'
saté	sati 'shish kabob'
ḍónpét, ḍònpét	ḍònpit 'purse'
kósér	kusir 'coachman'
ésa	ísa 'evening prayer'
gincó	gincú 'rouge'
sótó	sutu 'kind of soup'
tókó	tuku 'shop'
manḍór	manḍur, manḍòr 'foreman'

Segmental symbol clusters

A. Vowel clusters.

All but əV occur. For examples see below.

B. Consonant clusters.

1. Morpheme medial.

a. Geminates.

Any consonant but q can follow itself, i.e. can occur doubled. Such a sequence is a <u>geminate</u>. Geminated aspirates are written CCh, e.g. bbh, ggh. Phonetically these are long stops followed by aspiration, but they plainly pattern as the geminates of aspirates. Examples of geminates are given below in this appendix.

b. nC

There are a handful of examples of nasal plus stop clusters other than nC, e.g. taŋdhaŋ 'dance' (the competing form tandhaŋ also occurs). Some of these others are to be found below in this appendix.

There is also a root type - reduplicated monosyllable - e.g. baŋ+baŋ 'wing' which results in other nasal plus stop sequences. These will be discussed more fully in Chapter III.

c. $C_s C_r$

d. Other two symbol clusters.

Below are to be found all consonant clusters occurring in the corpus. Doubtless there are others which can be found in Kiliaan's dictionary but which did not appear in my sample.

e. Three symbol clusters.

$$nC_sC_r$$
$$str$$

2. Morpheme initial.

Initial consonant clusters occur in native words only as a result of the elision rules (see above, pages 31-33). A few other words exhibit initial C_sC_r clusters, e.g. prupagànḍa 'propaganda'; platína 'platinum'. Many speakers, however, insert the symbol a between the first two consonants of these words, e.g. palatína.

Consonant Clusters

pp	sappar	'name of a month'
pd	apdullà	'Abdullah'
pdh	apdhi	'slave'
ps	tapsíòn	'station'
pr	kapra	'usual'
pl	taplaq	'table-cloth'
br	tabràq	'collide'
bl	kíblàt	'direction of Mecca'
bhr	ghubhra	'become worse'
bbh	sabbhan	'each'
tt	sattu	'Saturday'
tr	sutra	'silk'
tm	patmí	'first wife'
dr	sadrika	'iron'
ddh	dhaddhi	'become'
ṭṭ	ṭaṭṭaŋ	'wide open'
ḍḍ	ḍaḍḍaŋ	'wide open'
ḍḍh	baḍḍha	'place'
cc	buccuq	'rotten'
zzh	azzhaq	'don't'
zhr	bhazhra	'lucky'
kk	pikkir	'think'

47

kt	bhakta	'carry'
ks	paksa	'force'
kj	pakjaq	'kind of sandal'
kn	pɛ́knɛ́k	'picnic'
gl	zigləm	'deep hole'
ggh	ghagghar	'fall'
ghr	aghrəm	'kind of snack'
ghl	zhughlaŋ	'ditch'
np	anpun	'already'
nb	anbu	'stop'
nbh	ghanbhar	'picture'
nt	tantu	'certain'
nd	undərnimən	'plantation'
ndh	mandhi	'effective'
nʈ	inʈiŋ	'light, easy'
nɖ	ənɖaq	'be willing'
nɖh	manɖhap	'low'
nc	ghancaŋ	'swift'
nz	banzir	'flood'
nzh	zhanzhi	'promise'
nk	sanka	'think, believe'
ng	gangu	'annoy'
ngh	sanghup	'promise'
nn	ɖinnaq	'here'
ns	bɛnsɪn	'gasoline'
mm	ɖhammaŋ	'light'
ññ	baññaq	'many'
ŋŋ	laŋŋiq	'sky'
ŋl	aŋlu	'sick'
ŋr	uŋrut	'perform in turn'
ŋs	kaŋsi	'until'
ht	ihtiar	'(way) of performing'
hl	ahlɪ	'expert, right person'
hr	mahrɛ́p	'evening prayer'
hj	cahja	'light'
qb	ghaqbur	'mix'

qḍ	saqḍəŋ	'dizzy'
qz	laqzun	'corpse'
ql	saqluj	'mix'
qm	maqmur	'prosperous'
qs	maqsiat	'forbidden by Islam'
qw	daqwa	'accuse'
sdh	lusdhuŋ	'jump out'
st	asta	'hand'
sṭ	masṭi	'must'
sz	maszit	'mosque'
sk	miskin	'poor'
sgh	masghi	'although'
sl	éslam	'Islam'
sr	asriŋ	'often'
sm	asma	'name'
sn	tarisna	'love'
ss	assin	'salty'
jj	majjit	'corpse'
ww	awwal	'beginning'
rp	sarpa	'garbage'
rb	kurba	'rinse'
rbh	kərbhuj	'water buffalo'
rt	arti	'meaning'
rd	sardin	'sardine'[17]
rḍ	marḍa	'hot coal'
rk	larkaŋ	'sharp edge'
rgh	argha	'price'
rc	parcaza	'believe'
rz	parzazi	'prijaji'
rzh	gharzhi	'tailor'
rl	parlu	'necessary'
rr	R+arrấn	'spiritless(ly)'
rm	dhurmas	'wash'
rn	barna	'color'
rŋ	arŋit	'rancid'
rq	kurqan	'Koran'
rs	bhərsi	'clean'

ld	kuldi	'larynx'
lp	alpuq	'crumbling'
lbh	dhilbhas	'throw down'
lz	mulza	'noble'
lk	pəlkaq	'thirsty'
lg	cəlgək	'gulp'
lgh	tulghəs	'branchless (tree)'
lm	calmut	'filthy'
ls	ghalsat	'scratch'
lw	halwa	'halvah'
lh	alhaŋ	'thirsty'
ll	ghallu	'previous(ly)'

The following list gives examples of reduplicated monosyllables ($C_1VC_2 + C_1VC_2$) producing clusters different from those found above:

təp+təp 'exact'		ɖaŋ+ɖaŋ	'eagle'
cap+cap 'drip'		maŋ+maŋ	'doubtful'
lat+lat 'spread'		ñiq+ñiq	'frayed'
bhət+bhət 'wrap around'		lus+lus	'release'
cək+cək 'house lizard'		ɖhil+ɖhil	'cut across grain'
zik+zik 'gallop'		ŋul+ŋul	'toothless'
kun+kun 'order'			

Three-consonant clusters are limited to nC_sC_r and str. Examples follow:

npl	canplaŋ	'tasteless'
nbr	anbri	'in order to'
ntr	təntrəm	'quiet'
nzhr	anzhra	'come frequently'
nkr	zhankrik	'cricket'
str	istri	'woman'

Following are examples of irregular C_nC:

tuŋtaŋ 'turn upside down'

karaʈuŋʈəŋ 'with no living relatives'

ɖanɖiŋ 'hum'

puŋpaŋ 'defy'

píŋpuŋ 'pingpong'

zhuŋzhaŋ 'push forward'

N-paʈuŋʈaŋ 'disobedient'

50

taŋdhaŋ 'dance'

Canonical Form

In the following discussion of canonical morphemic forms, elided, reduplicated, shortened, and compound forms are not considered. Reduplicated monosyllables and infixed reduplicated monosyllables are included, but plus juncture has
not been written in these examples. Bound morphemes are indicated by preceding
or following juncture symbols.

A. One syllable $(C_1)(V)(C_2)$

All of these, except for a few obvious borrowings, are particles and bound
morphemes.

      a. C   -n, -q 'extensions'

      b. V   i 'in', -a 'future'

      c. VC   -an 'suffix', is 'ice'

      d. CV   si 'which, who', -na 'his, her, its'

      e. CCV   pra 'pre-' (only in recently borrowed words)

      f. CVC   nəŋ 'in', san 'when', mun 'if', taq 'not'

B. Two syllables. $(C_1)V(C_5)(C_3)(C_4)V(C_2)$

The majority of root morphemes, and a few affixes are of this shape. These
will be divided into two subclasses:

1. With one or no medial consonant: $(C_1)V(C_4)V(C_2)$

      a. VV   ła 'yes', -ła 'here'

      b. CVV   sai 'good', pau 'mango', bau 'smell'

      c. VVC   aiŋ 'water', ias 'decorate', aup 'shady'

      d. VCV   apa 'what', uza 'chase away', -aghi 'a suffix'

      e. CVVC main 'play', zhaiq 'sew', buaŋ 'throw away'

      f. CVCV mata 'eye', ghula 'sugar', ghighi 'tooth'

      g. VCVC anaq 'child', iŋaq 'remember', ubaŋ 'money'

      h. CVCVC ghabaj 'make', kakan 'eat', taŋis 'weep'

      i. CC... Only as the result of elision.

51

2. With two or three medial consonants: $(C_1)V(C_5)C_3C_4V(C_2)$

   a. with medial geminate: matta 'ripe', cuccu 'stab repeatedly',
   sabbhar 'patient', dhaddhi 'become', ghallu 'previously',
   bugghik 'back', uddhi 'try', pissi 'money', luppa 'forget',
   laŋŋiq 'sky'

   b. nasal plus stop: bhəndər 'true', mantu 'son-in-law', sanghup
   'promise', səndhəŋ 'always', manzhəŋ 'to stand'

   c. clusters given above on pages 47-50: daqwa 'accuse', bhərsi
   'clean', bhakta 'carry', cahja 'light'

   d. reduplicated monosyllables: baŋbaŋ 'wing', təptəp 'exact',
   latlat 'spread', ñiqñiq 'frayed', kurkur 'scratch', səpsəp
   'suck', ŋulŋul 'toothless'

   e. d with vowel differences. Few of these occur: naŋniŋ 'kind of
   plant', puŋpaŋ 'defy', pɽŋpuŋ 'pingpong', zhuŋzhaŋ 'push forward'

   f. nasal plus stop plus liquid: anbri 'in order to', anzhra 'come
   frequently', zhankrik 'cricket'

   g. str: istri 'woman'

C. Three syllables. There are fewer of these than two syllable morphemes.

   1. The majority of three syllable morphemes are of the form
$(C_1)VC_xV(C_5)(C_3)C_4V(C_2)$ or $(C_1)V(C_5)(C_3)C_4VC_xV(C_2)$ where C_x equals C_n (nasals),
C_r (liquids), $_q$ (glottal stop), or $\emptyset$ (zero), and the vowel immediately preceding
C_x is /a/ or /u/. In other words, this is the same as the two syllable type with
an infixed VC_x either after the first consonant (first type) or before the last
vowel (second type).

   a. first type without cluster: calakaq 'accident', zhuraghan 'boat
   captain', cuməṭi 'whip', ghumighil 'malaria', gharaa 'eclipse'

   b. first type with cluster: sarunḍut 'fall over with sleepyness',
   kamuḍḍhi 'helm', kalanbu 'mosquito net', tarisna 'love', manussa
   'human being'

c. second type without cluster: kubhiri 'castrated', kubasa 'power'

d. second type with clusters: canḍila 'window', tanbhuru 'jealous', sanpian 'you'

e. type one or two: malulu 'only'

2. Many three syllable plant and animal names and onomatopoetic words begin with the syllable ka: kaluaŋ 'bat', kapiṭiŋ 'crab', kasunbha 'a plant (Bix Orellana)', kalətik 'coconut oil', karitik 'crackle', karusu 'rustling noise'.

3. Many three syllable forms beginning with ka have adjective-like meanings, but the remaining part of the word does not recur: katunḍu 'sleepy', katuruq 'leaking', kaunaŋ 'famous', katumu 'filthy'.

4. Similarly with ta: takiṭas 'late'.

5. Reduplicated monosyllables with infixed -al-, -ar-: tarəmtəm 'peaceful', dalaŋdaŋ 'tall and thin'.

6. Other than 1-5. Very few. ghanḍhiba 'bow', parcaza 'believe'.

D. Four syllable morphemes. Extremely few.

1. Borrowings from European languages (sometimes through Indonesian): prupagànḍa 'propaganda', kupɔ́rasi 'cooperative'.

2. Three syllable type plus affix where stem does not occur by itself: paliŋpiŋən 'deafened' (*paliŋpiŋ does not occur).

3. Others: muttiara 'pearl', kaniaza 'mistreat'.

Some Symbol Frequencies

The following lists show list frequencies for initial and final segmental symbols in Madurese roots. The initial list is based on some three thousand roots, the entire corpus. The final list is based on a sample of about eight hundred roots. Where percentages are the same, the absolute descending order has been kept (i.e. not rounded off).

53

	initial		final
s	10 o/o	a	18 o/o
k	9	q	14
t	8	ŋ	9
p	8	i	9
b	7	u	9
a	6	n	9
l	5	r	6
m	5	s	6
gh	4	k	6
bh	4	t	5
r	4	l	4
c	3	m	2
u	3	p	2
zh	2	j	less than 1 o/o
i	2		
dh	2		
ə	1		
ḍ	1		
z	1		
n	1		
g	1		
h	1		
ḍh	1		
ŋ	1		
ñ	less than 1 o/o		
d	"		
ṭ	"		
w	"		
j	"		

APPENDIX 4

Initial VV roots

The following are all the initial VV roots in the corpus and in Kiliaan's dictionary. Rule J-2 applies to these words and certain of their derivatives.

aiŋ	'water'
ain	'name of Arabic letter'
aip	'insult'
auŋ	'meow'
aup	'take shelter'
ia	'scream'
ias	'decorate'
iuŋ	'meow'
iəm	'whinny'
uiŋ	'nod head'
uit	'pry out'

The forms listed in the following table exemplify developments of all possible combinations through D_N, formulaically $V_1 D_N V_2$. The vowels in the left hand column are V_1 and the vowels at the head of the columns are V_2. For each vowel in the left hand column two sets of words are given. The first set has higher vowels and the second set has lower vowels. Each set is ordered as follows:

$$V_1 V_2$$
$$V_1 q V_2$$
$$V_1 r V_2$$
$$V_1 l V_2$$
$$V_1 s\text{-} V_2$$
$$V_1 j\text{-} V_2$$

n.e. means no example can be found for this cluster.

--- means the cluster is impossible.

The forms are in the intermediate stage just after the application of rule P-2.

a	i
a	báá 'flood'	bháí 'just'
ñàbáqá 'will place'	ŋaḍáqí 'to face'
báráq 'west'	ḍárí 'from'
bhálá 'family'	àbálí 'return'
páŋàbásán 'view'	ŋàbásí 'to look at'
pànghábáján 'work	n.e.
páàq 'chisel'	àèŋ 'water'
mókkàqá 'will open'	ŋànkàqè 'to serve (people)'
pàráq 'almost'	àrè 'day'
sálàŋ 'mutually'	màlèŋ 'thief'

56

	a	i
a	kəmàsàn 'gold-smith'	ŋàttàsè 'to overcome'
	pənàjjà 'his jar'	èpàsànpàjè 'be hung on a shelf'
i	ɖíá 'here'	ŋàzhíí 'to sell at a price'
	kàdhíbíqán 'alone'	ŋànghíqí 'to embroider'
	bíráŋ 'shy'	Ghírí 'name of a town'
	zhílá 'tongue'	àghílí 'to flow'
	ñàbísá 'will visit'	n.e.
	---	---
	cèà 'tasteless'	lèèr 'neck'
	kòpèqàn 'kite'	ñàkèqè 'to hurt (mentally)'
	tèràq 'glow'	mèrà 'red'
	kèlàp 'lightning'	pèlè 'choose'
	ŋèrèsà 'will slice'	èkàmàrèŋèsè 'is horrifying to'
	---	---
u	ghúá 'cave'	màbúí 'be silent'
	R+òngúqán 'keep nodding'	àbhúndhúqí 'wrap up'
	zhúráŋ 'valley'	ghúríŋ 'fry'
	búlán 'moon'	ghúlí 'movement'
	kàbhághúsán 'goodness'	nəbhúsí 'ransom back'
	ŋànghújá 'will use'	ŋànghújí 'to use'
	tòà 'old'	màssòè 'to wash'
	tàkòqà 'will be afraid'	sòqè 'the more...'
	kòràŋ 'less'	òrèŋ 'person'
	pòlà 'perhaps'	pòlè 'again'
	pàŋàntòsàn 'waiting place'	ŋàpòsè 'to cajole'
	àpòjjà 'his fire'	ŋàpòjè 'to urge on, fire up'
ə	---	---
	---	---
	bə́ráq 'heavy'	àbə́ríq 'to give'
	bə́lá 'split'	bə́lí 'buy'
	bə́lə́sán 'answer'	èbə́lə́sí 'be answered'
	---	---
	---	---
	---	---
	pəràŋ 'war'	sərèŋ 'often'
	kəlàs 'class'	məlè 'to buy'

57

     a   i

	a		i
ə	bátəssá 'its border'		màləsè 'to answer'
	---		---
	u		ə
a	bháɗ 'smell'		R+búzáən 'spotted with water stains'
	n.e.		R+pəgháqən 'keep on breaking'
	zhárúm 'needle'		bhárəŋ 'servant'
	bálún 'cotton'		ɗáləm 'inside'
	---		n.e.
	---		n.e.
	pàð 'mango'		pàcàcàən 'talkative'
	n.e.		n.e.
	pàrò 'half'		sàrəŋ 'with'
	màlò 'ashamed'		màləm 'night'
	---		n.e.
	---		---
i	aɗíút 'wave (vb.)'		ɗíəm 'silent'
	n.e.		kàbháríqən 'very early'
	bhírú 'green'		pàləghírən 'amusement'
	àbhílúk 'to turn'		bíləs 'ant'
	---		n.e.
	---		---
	cèòm 'kiss'		èəm 'whinny'
	n.e.		kàsàkònèqən 'too little'
	tèròn 'faded'		tèrəp 'extinguished'
	cèlòq 'sour'		sèlləm 'sink'
	---		n.e.
	---		---
u	dhúúm 'distribute'		ɗhúəs 'roar (wind)'
	---		n.e.
	búrú 'to run'		ghúrəm 'kind of ant'
	búlú 'body hair'		ɗúləmànnà 'day before yesterday'
	---		n.e.
	---		n.e.
	tòòt 'knee'		R+bənkòən 'wins on home ground (of cock)'
	---		n.e.
	tòròn 'descend'		kòrən 'group (of houses)'
	pòlò 'island'		n.e.
	---		n.e.

	u	ə
u	---	n.e.
ə	---	---
	---	---
	zhə́rǔk 'citrus fruit'	ghə́rə́m 'molar'
	bə́lǔq 'eel'	ghə́lə́m 'to want'
	---	kàpə̀ḍhə̀sə́n 'very highly spiced'
	---	---
	---	---
	---	---
	tə̀rð 'want to'	lə̀rə̀s 'correct'
	pə̀lð 'sweat'	cə̀lə̀ŋ 'black'
	---	kàmàlə̀sə́n 'very lazy'
	---	---

The following table shows the effect of P-1 rules across $D_{N_1}D_{N_2}$, that is across clusters of D_N.

n.e. means no example occurs in the corpus, and X indicates an impossible combination. The syllables concerned are underlined for the sake of clarity.

	r	l	q	-s	-j
r	ghǔb<u>hárrá</u> 'his going home'	<u>pàrlð</u> 'need'	<u>kòrqàn</u> 'Koran'	X	X
l	n.e.	<u>ghállǔ</u> 'before'	n.e.	X	X
q	<u>ḍáqrámmà</u> 'how'	<u>sàqlòj</u> 'mix'	X	X	X
s-	X	X	X	bhá<u>ghǔssá</u> 'its goodness'	X
j-	X	X	X	X	kə̀r<u>bhǔjjá</u> 'his water-buffalo'

Some examples of $D_H V_1 D_{N_1} V_2 D_{N_2} V_3$ are given below; in these, the P-1 rules are effective across three syllables:

baariq → <u>bááríq</u> 'yesterday'

gharaa → gháráá 'eclipse'

bhurus-na → bhurus-sa → bhúrússá 'his dog'

zha-lauq → zháláúq 'to the south'

APPENDIX 6

Elisions

The following lists give examples of words which undergo elisions.   *indicates a rare or unsure elision.

1) $CVC_r \rightarrow CC_r$

<u>l</u>   <u>r</u>

p	palappa 'spices'	pariksa 'examine'
b	balandha 'Dutch'	baramma 'how'
bh	bhaləŋər 'naughty'	bharana 'to get worse'
t	taləkən 'service for dead'	tarima 'receive'
d	d-al-aŋ+daŋ 'tall and thin'	darigu 'flour'
dh	dhalima 'pomegranate'	dharami-an 'rice stalk'
ḍ		a-ḍarakkaŋ 'with feet wide apart[16]
c	calaṭṭuŋ 'manure'	carita 'story'
z	zaliṭən 'black w. dirt'	zarukkuŋ 'sit with raised knees'
zh	zhaluzzhuq 'stuttering'	a-zh-ar-ək+zhək-an 'stand around'
k	kalanbhi 'upper garment'	karitik 'crackle'
g	galinḍiŋ 'roll'	R+garudus 'too quickly'
gh	ghalaḍhak 'bridge'	ghə̀ruŋ-an 'throat'
m	malarat 'miserable'	marə̀nəs 'to grumble'
n	nalika-na 'when'	narima 'to receive'
ñ	ñalaṭak 'disorderly'	ñarupuq 'pimpled'
ŋ	ŋaləñər 'uncomfortable feeling (in throat)'	ŋarusu 'roaring noise'
s	salamət 'safe'	sərina 'because'

61

2) $CVC_n \rightarrow CC_n$

	$\underline{m}$	$\underline{n}$	$\underline{\tilde{n}}$	$\underline{\eta}$
p		punapa 'what'	*pa-ñakit†	
t	*tamuni 'afterbirth'	tanikər 'marble'		taŋiri 'kind of fish'
dh		*dhaniliŋ 'crazy'		
c	camara 'Casuarina'			
z	zumandil+awwal 'name of a month'	zanila 'window (rarely used)'		
k	kamiri 'kind of nut'	*kaniaza 'mistreat'		
gh	*ghumighil 'malaria'			
s	sa-mankin 'now'	sanapan 'rifle'		saŋaza 'purposely'

3) $CVC_G \rightarrow CC_G$

The examples given below have been developed from CiV and CuV by rule P-9.

	$\underline{i}$	$\underline{w}$
p	pèjàrà 'take care of'	pòwàsà 'fast'
b	bíjásá 'common'	
k	kèjàè 'Moslem leader'	kòwàcí 'kind of nut'
m	mèjàrà 'to take care of'	mòwàrà 'river mouth'
s		sòwàrà 'voice'

4) $CVC_s \rightarrow CC_s$

	dental	velar
s	*sa-tia 'now'	sakucí 'sloop'
		*sa-ghamiq 'twenty five'

† From paŋ-sakit

62

APPENDIX 7

Orthography

The main differences between the transcription used here and present day
Madurese orthography are as follows:

1. For the most part higher and lower alternants of vowels are written out.
Both alternants of /a/ are written a, however.

symbol	alternant	orthography	example	
			transcription	orthography
i	í	i	bhiru	biru 'green'
i	è	è (or é)	pili	pèlè 'choose'
u	ú	u	buru	buru 'run'
u	ò	o	pulu	polo 'island'
a	á	a^{21}	baba	baba 'under'
a	à	a	mata	mata 'eye'
ə	ɔ́	e	kubhəŋ	kobeng 'around'
ə	ə̀	e	nəŋ	neng 'in'
é		è (or é)	kósér	kosèr 'driver'
ó		o	kósér	kosèr 'driver'

2. Gemination is always written out. For example, bəli is spelled belli
'buy'.

3. Nasal plus stop is always written out as generated. For example, anpun
is spelled ampon 'already'.

4. Generated j and w are always written out except when between prefix and
root. For example:

transcription	orthography
siaŋ	sèjang 'daylight'
suara	sowara 'voice'
N-bəli-aghi	mellèjagi 'to buy'

5. In handwritten and typewritten Madurese no distinction is usually made

63

between dental and alveolar stops; they are both written t, d, dh. In printed Madurese alveolar stops are usually sub-dotted as in the present transcription.

6. No distinction is now made between voiced and aspirated stops; they are all written b, d, ḍ, dj respectively. Before 1940 they were distinguished as they are here, the aspirated stops being written with voiced stop plus h. Some people still continue this practice.

transcription	orthography
baba	baba 'under'
bhabhar	babar 'to give birth'
baza	badja 'grandchild'
bazha	badja 'steel'
bhaza	badja 'crocodile'

7. Individual symbols and clusters:

transcription	orthography	example transcription	orthography
ŋ	ng	uriŋ	orèng 'person'
ŋŋ	ngng	laŋŋiq	langngè' 'sky'
c	tj	caca	tjatja 'talk'
z	dj	zikar	djikar 'wagon'
zh	dj	zhalan	djalan 'road'
zzh	ddj	azzhaq	addja' 'don't'
zz	ddj	nazzan	naddjan 'although'
ñ	nj	ñata	njata 'clear'
ññ	nnj	baññaq	bannja' 'much'
q	'	kuliq	kolè' 'skin'
		liir	lè'èr 'neck'
		i-pati-i	èpatè'è 'be killed'

As can be seen from the last two examples, glottal stop is written when generated except when it occurs between prefix and root. However, it is written when it is part of a reduplication, e.g. R+bua-an is spelled wa'-buwa'an 'fruits'.

8. Results of J-Rules are written out.

transcription	orthography
uruk-a	orogha or oroga 'will add'
bhutuk-na	bhutoggha or butogga 'his fertilizer'

9. A hyphen is placed between the reduplicated syllable or syllables of R
and Rt and what follows.

	transcription	orthography
	R+aliq	lè'-alè' 'younger siblings'
	a-R+taña	anja-tanja 'keep on asking'
	Rtm+bua-an	buwa'-buwa'an 'fruits'
	Rtw+sakula-an	sakola'an-sakola'an 'schools'

Sometimes a raised ^{2} is used for Rt reduplications. For example, buwa'^{2}an;
sakola'an^2.

FOOTNOTES

1. See M. Halle, <u>The Sound Pattern of Russian</u> 19-75, ('s Gravenhage, 1959),
The Strategy of Phonemics, <u>Word</u> 10.197-209 (1954) and N. Chomsky and M.
Halle, <u>The Sound Pattern of English</u> (New York, 1968). The literature on
this subject has become too long to list in its entirety.

2. Jakobson, Fant, and Halle, Preliminaries to Speech Analysis, the distinctive
features and their correlates, <u>MIT Acoustics Laboratory</u>, <u>Technical Report</u>
#13 (May, 1952).

3. This has been recognized in the Chomsky and Halle work mentioned in fn. 1.
For example, Madurese has five stop positions (labial, dental, alveolar,
palatal, and velar). This apparently cannot be handled by the distinctive
feature method as presented so far. In personal communications Halle has
suggested that alveolar be treated as retroflex, but this is neither phonetically accurate, nor could this feature be used elsewhere in the language.

   For other objections to this approach see: Y. Bar-Hillel, Three
Methodological Remarks on Fundamentals of Language, <u>Word</u> 13.323-34 (1957)
and C. Ferguson, review of Halle, The Sound Pattern of Russian, <u>Language</u>
38.284-97 (1962).

4. For earlier remarks on this subject see: K. Pike, Grammatical Prerequisites
to Phonemic Analysis, <u>Word</u> 3.155-72 (1947) and K. Pike, More on Grammatical
Prerequisites, <u>Word</u> 8.106-21 (1952).

5. For a discussion of biuniqueness and related topics see N. Chomsky, <u>Current
Issues in Linguistic Theory</u> 78ff (The Hague, 1964).

6. C. Fries and K. Pike, Coexistent Phonemic Systems, <u>Language</u> 25.29-50 (1949).

7. B. Bloch, Phonemic Overlapping, <u>American Speech</u> 16.278-84 (1941), reprinted
in M. Joos (ed.), <u>Readings in Linguistics</u>, 93-96 (Washington, 1957).

8. For discussions of morphemes and cutting see pages 69-70.

9. Since loan words not occurring in the corpus or new loan words may appear,
    one can only approximate the number of foreign sounds.

10. There can be no ambiguity since the cluster consonant plus h does not other-
    wise occur without intervening juncture. Geminated aspirates (C_aC_a) will be
    written CCh. For example, bbh, ddh, ggh.

11. Loan words are usually characterized by a special set of vowels (non-alter-
    nating or special) and/or by foreign consonants. There are, however,
    borrowed words which are only detectable by comparative, historical, or
    extra-linguistic means. These are generally not under consideration here.

12. My corpus consists of approximately three thousand roots and their deriva-
    tives. It is difficult to say however what percentage of the entries in
    Kiliaan's dictionary would fit this statement, since many specifically West
    Madurese words are included, and this dialect has a lot more loan words than
    the dialect being considered here. A guess is that ninety percent would
    still require only the four vowels under discussion.

13. The terms alternating and non-alternating were chosen since the former show
    their typical alternating vowel qualities in morphophonemic alternations as
    well as elsewhere. For a discussion of the similar problems raised by loan
    words in Turkish, see: R. B. Lees, The Phonology of Modern Standard Turkish
    10-15 (= vol. 6 Uralic and Altaic Series) (Indiana University, 1961) and the
    review of it by K. E. Zimmer, Word 21.126-8 (1965).

14. The existence of a contrastive ə is doubtful. It does not occur in the
    corpus, and it would be difficult to say where it could be borrowed from.
    It is included here to indicate that the slot is ready should a loan con-
    taining it occur. Non-alternating ɔ́ occurs in some Indonesian words, e.g.
    kupɔ́rasɩ → [kɔpə̂rasi] 'cooperative'. Also, contrary to Madurese rules
    (P-3 below) the r of this word was not geminated by my bilingual informants.

15. The location of stress is largely, perhaps completely, predictable in terms

of syntax and internal intonation. This must await further work.

16. One doubtful case occurs in the corpus. As a result of the elision rule
    (P-12) a-ɖrakkaŋ appears in my notes from a-ɖarakkaŋ 'with wide spread feet',
    but I did not take careful note of this at the time.

17. One possible example of this is sardin or sarɖin 'sardine'. I am unsure
    which is the correct form or, in fact, whether there is any contrast be-
    tween dental and alveolar stop after r. The word marɖa 'live coal'
    definitely contains a phonetic alveolar stop, but sardin is the only possi-
    ble, but unsure, case of r plus dental.

18. Although this rule has the same junctures on both sides of the arrow, they
    are word junctures and therefore it is not located in the J-Rules. This
    rule must be located here since the ê qualities must be known.

19. The qualities of á gave early Dutch writers on Madurese a great deal of
    difficulty. Some of them described it as a high front rounded vowel! Only
    Kiliaan (1:19f) clearly understood its phonetic nature.

20. But never as high as ə.

21. Rarely written ǎ. Sometimes written å in the Dutch literature on Madurese.

CHAPTER III

MORPHOLOGY I

Elements

Morphology is the study of words and their constituent elements. Word, in Madurese, can be defined in terms of junctures and of initial and final elements. The Madurese word is enclosed between word (#) junctures in the following environment:

$$\cdot \left| \left\{ \begin{matrix} \text{(suffix)} \\ \text{(extension)} \end{matrix} \right\} \# \text{ word} \# \left\{ \begin{matrix} \text{(Prefix)} \\ \text{(proclitic)} \\ \text{(extension)} \end{matrix} \right\} \right|$$

where the suffix or extension is part of the preceding word and the prefix, proclitic, or extension is part of the following word.

There are also limitations on what elements occur at the beginning or end of a word in Madurese, e.g. only roots or a listable number of extensions and suffixes occur as the final element in a Madurese word.

A minimum component of a word is a root, affix, extension, or proclitic. Maximally a word consists of affixes plus extensions, plus proclitics, plus roots.

The terms affix and extension are defined by lists given below. Proclitics are a finite number of elements which are joined to what follows by either word or dot juncture. They are therefore independent words or, in fast speech, part of a larger word. All proclitics are listed below. A root is the form left when all affixes, extensions, and proclitics have been stripped from it, e.g. in i-pa-N-bəli-aghi 'to be bought for' i-, pa-, N-, and -aghi are affixes and bəli 'buy' is the root.

Many affixes, extensions, or parts of affixes of the same shape behave the same way in respect to other elements in the same word. These affixes, exten-sions, or partial affixes will be called <u>affix-forms</u>.[1] For example, affix-form pa- consists of several affixes: 'noun former; causative verbal', among others, as well as part of such affixes as pa- -an 'locational noun', and R+N-pa- 'to pretend to'. Similarly the affix-form N- consists of among others 'active tran-sitive; various intransitive affixes; basic stem marker' and is part of, for example, N- -i 'to act like, look like'.

It is in the above respect that the present approach to the morphology is most similar to the approach to the phonology presented above, i.e. affix-forms and phonologic symbols both ignore to some extent considerations of contrast and are grouped according to form and behavior in respect to adjacent elements or symbols.

Cutting has been done with a view to separating by junctures all recurrent partials except where they are unique cases, e.g. baɖa 'there is'; taɖaq 'there isn't'; taq 'not' and ari 'day'; baariq 'yesterday', or not clear as in some paradigmatic sets of substitutes, e.g. apa, napi, punapa 'what' (different style levels); sapa, sira, pasira 'who' (same style levels respectively).

Submorphemic analysis

Roots

Some roots occur without cooccurring overt non-roots (affixes, extensions, or proclitics). Such a root will be regarded as containing a null affix (<u>not</u> a zero affix).[2] Examples follow:

> anaq 'child'
> pəɖhaŋ 'sword'
> ənəm 'six'
> ɖatəŋ 'to come'
> intar 'to go'

Other roots occur only if accompanied by some overt non-root. For example:[3]

root	example derivative
bəlas	bəlas-an 'teens'
atus	nəm.atus 'six hundred'
assa	N-assa-i 'to wash'
alun	R+alun 'town square'[4]

The majority of Madurese roots conform to the shapes outlined above (Appendix 3). There exist a few roots in the form of reduplicated monosyllables which contain clusters which are in contrast to the homorganic nasal quality rules given above, e.g. baŋbaŋ 'wing' instead of the expected *banbaŋ → *bámbáŋ. However, in other respects they do not act like reduplicated words; for instance, like other roots they occur reduplicated, e.g. R+baŋbaŋ 'wings'. The placing of the affix N- is also different from that of other words containing reduplications, e.g. reduplicated R+N-kalaq 'to keep on taking' as opposed to N-capcap 'to drip'. The latter in turn can be reduplicated to form R+N-capcap 'to keep on dripping'. Reduplicated monosyllables will be written out in full with a plus juncture between the syllables,[5] for example:

> baŋ+baŋ 'wing'
> bhət+bhət 'wrap around'
> cap+cap 'drip'
> zhuŋ+zhuŋ 'lift up'
> kun+kun 'order'

A small number of reduplicated monosyllable roots have -ar- or -al- infixed immediately after the first consonant of the first syllable. For example:

> b-ar-iŋ+biŋ 'stand on end (hair)'
> d-al-aŋ+daŋ 'tall and thin'
> s-al-at+sat 'skip over the water'
> t-ar-ip+tip 'front part of the house'
> t-ar-əm+təm 'peaceful'
> zh-ar-ək+zhək 'stand around'

A few roots are incompletely reduplicated monosyllables with vowel variation of the form $C_1uC_2+C_1aC_2$. Only three occur in the corpus:

> ɖhuk+ɖhak 'broken down'

71

luq+laq 'talk brokenly'

suŋ+saŋ 'upside down'[6]

There are a few cases of other vowel variation:

ɖaŋ+ɖiŋ 'hum'

piŋ+puŋ 'pingpong'

There are a few words whose roots are in doubt, i.e. there are not enough

forms to determine the root unambiguously. For example:

paŋanzhur 'hunter' where the root is *anzhur, *ŋanzhur
    or *kanzhur preceded by the prefix paŋ- 'agent'.

pañaras 'check' where the root is *caras, *saras or
    *ñaras preceded by the same prefix as in the last
    example. cf. paŋ-anbhuŋ 'nose' with the root
    anbhuŋ 'smell'.

In other cases the underlying form is clear, but it does not occur in other

environments.[7] For example:

panzhalin 'rattan', but *zhalin does not occur elsewhere.

matalaŋŋaghi 'to buy (something for someone else)', but
    *talaŋ does not occur elsewhere.

<u>Root variants</u>

A given root may be associated with one or more other roots which are

similar in shape and meaning. Many of these are competing forms or originally

dialectal forms now also used in East Madura. In some cases there has been

specialization of meaning.

1. Sound symbolism.

    a. Already mentioned in the phonology is the case of West Madurese:

    u...u or i...i 'ordinary degree of the quality'

    R+ú...ú or R+í...í 'high degree of the quality'.

For example:

kiniq 'small'

R+kiníq 'very small'

Such forms, however, are not in general use in the standard dialect. A similar alternation occurs in Javanese, and this may have been borrowed by West Madurese.

   b. Not restricted to one dialect are cases of:

   i...i 'lesser degree'
   u...u 'higher degree'
   galindiŋ 'roll (of something small)'
   galunduŋ 'roll (of something large)'
   maniqniŋ 'swollen (to a small degree)'
   manuqnuŋ 'swollen (to a large degree)'

No cases containing only a single vowel occur.

2. Competing and specialized forms.

   a. About 25 roots in the corpus have variants with final glottal stop or with final stop (p, t, k). For the most part these are competing forms, the variant ending in glottal stop being more common, but in some cases there has been specialization of meaning. With several exceptions the stop variant occurs only before a suffix, and not as word final.

q	p
udiq 'live'	
N-udiq-i 'to kindle (fire)'	par-udip-an 'kindling'
ucaq 'say'	
ka-ucaq-a 'once upon a time'	ka-ucap-a 'once upon a time'

q	t
kuliq 'skin'	N-kulit 'to skin (something)'
bəraq 'heavy'	
ka-bəraq-an 'with difficulty'	ka-bərat-an 'faeces'[8]
buaq 'load'	
N-buaq 'be loaded'	N-buat 'be loaded'
	buat-an 'load (noun)'
zhaiq 'sew'	
zhaiq-an 'sewing'	zhait-an 'sewing'

<u>q</u>	<u>k</u>
anaq 'child'	pa-r-anak-an 'womb'
tariq 'pull'	tarik 'taut'
N-tariq 'to pull'	N-tarik 'to pull taut'

b. Some roots have variants with medial ss and cc.

bassu	baccu	'wash'
assin	accin	'salty'
assəm	accəm	'tamarind'

One case of single s varying with single c also occurs.

lisəŋ	licəŋ	'black on bottom of pot'

c. Some roots have initial Cu varying with Ca. With a few exceptions the former are more usual in East Madurese.

cuməṭi	caməṭi	'whip'
kubhiri	kabhiri	'castrated'
kucanba	kacanba	'shelled peas'[9]
kuciba	kaciba	'disappointed'
punapa	panapa	'what'
lumari	lamari	'wardrobe'
sumili	samili	'although'

One variant root seems to have developed to a redupicated form. R+sapu → pu+sapu 'brush' (root: sapu 'wipe', R+ 'instrument') with the variant pasapu 'brush'.

d. A few roots have initial V varying with initial mV.

uŋəl	muŋəl	'voice'
ənkin	mənkin	'later'
ənəm	mənəm (rare form)	'six'

e. Two roots beginning in bh have variants with a prefixed san.

bhazaŋ	sanbhazaŋ	'pray'
bhəli	sanbhəli	'slaughter'

f. Some particles and pronouns have variants with initial a.

naŋiŋ	anaŋiŋ	'but'
rua	arua	'that'
ria	aria	'this'

g.   There are also many non-recurring types of variation.

initial consonant

curik	kurik 'match'
ghənḍhi	kənḍhi 'jar'
ñiḍḍha	ŋiḍḍha 'sound (asleep)'
ñəlu	ŋəlu 'have a headache'
zhəbhiŋ	cəbhiŋ 'young girl'
ukkal	bukkal 'open up'
urup	purup 'exchange'
asra	pasra 'hand over'
addhək	paddhək 'build'
panḍi	manḍi (substandard) 'bathe'

medial consonant

calun	callun 'candidate'
dhibiq	dhiriq 'self'
ḍhimin	ḍhiŋin 'beforehand'
ruba	rupa 'shape'
paturuq	panturuq 'have someone buy (something)'

medial vowel

təkuq	təkiq 'gecko'
ḍhinḍha	ḍhənḍha 'fine'
panḍaq	pinḍaq 'short'
linka	lanka 'step'
linghi	lunghu 'sit'

More than two variants

ḍiccil	ḍuccul	ḍiccal 'loosen'	
ghaluḍuq	kaluḍuq	ghaluñuq 'swallow'	
ghanḍhiŋ	bhanḍhiŋ	tanḍhiŋ 'compare'	
ammaŋ	nammaŋ	ḍhammaŋ 'light (weight)'	
maski	masghu	masghi	makki 'although'
ghallu	dhallu	ghillu	dhillu 'beforehand'

Extensions[10]

Extensions are single symbols without clear meaning immediately prefixed or suffixed to the root. They are in contrast or free variation[11] with their absence. They will be called contrastive extensions and free variation extensions respectively.

Extensions are phonologically part of the root since they always reduplicate with the root (see rules above). In the following examples the extension has been underlined for ease of reading:

R+ghiba-n̲ → bán̲+ghíbán̲ 'gift'
R+N-asta-n̲-i → tán̲+ŋàstán̲è 'to hold (a job)'

The extensions are grouped into three affix-forms: k-, q-, and -n. In the following examples the root has also been given:

k-   anaq 'offspring'   R+k-anaq 'child' in contrast
    to R+anaq 'offspring (pl.)'.

q-[12]   əla 'already'   sa-q-əla-na 'after' in free
    variation with sa-əla-na 'after'.

        ənəŋ 'stay'   i-pa-q-ənəŋ 'given a place to
    stay' in contrast to i-pa-ənəŋ 'made to keep quiet'.

-n   sari 'sleep'   a-sari-n 'to sleep' in free
    variation with a-sari 'to sleep'

        təmu 'meet'   a-R+təmu-n 'to meet (by pre-
    arranged plan)' in contrast to a-R+təmu 'to meet (by accident)'.

        paru 'half'   i-pa-paru-n 'to be sharecropped'
in contrast to i-pa-paru 'to be divided in half'.[13]

Other elements of the same shape and behaving the same way as extensions are in complementary distribution with their absence, i.e. the extended form of the root is in complementation with the unextended form, or with some affix-form, e.g. k- with ka- and -n with -an. These elements, which will be called complementary extensions, are: r-, k-, q-, -n. The last three will be regarded as belonging to the same affix-forms as the extensions of the same shape respectively. The first element in the list, r-, is an affix-form of its own. Like extensions, they reduplicate along with the root. Examples follow:

r-

anaq 'child'   N-pa-r-anaq-i 'deliver a child'
        i-ka-r-anaq-i 'be brought up'

r-

apa 'what'   a-r-apa 'how'

                  i-ka-r-apa 'done what to?'

k-

ənɖaq 'want'   i-k-ənɖaq-i 'be wanted'

                    ка- -i 'transitive former'

asi 'love'   Rf+k-asi 'favorite'

q-

ɬa 'yes'   i-q-ɬa-i 'be agreed to'

                  pa-q-ɬa-na 'his agreeing'

-n

dhuka 'anger'   i-dhuka-n-i 'be angered at'

                    -i 'transitive former'

cina 'Chinese'   pa-cina-n 'Chinese quarter'

                  pa- -an 'locational noun'

Proclitics

All proclitics are particles,[14] and most of them are monosyllabic. Several proclitics (ɖaq 'to', and taq 'not') are of such a shape that their behavior with respect to a following word cannot be determined solely on the grounds of the phonologic rules of the preceding chapter. These words have been assigned to the class of proclitics for other reasons: both taq and ɖaq act like proclitics in respect to a following word beginning with (ə)[15] and taq is also stem-forming.[16] The following proclitics occur:[17]

ka 'to'	namuŋ 'only'
zhuŋ '-er'	naŋiŋ 'but'
ban 'and'	mun 'if, when'
san 'when'	taŋ 'my'
ghan 'up to'	saŋ 'my'
niŋ 'only'	taq 'not'
nəŋ 'in'	ɖaq 'to'
miq 'perhaps'	pas 'then'
salaŋ 'mutual'	i 'in, at'

Certain forms of the numbers are also proclitic.

Affixes and affix-forms

Affixes are of four kinds: prefixes, which appear before the root; infixes, which appear immediately after the first consonant of the root; suffixes, which appear after the root; and circumfixes, part of which occurs before and part after the root. Examples follow:

	affix	root
prefix:	a-rassa 'to feel'	rassa 'feel'
	paŋ-təmu 'opinion'	təmu 'meet'
	ta-bassa 'very wet'	bassa 'wet'
infix:	gh-um-antuŋ 'to depend'	ghantuŋ 'hang'
	zh-al-imət 'be quiet'	zhimət 'be quiet'
suffix:	kuniŋ-an 'brass'	kuniŋ 'yellow'
	bhərsi-i 'clean!'	bhərsi 'clean'
	bəli-aghi 'buy (for someone)!'	bəli 'buy'
circum-fix:	ka-baḍa-an 'situation'	baḍa 'there is'
	pa-bhaku-an 'tobacconist'	bhaku 'tobacco'
	ka-kuriŋ-ən 'be too little'	kuriŋ 'not enough'

Morphophonemics

This section gives the rules or lists for alternations which are not handled by the J-Rules and P-Rules of Chapter II.

Roots

1. Some dissyllabic roots of the form $əC_1V(C_2)$ become $C_1V(C_2)$ under conditions which are not entirely clear.[18] It is interesting to note that most of the roots which act this way are obvious recent borrowings. Besides this type there are two roots: əla 'already' and ənəm 'six' which lose their initial ə under unique conditions. Following is the list of roots in the corpus which lose initial ə:

əbàŋ 'bank'	əgàs 'gas'
əpak 'pack'	əlis 'lesson'
əsak 'pocket'	əpis 'plague'
əzas 'jacket'	əmas 'gold'

əzắs 'jacket'   ərim 'brake'
əpếl 'pill'   əsiŋ 'zinc'
əkar 'map'   ət̪i 'tea'
əlap 'cloth'   əcap 'print'
əlˤt 'member'   əcit 'paint'
əsip 'boss'

In the examples given below, such roots will be referred to as (ə) roots.

As far as can be determined, the rules for (ə) roots are as follows; these rules are not ordered:

    a. q.(ə) → q.ə <u>or</u> → -q

Thus, in this environment ə is in free variation with zero. For example:

    ɖaq.(ə)bàŋ → daq.əbàŋ; or → ɖaq.bàŋ 'to the bank'.

    b. For some words, a preceding proclitic ending in the symbol a develops a glottal stop, whereupon in some cases the (ə) → zero, but in other cases it more frequently → ə. For example:

    ka.(ə)bàŋ → ka-q.(ə)bàŋ → kaq.bàŋ 'to the bank'

    sa.(ə)zham → sa-q.(ə)zham → saq.zham 'one hour'

    sa.(ə)sak → sa-q.(ə)sak → usually saq.əsak; → (rarely)
        saq.sak 'one pocket'.

The extent to which these two types occur is not clear. An example also occurs before a non-(ə) root after the proclitic sa. 'one':

    sa.kếlu → sa-q.kếlu → saq.kếlu 'one kilogram'.

    c. In some words, in fast speech, the consonant after the (ə) is doubled with loss of (ə) after the proclitic numbers ending in a vowel. For example:

    sa.(ə)zham → sazzham 'one hour'[19]
    ɖu.(ə)zham → ɖuzzham 'two hours'
    sa.(ə)pak → (rarely) sappak 'one pack'
    sa.(ə)sak → (rarely) sassak 'one pocket'

    d. (ə) becomes zero or ə after pause (including any internal intonation involving pause). For example:

79

(ə)zham-na i-pa-bəciq. → zham-na i-pa-bəciq; or → əzham-na
i-pa-bəciq. 'His clock has been fixed.'

e. The corpus, however, shows some cases of (ə) → zero in other environments than those listed above. The conditioning factor or factors in these examples are not clear. Perhaps loss of (ə) is always possible in rapid speech.

N-turuq (ə)zham paŋ-azhar-an → N-turuq zham paŋ-azhar-an,
or N-turuq əzham paŋ-azhar-an 'to follow the lesson
hours'.

paŋ-sakit (ə)pis → paŋ-sakit pis 'the plague'
untal (ə)pél → untal pél 'swallow a pill'
miññaq (ə)gas → miññaq gàs 'kerosene'
N-pa-kakan (ə)rim → N-pa-kakan rim 'to apply the brakes'
R+(ə)zham-an → R+zham-an, or → R+əzham-an 'for hours and hours'

f. The special case of ənəm 'six' will be treated under the morphology of the numbers (see below page 199).

g. əla 'already' is an unclear special case. Loss of initial ə occurs after dot juncture, after pause, and after many full words in fast speech. For example:

mun.la 'when already'
la paraq 'already almost'
sumili-a la 'although already'

Since the conditioning of (ə) roots is not clear, in the examples given from now on they will be written as they appear in the corpus.

2. The names of two of the directions have alternate forms after the prefix ZA- 'in the..., to the...'.

Form in isolation	ZA-
timur 'east'	za-dhimur 'in the east'
ḍaza 'north'	zha-raza 'in the north'

3. A finite number of roots have forms which are in complementary distribution with the form cooccurring with one of the complementary extensions k-, r-, q-, -n. Examples follow:

root		extended form	sample derivation
r-	anaq 'child'	r-anaq	i-ka-r-anaq-i 'be brought up'
	apa 'what'	r-apa	a-r-apa 'how'
k-	əmas 'gold'	k-əmas	pa-k-əmas-an 'gold smithy'
	ucaq 'say'	k-ucaq	i-k-ucaq-aghi 'be said'
q-	ɩa 'yes'	q-ɩa	i-q-ɩa-i 'be agreed to'
-n	dhuka 'anger'	dhuka-n	i-dhuka-n-i 'be angered at'

4. Miscellaneous. The allomorphs appearing below occur only in the given derivative:

root	derivative
anaq 'child'	R+ənaq-an 'doll'
uriŋ 'person'	ka-s.uraŋ 'one person, alone'

5. A few roots show optional close juncture with a preceding R, proclitic, or word. The roots involved are: aḍaq 'front', agghu or lagghu 'morning',[20] and agghiq or lagghiq 'more, in addition'. For example:

R+agghu-q → ghúqàgghúq 'in the future'
R-agghu-q → ghúqágghúq 'in the future'

R+aḍaq → ḍáqàḍáq 'at first'
R-aḍaq → ḍáqáḍáq 'at first'

ḍua-q agghiq → ḍúwáqàgghíq 'two more'
ḍua-q-agghiq → ḍúwáqágghíq 'two more'

6. Morphophonemics of the substitutes will be given below.

7. Morphophonemics of the numbers will be given below.

Proclitics

Monosyllabic proclitics ending in the symbol a develop a final q before a lost ə; see above page 79. For example:

ka.əbàŋ → kaq.bàŋ 'to the bank'

Affixes and affix-forms

1. The affix-forms ka- and -an are in complementary distribution with the

complementary extensions k- and -n respectively. For example:

extension	affix	derivative with complementary extension
k-	ka- -i	i-k-ǝnḑaq-i 'be wanted'
-n	ka- -an	ka-tunu-n 'burned'

2. Reduplications

Reduplications are considered prefixes because the overt form of R and Rf appears before the root. Total reduplication (Rt) will also be included here.

There are a few cases of irregular reduplication in which the vowel of the R syllable is /a/ no matter what the vowel of the root syllable. The quality of this /a/ (higher or lower), however, is the same as the quality of the final root vowel. These will be written out in full where they occur. For example:

car+kacir 'mixed up' → cȧr+kȧcȇr

a-lar+ghǝlur 'men and women together' → alȧr+ghȯlȗr

jak+riuk 'splash around' → jȧk+rȇjȯk [also normal
    R+riuk → jȯk+rȇjȯk]

das-garudus 'fast and sloppy' → dȧs+gȧrȗdȗs [also normal
    R+garudus → dȗs+gȧrȗdȗs]

ḑhat+inḑhit 'be of the same (age)' → ḑhȧt+ȇnḑhȋt

A few irregular cases of Rt also occur:[21]

(anaq) untaη+antiη 'only (child)'

tindhak+tandhuk 'behavior'

unghu-an+unghu 'really'

In the last example, the affix -an is not in its usual position in respect to the reduplication.

One uniquely reduplicated root is formed from aḑu 'an exclamation of pain'. Derivatives are formed from this root, e.g. R+aḑu-an 'keep on saying aḑu'. There is also a form aḑuḑu 'groan' which in turn has derivatives, e.g. N-aḑuḑu 'to groan', pa-N-aḑuḑu-na 'his groaning', and which is reduplicated in the normal way: R+N-aḑuḑu → ḑȗ+ηaḑȗḑȗ 'to keep on moaning'.

3. Shortening

Some irregular forms occur in the address form of kinship words.

	Full	Shortened Irregular
	ibhu 'mother'	bhuq [also regular bhu]
	ñai 'grandmother'	ñi
	kai 'grandfather'	ki
	kaɩ 'father (nobility)'	ɩq

4. Suffix -i

-i-a → -an-a, i.e. the suffix -i 'verbal suffix' obligatorily becomes -an when followed by -a 'future'. Examples:

i-bhərsi-i 'be cleaned'
i-bhərsi-i-a → i-bhərsi-an-a 'will be cleaned'

N-ka-təru-i 'to want'
N-ka-təru-i-a → N-ka-təru-an-a 'will want'

i-ka-suka-n-i 'is wanted'
i-ka-suka-n-i-a → i-ka-suka-n-an-a 'will be wanted'

5. Prefix paŋ-

The prefix paŋ- obeys the following unordered rules:

a. paŋ-V → paŋ-V

paŋ-arəp → paŋ-arəp 'hope'
paŋ-asi → paŋ-asi 'love potion'

b. paŋ-C_{v1} → paC_n^{h22}

paŋ-puti → pamuti 'bleach'
paŋ-təmu → panəmu 'opinion'
paŋ-cukur → pañukur 'razor'
paŋ-kəraq → paŋəraq 'slicer'

No examples for paŋ-ʈ occur in the corpus.

c.

$$\text{paŋ-} \begin{bmatrix} C_v \\ C_a \end{bmatrix} \to \text{pan-} \begin{bmatrix} C_v \\ C_a \end{bmatrix}$$

paŋ-bagi-an → pan-bagi-an 'distribution'
paŋ-ɖɖra-an → pan-ɖara-an 'egg-laying (chicken)'
paŋ-zaga → pan-zaga 'guard'
paŋ-bhantu → pan-bhantu 'helper'
paŋ-zhaiq → pan-zhaiq 'tailor'

$$\text{paŋ-ghabaj-an} \rightarrow \text{pan-ghabaj-an 'work'}$$

Note that n will then become homorganic to the following consonant by the rules of Chapter II.

No examples occur in the corpus for: paŋ- before d, g, dh, ḍh.

d. $\text{paŋ-C}_n \rightarrow \text{pa-C}_n$
$\rightarrow \text{paŋ-C}_n$

The latter development is less common.

$$\text{paŋ-nisər} \rightarrow \text{pa-nisər, or (rare)} \rightarrow \text{paŋ-nisər 'pity'}$$

e. $\text{paŋ-C}_r \rightarrow \text{paŋ-C}_r$

$\text{paŋ-rasa} \rightarrow \text{paŋ-rasa 'feeling'}$

$\text{paŋ-ladhin} \rightarrow \text{paŋ-ladhin 'servant'}$

f. $\text{paŋ-s} \rightarrow \text{pañ}$

$\text{paŋ-sakit} \rightarrow \text{pañakit 'sickness'}$

No examples of paŋ- followed by h, j, or w occur.

6. The prefix N- obeys the following unordered rules:

a. $\text{N-V} \rightarrow \text{ŋ-V}$

$\text{N-aku} \rightarrow \text{ŋ-aku 'to confess'}$

$\text{N-inəp} \rightarrow \text{ŋ-inəp 'to spend the night'}$

$\text{N-əcap} \rightarrow \text{ŋ-əcap 'to print'}$

$\text{N-uan} \rightarrow \text{ŋ-uan 'to herd'}$

b. $\text{N-C}_{vl} \rightarrow \text{C}_n^{h22}$

$\text{N-pəḍhaŋ} \rightarrow \text{məḍhaŋ 'to hit with a sword'}$

$\text{N-tutup} \rightarrow \text{nutup 'to close'}$

$\text{N-ṭaṭṭaŋ} \rightarrow \text{naṭṭaŋ 'to be wide open'}$

$\text{N-cucu} \rightarrow \text{ñucu 'to stab'}$

$\text{N-kirim} \rightarrow \text{ŋirim 'to send'}$

c.
$$\text{N-} \begin{bmatrix} \text{C}_n \\ \text{C}_r \end{bmatrix} \rightarrow \text{a-} \begin{bmatrix} \text{C}_n \\ \text{C}_r \end{bmatrix}$$

$\text{N-ñata-aghi} \rightarrow \text{a-ñata-aghi 'to prove'}$

$\text{N-ŋəm+ŋəm} \rightarrow \text{a-ŋəm+ŋəm 'to hold in the mouth'}$

$\text{N-miññaq-i} \rightarrow \text{a-miññaq-i 'to oil'}$

84

N-nanghala → a-nanghala 'to plow'

N-rusak → a-rusak 'to break'

N-laku-n-i → a-laku-n-i 'to work on'

Two exceptional cases of $N-C_n → C_n$ occur. They are: N-naiq-i → naiq-i 'to climb on'; N-mula-i → mula-i 'to begin'. For ease of reading they will be transcribed without N- throughout this grammar.

    d. N-s → ñ

       N-suun → ñuun 'to request'[23]

No cases preceding roots beginning with w occur in the corpus, but since such roots usually have variants beginning with b, the N- formation is ambiguous. For example, both bakkil and wakkil 'represent' occur as do both N- forms: makkil-i and a-bakkil-i 'to represent', but is the former to be derived from bakkil or wakkil?

    e.

$$N- \begin{bmatrix} C_v \\ C_a \\ h \end{bmatrix} \rightarrow \quad C_n^h$$

$$\text{or} \quad \rightarrow a- \begin{bmatrix} C_v \\ C_a \\ h \end{bmatrix}$$

$$\text{or} \quad \rightarrow an- \begin{bmatrix} C_v \\ C_a \\ h \end{bmatrix}$$

N- plus voiced or aspirated stop or h becomes either homorganic nasal as for the voiceless stops, or a- plus the original symbol, or an- plus the original symbol. The choice depends on the following root. Some roots exhibit two of the three possibilities (in free variation); some roots have two possibilities with one predominating; and some roots have specialization of meaning of one or the other alternant. The an- alternant is very rare.[24] The appendix below gives the developments of N- plus all roots in the corpus beginning with voiced or aspirated stop or h.

The following table summarizes the data in the appendix.

Initial consonant	Total number of cases	a-	Nasal	Both a-, nasal	an-	Both a-, an-
b	47	16	22	7[1]	0	1[2]
d	2	2	0	0	0	0
ḍ	4[3]	2	1	1	0	0
z	3	3	0	0	0	0
g	2	2	0	0	0	0
bh	33	26	1	2	0	4
dh	18	11	1	5[4]	1	0
ḍh	5	5	0	0	0	0
gh	25	21	1	1	2	0
zh	16	11	2	0	1[5]	2
h	4	1	1	2	0	0
Totals	159	101	30	17	4	8

Notes to table

1. Some are rare: e.g. a-baḍḍha-i 'to place'.

2. Specialization of meaning in an-buza-i 'to salt'.

3. ḍapaq has N-ḍapaq → napaq 'to reach'; N-ḍapaq-aghi → napaq-aghi, or → a-ḍapaq-aghi 'to convey'

   There is also ambiguity in nunpa 'to spill' since both ḍunpa and tunpa occur as roots.

4. Rare forms: N-dhalatin-i → naladhin-i 'be patient with'; N-dhilbhas → a-dhilbhas 'to throw down'

5. an-zhala only occurs in an-zhala sutra 'act deftly, trickily', zhala 'fishing net', sutra 'silk' [literally 'use a silk fishing net'].

Roots beginning with b have an approximately even number of nasal and a-alternants. The latter is more common when a suffix also occurs.

> b: N-baca → maca 'to read'
>
> N-baliq → a-baliq 'to turn over (transitive)'
>
> N-bassa-i → massa-i, or → a-bassa-i 'to wash (transitive)'
>
> N-baḍḍha-i → maḍḍha-i, or → a-baḍḍha-i (less common) 'to place'

In some cases, different derivatives of the same root show different alternants.

> N-bagi → mági 'to distribute'
>
> N-bagi-aghi → a-bagi-aghi 'to distribute (for someone)'

There is one case of an- and a- on the same root. The former has become specialized in meaning.

> N-buza-i → an-buza-i 'to salt' only in the expression
> an-buza-i saghara 'to salt the sea (i.e. do something
> useless)', as opposed to the more general N-buza-i →
> a-buza-i 'to salt'.

The majority of roots beginning with d, ḍ, z, g have the a- alternant, but the total number of examples is small.

> d: N-daqwa → a-daqwa 'to accuse'
>
> ḍ: N-ḍiccil-i → a-ḍiccil-i 'to loosen'
>   N-ḍapaq → napaq 'to reach'
>   N-ḍapaq-aghi → napaq-aghi, or → a-ḍapaq-aghi 'to convey'
>
> z: N-zagal → a-zagal 'to butcher'
>
> g: N-gangu → a-gangu 'to annoy'

The majority of roots beginning with aspirated stops take the a- alternant, but there are some cases of nasal and of an-.

> bh: N-bhaḍhi → a-bhaḍhi 'to make'
>   N-bhəḍhil → məḍhil 'to shoot'
>   N-bhatək → a-bhatək, → matək 'to strike'
>   N-bhabhaza-i → a-bhabhaza-i, or → an-bhabhaza-i 'to endanger'
>
> dh: N-dhuddhuq → nuddhuq 'to point'
>   N-dhuum → a-dhuum 'to distribute'
>   N-dhabuq → nabuq, or → a-dhabuq 'to pluck'
>   N-dhaddhi-aghi → an-dhaddhi-aghi 'to bring about'
>
> ḍh: N-ḍhaar → a-ḍhaar 'to eat'
>
> zh: N-zhaiq → a-zhaiq 'to sew'
>   N-zhuzzhu → ñuzzhu, or → a-zhuzzhu 'to stick'
>   N-zhalan-aghi → a-zhalan-aghi, or → an-zhalan-aghi 'to
>   perform'
>
> gh: N-ghinḍhuŋ → ŋinḍhuŋ 'to carry on hip'
>   N-ghabaj → a-ghabaj 'to make'
>   N-ghiba → ŋiba, or → a-ghiba 'to carry'
>   N-ghaḍhu-i → an-ghaḍhu-i 'to possess'
>
> h: N-hurmat-i → ŋurmat-i 'to honor'

N-haram.aghi → ŋaram.aghi, or → a-haram.aghi 'to forbid'

When cooccurring with R, the choice appropriate to the root appears. The a- alternant appears before the reduplicated syllable, while the nasal and an- alternants occur after the reduplication. For example:

R+N-kakan → kan+ŋakan 'to have a bite to eat'

R+N-bhaḍhi → a-ḍhi+bhaḍhi 'to make'

R+N-ghiba → ba+ŋiba, → a-ba+ghiba 'to carry'

Dialect variants of N-

The above description holds for modern conversational East Madurese. Much variation occurs in the other dialects. Since little work was done on non-standard dialects, most of the following is taken from Kiliaan.

As has been mentioned above in the phonology in West Madurese (particularly Bangkalan) the following holds:

$$N-\begin{bmatrix} C_v \\ C_a \end{bmatrix} V_H \rightarrow C_n^h V_H$$

In other words, a nasal consonant replaces the stop but the following vowel retains its higher quality. Put more generally, the vowel following the initial root consonant retains its quality (higher or lower) when the preceding stop is replaced by a nasal consonant. (Kiliaan 1.36)

For example, in West Madurese: N-ghaŋsi → ŋáŋsi 'to sharpen'. cf. East Madurese: N-ghaŋsi → a-ghaŋsi 'to sharpen'.

In a total description of West Madurese, this could be handled by ordering the rules, i.e. the rules for vowel qualities would precede the N- rules.

According to Kiliaan (1.7-8), N- in West Madura sometimes becomes ən- before voiceless dental, or alveolar, and palatal stops, and s; and əŋ-, aŋ- or ə- before liquids (Kiliaan 1.9-10), as well as əŋ- before s and ən- before labial and velar stops (Kiliaan 1.10).

Some examples from Kiliaan (loc. cit.).

N-sakiq-i → ən-sakiq-i 'to hurt'

88

N-ʈuk+ʈuk → ən-ʈuk+ʈuk 'to knock'
N-ləzhur → əŋ-ləzhur, → ə-ləzhur 'to melt'
N-rusak → aŋ-rusak 'to destroy'

In another place, Kiliaan claims that N- → ən- before voiced and aspirated
stops, → ə or zero before nasals (cf. East Madurese N-naiq-i given above) and
ən- before liquids, but it is not clear what dialect he is discussing (Kiliaan
1.75f). Some examples:

N-dhabuq → ən-dhabuq 'to pluck'
N-nanghala → ə-nanghala, → nanghala 'to plow'

Kiliaan never clearly states whether all or any of the preceding possibilities are in free variation, are sub-dialectal variants, or just what their
position is.

According to Kiliaan (1.11) in the Kangean dialect N- → an- in all environments. For example:

N-buaŋ → an-buaŋ 'to throw away'
N-ləzhur → an-ləzhur 'to melt'

7. The affix-form a- obeys the following rule: V-a- → V- This holds for
all affixes of the shape a-, including the a- alternant of N-. Because of other
rules to be given below it will usually not be necessary to write a- in these
cases, except where the a- alternant of N- is involved. The following examples
only show the latter category:

pa-N-ghabaj-na → pa-ghabaj-na 'his making'
i-N-zhaiq-aghi → i-zhaiq-aghi 'to be sewed for'

8. The prefix ZA- 'in the..., to the...' only occurs before the names of
the directions where it has the following forms:

ZA-timur → za-dhimur 'in the east'
ZA-ɖaza → zha-raza 'in the north'
ZA-baraq → zhu-baraq 'in the west'
ZA-lauq → zha-lauq 'in the south'

9. The morphophonemics of affixes cooccurring with substitutes will be
treated below.

10. The morphophonemics of affixes cooccurring with numbers will be treated below.

APPENDIX TO AFFIX MORPHOPHONEMICS

All cases in the corpus of the affix-form N- for roots beginning with voiced
or aspirated stop and h are given below. In most cases other derivatives than
the one given here take the same form of N-; for example other derivatives of
N-bhəḍhil 'to shoot' → məḍhil also have the nasal form of N-. The few devia-
tions from this will be noted.

b   N-baba → maba 'to be below'
     N-baca → maca 'to read'
     N-baccu → maccu 'to wash'
     N-baddhan-i → a-baddhan-i 'to mock'
     N-badhana-i → a-badhana-i 'to act like a wedana'
     N-baḍa-aghi → a-baḍa-aghi 'to hold, have performed'
     N-baḍḍha-i → maḍḍha-i, a-baḍḍha-i (rare) 'to put someplace'
     N-baghi → maghi 'to give'
     N-bagi → magi 'to distribute'
     N-bakkil-i → makkili, a-bakkil-i 'to represent'
     N-bala → mala-i 'to speak to'
     N-balandha-i → a-balandha-i 'to act Dutch'
     N-balanzha-i → a-balanzha-i 'to pay expenses for'
     N-balau → a-balau 'to make blue, to blue (wash)'
     N-baləs → maləs 'to return in kind'
     N-bali-aghi → mali-aghi, a-bali-aghi 'to return'
     N-bali-i → a-bali-i 'to return for'
     N-baliq → a-baliq 'to turn over'
     N-bankaŋ-i → a-bankaŋ-i 'to denude'
     N-baraghat-i → a-baraghat-i 'to pay the costs of'
     N-baruŋ → a-baruŋ 'to work in a coffee-shop'
     N-bassa-i → massa-i, a-bassa-i 'to wet'
     N-batəs-i → matəs-i, a-batəs-i 'to bound, put a boundary to'
     N-bazar → mazar 'to pay'
     N-bazhiq-aghi → a-bazhiq-aghi 'to disgust'

b N-bəciq-i → məciq-i 'to deflower'

  N-bəɖhaq-i → a-bəɖhaq-i 'to powder'

  N-bəɖhi → məɖhi 'to be gritty'

  N-bəgha → məgha 'to soak'

  N-bəkas → məkas 'to order'

  N-bəlas-aghi → məlas-aghi 'to be pityful'

  N-bəli → məli 'to buy'

  N-bəriq-i → a-bəriq-i 'to give to'

  N-biddaŋ-i → a-biddhaŋ-i 'to boil'

  N-biɖɖhiq → miɖɖhiq 'to lead along'

  N-bilaŋ → milaŋ 'to count'

  N-bituŋ → mituŋ 'to count'

  N-biṭṭaq → miṭṭaq 'to open up'

  N-buaŋ → muaŋ 'to throw away'

  N-buaq → muaq 'to be loaded, to hold, contain'

  N-buɖi → muɖi 'to be back, in the rear'

  N-bukkaq → mukkaq 'to open, to be open'

  N-bulaŋ → mulaŋ 'to instruct'

  N-buŋu-i → a-buŋu-i 'to wake up'

  N-buruk → muruk, a-buruk 'to teach'

  N-buza-i → a-buza-i 'to salt'

  N-buza-i saghara → an-buza-i saghara 'to salt the sea (i.e. do something useless)'

  N-buzhəl-i → a-buzhəl-i 'to put a naval on (to something)'

bh N-bhabhaza-i → an-bhabhaza-i, a-bhabhaza-i 'to endanger'

  N-bhaɖhi → a-bhaɖhi 'to make'

  N-bhaghus-aghi → a-bhaghus-aghi 'to consider good'

  N-bhakta → a-bhakta 'to carry'

  N-bhakti-i → a-bhakti-i 'to be devoted to'

  N-bhalik → a-bhalik 'to turn backwards, inside out'

  N-bhanɖhiŋ → a-bhanɖhiŋ 'to compare'

  N-bhantal-i → a-bhantal-i 'to provide with a pillow'

  N-bhantiŋ → a-bhantiŋ 'to dash down'

  N-bhantu → a-bhantu 'to help'

  N-bharanku → a-bharanku 'to cradle in one's arms'

  N-bharəŋ-i → a-bharəŋ-i 'to accompany'

  N-bharis-i → a-bharis-i 'to line up, underline'

  N-bhasa-i → a-bhasa-i 'to speak to in alus language'

bh   N-bhatək → matək, a-bhatək 'to strike'

       N-bhaṭi → a-bhaṭi 'to profit'

       N-bhaṭik → a-bhaṭik 'to batik'

       N-bhəḍhil → məḍhil 'to shoot'

       N-bhəndhu-n-i → an-bhəndhu-n-i, a-bhəndhu-n-i 'to be angry at'

       N-bhənḍər-aghi → a-bhənḍər-aghi 'to exonerate, justify'

       N-bhərsi-i → a-bhərsi-i 'to clean'

       N-bhət+bhət → mət+bhət, a-bhət+bhət 'to wrap around'

       N-bhidha-aghi → a-bhidha-aghi 'to differentiate'

       N-bhilla-i → a-bhilla-i 'to defend (?)'

       N-bhuḍhu-aghi → a-bhuḍhu-aghi 'to consider stupid'

       N-bhukti-i → an-bhukti-i, a-bhukti-i 'to show as proof'

       N-bhundhuq → a-bhundhuq 'to wrap'

       N-bhunkak-aghi → a-bhunkak-aghi 'to make happy'

       N-bhunkar → a-bhunkar 'to overturn'

       N-bhuru-i → a-bhuru-i 'to hunt'

       N-bhurun-i → a-bhurun-i 'to chase down'

       N-bhutu-aghi → a-bhutu-aghi 'to need'

       N-bhuṭuk → a-bhuṭuk 'to fertilize'

d   N-daqwa → a-daqwa 'to accuse'

       N-darus → a-darus 'to read the Koran in a particular way'

dh   N-dhabuq → a-dhabuq, nabuq 'to pluck'

       N-dhaddhi-aghi → an-dhaddhi-aghi 'to bring about'

       N-dhalatin-i → a-dhalatin-i, nalatin-i (rare) 'to be patient with'

       N-dhallu-i → a-dhallu-i 'to go ahead of'

       N-dhan+dhan-i → a-dhandhan-i 'to dress'

       N-dhəkuŋ-i → a-dhəkuŋ-i 'to kneel over'

       N-dhika-aghi → a-dhika-aghi 'to order'

       N-dhilbhas → nilbhas, a-dhilbhas (rare) 'to throw down'

       N-dhina-aghi → a-dhina-aghi 'to let'

       N-dhinghal-aghi → a-dhinghal-aghi 'to leave behind'

       N-dhisa-i → a-dhisa-i, nisa-i 'act like a villager'

       N-dhua-i → a-dhua-i 'to pray over'

       N-dhuddhuq → nuddhuq 'to point'

       N-dhudhiŋ → a-dhudhiŋ, nudhiŋ 'to point'

       N-dhulit → a-dhulit 'to touch with the finger-tip'

       N-dhullu-i → a-dhullu-i 'to go ahead'

       N-dhuŋŋiŋ-aghi → a-dhuŋŋiŋ-aghi 'to narrate'

dh   N-dhuum → a-dhuum 'to distribute'

ḍ   N-ḍaḍḍar → a-ḍaḍḍar 'to open wide'

      N-ḍapaq → napaq 'to reach, arrive at'

      N-ḍapaq-aghi → napaq-aghi, a-ḍapaq-aghi 'to convey'

      N-ḍiccil-i → a-ḍiccil-i 'to take apart'

      N-ḍunpa → nunpa 'to spill'

ḍh   N-ḍhabu-i → a-ḍhabu-i 'to speak to'

      N-ḍhaar → a-ḍhaar 'to eat'

      N-ḍhil+ḍhil → a-ḍhil+ḍhil 'to open (seams)'

      N-ḍhinḍha-i → a-ḍhinḍha-i 'to fine'

      N-ḍhukun-i → a-ḍhukun-i 'to be a native doctor'

z   N-zaga → a-zaga 'to guard'

      N-zagal → a-zagal 'to butcher'

      N-zawap → a-zawap 'to answer'

zh   N-zhaba-aghi → a-zhaba-aghi 'to put into Javanese'

      N-zhaiq → a-zhaiq 'to sew'

      N-zhagha-i → a-zhagha-i 'to wake up'

      N-zhala sutra → an-zhala sutra 'to use a silk fishing net (i.e. to act
                                      craftily, deftly)'

      N-zhalan-aghi → an-zhalan-aghi, a-zhalan-aghi 'to set into motion'

      N-zhamu-i → a-zhamu-i 'to medicate'

      N-zhau-i → an-zhau-i, a-zhau-i 'to go away from'

      N-zhazhal → a-zhazhal 'to try'

      N-zhəmur → a-zhəmur 'to dry'

      N-zhual → a-zhual 'to sell'

      N-zhuŋ+zhuŋ → a-zhuŋ+zhuŋ 'to lift high'

      N-zhuraghan-i → a-zhuraghan-i 'to be a ship captain'

      N-zhuzhu → a-zhuzhu 'to feed'

      N-zhuzzhu → a-zhuzzhu, ñuzzhu 'to stick, prick'

      N-zhuzzhuq → a-zhuzzhuq, ñuzzhuq 'to touch with fingertip'

g   N-gangu → a-gangu 'to annoy'

      N-gazi → a-gazi 'to pay wages to'

gh   N-ghabaj → a-ghabaj 'to do, make'

      N-R+ghaḍhi → a-R+ghaḍhi 'to pawn'

      N-ghaḍhu-i → an-ghaḍhu-i 'to own, possess'

      N-ghagghar-i → a-ghagghar-i 'to fall on'

      N-ghanbhar → a-ghanbhar 'to draw'

gh   N-ghanpaŋ-aghi → a-ghanpaŋ-aghi 'to facilitate'

      N-ghandha-i → a-ghandha-i 'to put make-up on'

      N-ghantuŋ → a-ghantuŋ 'to hang'

      N-ghaŋsi → a-ghaŋsi 'to sharpen'

      N-gharap → a-gharap 'to work on'

      N-gharu → a-gharu 'to scratch'

      N-ghərpas → a-ghərpas 'to hit with a stick'

      N-ghərus → a-ghərus 'to iron'

      N-ghərzha → a-ghərzha 'to stamp on'

      N-ghətun-aghi → an-ghətun-aghi 'to surprise, amaze'

      N-ghiba → ŋiba, a-ghiba 'to carry'

      N-ghindhuŋ → ŋindhuŋ 'to carry on back or hip'

      N-ghindhuq → a-ghindhuq 'to insert'

      N-ghula-i → a-ghula-i 'to sugar'

      N-ghuluŋ → a-ghuluŋ 'to roll'

      N-ghuluq-i → a-ghuluq-i 'to roll around on'

      N-ghuna-aghi → a-ghuna-aghi 'to make use of'

      N-ghuntiŋ → a-ghuntiŋ 'to cut, shear'

      N-ghuŋ+ghuŋ → a-ghuŋ+ghuŋ 'to total'

      N-ghuriŋ → a-ghuriŋ 'to fry'

h   N-haram-aghi → ŋaram-aghi, a-haram-aghi 'to forbid'

      N-hiran-aghi → a-hiran-aghi 'to surprise'

      N-hurmat-i → ŋurmat-i 'to honor'

      N-huzzha-aghi → ŋuzzha-aghi, a-huzzha-aghi 'to speak about'

FOOTNOTES

1. The closest example in English would be to consider 'noun plural' and 'verb present singular' (-s, -z, -ɨz) an affix-form.

2. In cases where the root has no derivatives and is a particle, e.g. ɖari 'from', there is no point to positing a null affix.

3. Such roots are few and will not be distinguished in transcription from those which can occur alone.

4. That this is not a trisyllabic root *lunalun can be seen from the syllabification and from the lack of nasalization of the penultimate vowel: lõn/à/lõn.

5. Plus juncture is thus the juncture occurring within words across which none of the phonology rules are effective. This is true of CVCCVC where the medial CC is $C_n C_s$, e.g. baŋbaŋ; the plus juncture has been assigned to all roots of this shape, i.e. to all reduplicated monosyllables. Another possible analysis would have been to generate these roots <u>after</u> the nC_s rules.

6. Compare with saŋ+saŋ 'get entangled'.

7. This is, of course, the old problem of 'cranberry morphs'.

8. The meaning relation seemed reasonable to informants.

9. canba 'shelled peas' also occurs.

10. For various reasons similar elements have been considered the other way around, i.e. the lost part of reduced forms, e.g. ɖimma reduced to ɨmma. For details see pages 187-188.

11. The definition of free variation used here is that of Hockett in Problems of Morphemic Analysis, <u>Language</u> 23.328 (1947): (a) that one cannot predict, save perhaps statistically, which form will occur in a particular instance,

and (b) that the occurrence of one, rather than of the other, does not produce an utterance different in meaning.

12. It is possible to analyze the q- affix-form in a different way: namely to write such roots with an initial glottal stop, e.g. qəla, and then provide for these in the phonologic rules and canonic forms of morphemes.

One case of apparent assimilation of a reduplication to the following syllable occurs in the following example of free variation: daqwa 'accuse'; i-R+daqwa → èwádáqwá; i-R+q-daqwa → èwáqdáqwá 'to be accused often'. Other derivations from this root with R+ have the same free variation of +q- versus its absence.

13. Difficulties are caused by forms such as marḑuani 'to be in doubt', probably to be connected with the root ḑua 'two', though mar- does not elsewhere occur as a prefix; and borrowed words, e.g. paranaghan 'Eurasian' borrowed from Indonesian peranakan 'Eurasian'. Is this to be analyzed par-anak-an or pa-r-anak-an and connected with the root anaq 'child'? Also difficult is the case of triple free variation in ka-saksi-an, ka-saksi-n, ka-saksi-n-an 'witnessed' from saksi 'witness' and an affix (usually ka- -an) meaning 'passive'.

14. This class can be defined syntactically as words which cannot be predicates.

15. See pages 78-80.

16. See page 101.

17. Informants are unsure about kantus 'up to, until'.

18. There are also roots of the shape C_1VC_2 which never have the form $əC_1VC_2$, e.g. zham 'o'clock', hal 'matter', hak 'right'.

19. The occurrence of the three forms of sa.əzham 'one hour' are perhaps conditioned by speed and style; in order of increasing speed and less formal style they are: sa.əzham, saq.zham, sazzham.

20. The word lágghu-q 'tomorrow' occurs in West Madurese. Historically this may be from R-lagghu-q → ghúqlágghúq with apocopation of the first syllable as

sometimes happens in West Madurese. See page 33 above for discussion of elision in West Madurese.

21. It is also possible to consider the first two following examples compounds composed of root variants.

22. For the definition of homorganic see page 17.

23. In one case N- → a- before s: N-sanbhazaŋ.aghi → a-sanbhazaŋ.aghi 'to pray over'. Note that the root is a root variant of bhazaŋ 'pray'.

24. My impression is that the a- alternant is encroaching on both the an- and C_n alternants for roots beginning with voiced or aspirated stops.

CHAPTER IV

MORPHOLOGY II

Derivation

The elements of a word are said to <u>cooccur</u> with each other. There are the following general restrictions on cooccurrence:

1. Prefix. Various prefixes cooccur. The possible combinations and their internal order will be discussed below beginning on page 103.

2. Infix. Only one infix occurs in a word.

3. Suffix. Not more than two suffixes cooccur in the same word except in rare cases which are gramatically on the border-line.[1] The second of the two cooccurring suffixes can only be -a 'future, irrealis' or -na 'definite, 3rd person pronominal', but these two cannot cooccur, i.e. neither *-a-na nor *-na-a occurs.

4. Superfix. Not more than one superfix occurs per word.

5. Reduplication. No more than one of the same type of reduplication occurs per word (except for certain derivatives of the numbers); thus R plus R, Rf plus Rf, and Rt plus Rt do not occur.

6. Shortening (S) does not cooccur with any other affix.

7. The cooccurrence of extensions and proclitics with other elements is quite restricted. The occurring combinations will be discussed below beginning on page 103.

Words are built from roots by the addition of other elements. This building is done in an order, i.e. words show immediate constituent structure.

A word containing the elements abc where b is a root and a and c are non-roots can be analyzed into immediate constituents in one of the following

99

ways: a[bc], i.e. a is prefixed to bc; [ab]c, i.e. c is suffixed to ab; or
[a]b[c], i.e. ac is circumfixed to b. The expression <u>last added element</u> will
mean that element which is the last to be built onto the rest of the word, e.g.
in the above examples the last added elements are a, c, and ac respectively.[2]

   A word which contains a non-root element as its last added element is a
<u>derivative</u>, e.g. bəlas-an 'teens', ka.luar 'to go out'. The process of forming
derivatives is <u>derivation</u>. The form to which the last non-root element has been
added is a <u>stem</u>, e.g. bəlas is the stem of bəlas-an and luar is the stem of
ka.luar.

   In both the examples given in the previous paragraph the stem is the same
shape as the root. The following example shows that this is not necessarily
true; the stem of a-R+taña 'to keep on asking' is a-taña 'to ask'. The latter
in turn is a derivative whose stem is taña (= root). Such an analysis, going
back to the root by succeedingly smaller stems, will be called the <u>derivational</u>
<u>history</u> of a word. Examples follow; in each of these examples a word serves as
the stem for the derivative on the following line:

root	pəɖhaŋ
+null	pəɖhaŋ 'sword'
+N-	N-pəɖhaŋ 'to strike with a sword'
+pa- -na	pa-N-pəɖhaŋ-na 'his striking with a sword'
root	tau
+null	tau 'to know'
+taq.	taq.tau 'not know'
+R+N-pa	R+N-pa-taq.tau 'to pretend not to know'
+pa- -na	pa-R+N-pa-taq.tau-na 'his pretending not to know'
root	kutəp
+null	kutəp 'throw'
+salaŋ.	salaŋ.kutəp 'throw at each other'
+N-pa-	N-pa-salaŋ.kutəp 'make (them) throw at each other'
+R+	R+N-pa-salaŋ.kutəp 'make (them) continually throw at each other'
+pa- -na	pa-R+N-pa-salaŋ.kutəp-na 'his making (them) continually throw at each other'

An element will be said to be <u>stem-forming</u> if it cooccurs with another element to form a stem. Most roots and affixes, all extensions, and some proclitics are stem-forming, e.g. the prefix a- is stem-forming because it cooccurs with taña 'ask' to form a-taña 'to ask' which is the stem for a-taña-a 'will ask'. Similarly, the proclitic ka. 'to' is stem-forming because it cooccurs with luar 'outside' to form ka.luar 'to go outside' which is the stem for pa-ka.luar 'extract!'.

The stem-forming proclitics are salaŋ 'mutual', zhuŋ '-er', taq 'not', ka 'to' and the proclitic form of the numbers.[3]

Stems are <u>radical</u>, <u>affixal</u>, <u>proclitic,</u> and <u>extended</u>. Radical stems have a root as their last added element. Affixal stems have an affix as their last added element. Proclitic stems have a proclitic as their last added element. Extended stems have a contrastive or free variation extension as their last added element. Extended stems do not cooccur with a null affix, i.e. they must occur in some overt derivative. Examples of the various kinds of stem follow:

	<u>stem</u>	<u>derivative</u>
radical	bəlas	bəlas-an 'teens'
affixal	a-taña	a-taña-a 'will ask'
proclitic	ka.luar	pa-ka.luar 'extract'
extended	tai-n	N-tai-n 'be rusty'

An <u>inflection</u> is a set of affixes each of which cooccurs with the same stem. The inflected forms, each consisting of a stem plus a member of the inflection set, have some syntactic environments in common and certain ones distinct.[4]

Madurese has only one inflection. This inflection only cooccurs with radical and affixal stems. The glosses given below are not meant to be exhaustive. The last form, without prefix, will be called the <u>stem form</u>.

<u>inflection</u>	<u>radical stem</u>	<u>affixal stem</u>
N-stem	N-kakan 'to eat'	N-pa-rusak 'to break'
i-stem	i-kakan 'be eaten'	i-pa-rusak 'be broken'
stem	kakan 'eat!'	pa-rusak 'break!'

The form in N- will be used to stand for the entire inflection when such forms are quoted, e.g. N-kakan will be used to represent N-kakan, i-kakan, and kakan.

A compound is a word containing a sequence of two or more roots, shortened roots, and/or derivatives.[5]

Compounds

Madurese compounds are of two kinds: full root and shortened root. The root parts of compounds are joined by close juncture, e.g. kuraŋ-azhar 'rude'.

Full root compounds are uncommon.

> kuraŋ-azhar 'rude' [kuraŋ 'not enough'; azhar 'learn']
> i-pədhəm-pati-aghi 'be worked to death' [pədhəm 'with eyes closed'; pati 'death']

One full root compound contains a root with complementary extension: ḍhukun-r-anaq 'midwife' [ḍhukun 'native doctor'; anaq, r-anaq 'child'].

In shortened root compounds the first root appears in shortened form (S; see page 30 above). For example:

> sap-laṭi 'handkerchief' [usap 'wipe'; laṭi 'lip']
> riŋ-tua 'parents' [uriŋ 'person'; tua 'old']
> zhuq-ənpul 'pinky' [tuzhuq 'finger'; ənpul 'pinky']
> sar-suri 'afternoon market' [pasar 'market'; suri 'afternoon']
> naq-putu 'descendents' [anaq 'child'; putu 'grandchild']

One such shortened root is assimilated to the following root: sat-tanaŋ 'handkerchief' [usap 'wipe'; tanaŋ 'hand'].

One case of unique shortening occurs in: zhur-tulis 'clerk' [zhuru 'skilled worker'; tulis 'write'].

In some words which seem to be shortened compounds one or both parts are unclear, or the semantic connection is obscure. For example:

> nin-bharaq 'west monsoon' [? aŋin 'wind'; baraq 'west']
> tar-puti 'white headcloth' [? latar 'background'; puti 'white']
> tar-cələŋ 'black headcloth' [? latar 'background'; cələŋ 'black']
> zhaŋ-sira 'pillow' [? zhaŋ; sira 'head']
> pak-ḍaŋ+ḍaŋ 'crossroads' [? tapak 'palm'; ? ḍaŋ+ḍaŋ 'eagle']

The full root compound tapak-ɗaŋ+ɗaŋ 'crossroads' also occurs.

Two other words, used mostly by Madurese speakers living on Java, have both parts shortened: bhu-liq 'younger sister of parent' [ibhu 'mother'; aliq 'younger sibling'] and paq-lĭq 'younger brother of parent' [əpaq 'father'; aliq 'younger sibling']. Note that the latter compound retains the ĭ quality of the former.

Derivatives

Madurese derivatives are presented in five categories: verbals, nouns, particles, substitutes, and numbers. Within each category affix-forms are given in such an order that, in general, no forward reference need be made. Each affix-form is then subdivided into a number of classes depending on form of stem, meaning of stem, meaning of derivative, and, if necessary, derivational history. Combinations of the affix-form being discussed with previously mentioned affix-forms, i.e. where a derivative serves as stem for another derivative, are then given.

Single words are generally exemplified simply by giving the stem and the derivative, e.g. tiɗuŋ 'to sleep', ta-tiɗuŋ 'to fall asleep'. Where partial or complete sentences are given as examples the following system is used: each word in the Madurese sentence is assigned a number. The English translation follows. After that, in square brackets, each word in the original sentence is mentioned by number and glossed. Only the stem or basic derivative[6] of the affix being exemplified is given. For example, the following sentence illustrates the suffix -a:

> sinkuq intar-a ka pasar. 'I'm going to the market'.
>   1   2   3   4
> [1. sinkuq 'I', 2. intar 'to go', 3. ka 'to',
> 4. pasar 'market']

The abbreviation rel. particle [= relative particle] will be used to gloss the word si.

VERBALS

A verbal is a stem which cooccurs with the suffix -a 'future, irrealis'.[7]
A verbal is transitive or intransitive. Transitive verbals have the three form
inflection discussed on page 101 above. Intransitive verbals are not inflected.

Verbal derivatives are as follows:

-a

The suffix -a is not stem-forming. By definition it cooccurs with any
verbal stem. The morphophonemics of -i before -a have been discussed above on
page 83 . It should be noted again that -i-a → -an-a. For some speakers,
-i-a → -an-a-a. This is considered substandard by educated Madurese.

-a has a range of meanings covering such categories as: 'future, conditional,
contrary to fact, wished for, possible'.

1) Future.

        sinkuq intar-a ka pasar. 'I'm going to the market.' [1. sinkuq
           1   2   3   4
          'I', 2. intar 'to go', 3. ka 'to', 4. pasar 'market']

-a derivatives from proclitic stems:

        sinkuq ka.aḍaq-a. 'I'm going up front.' [1. sinkuq 'I',
           1   2
          2. ka.aḍaq 'to the front']

        sinkuq ka.kuṭṭa-a. 'I'm going to the city.' [1. sinkuq 'I',
           1   2
          2. ka.kuṭṭa 'to the city']

2) -a cooccurs with the verbals N-pinta, and N-suun in the meaning 'polite
request'.

        N-suun-a kupî bisaus. 'I'd just like coffee'. [1. N-suun 'to
           1   2   3
          request', 2. kupî 'coffee', 3. bisaus 'just']

3) Certain auxiliaries are usually followed by verbal plus -a. These are:
təru, ka-suka-n 'to want, to be about to', parlu 'need to, have to', N-aghaq 'be
on the point of', bhakal, bhaḍhi 'will, be going to', a-zhanzhi 'to promise to'.

        sinkuq təru R+zhalan-an-a. 'I'm going for a walk.' [1. sinkuq
           1   2   3

104

'I', 2. təru 'going to', 3. R+zhalan-an 'to take a walk']

bhakal i-ka-ghabaj-a təpuŋ. 'It will be made into flour.'
　1　　　　2　　　　　3
　　[1. bhakal 'will', 2. i-ka-ghabaj 'be made into', 3. təpuŋ 'flour']

4) Certain particles are usually followed by verbal plus -a. Some of these are: paraq, R+ḍaraq, lagghiq 'almost'.

　　paraq mari-a 'almost finished'
　　lagghiq N-pati-a 'almost died'
　　paraq taq i-kəniŋ-a abas 'almost couldn't be seen' [1. taq 'not',
　　　　　1　　　2　　　3
　　2. i-kəniŋ 'be able', 3. abas 'see']

5) Some verb phrases are followed by verbal plus -a. Among these are: luppa si 'forget to', takuq si 'be afraid to'.

　　ka-bhunkak-an-na taŋ aliq / ta-libat + kaŋsi luppa si N-kakan-a.
　　　　1　　　　　　　2　　3　　　4　　　　5　　6　　　7
　　'Brother's joy was so great that he forgot to eat.'
　　[1. ka-bhunkak-an-na 'his joy', 2. taŋ 'my', 3. aliq 'younger
　　sibling', 4. ta-libat 'very much', 5. kaŋsi 'so that', 6. luppa
　　si 'forget to', 7. N-kakan 'to eat'].

6) The particle ghiq 'yet' followed by a verbal plus -a means 'just about to'.

　　antus ghallu + sinkuq ghiq a-kəmi-a. 'Wait a minute; I'm going to
　　　1　　2　　　　3　　4　　5
　　urinate.' [1. antus 'wait', 2. ghallu 'first', 3. sinkuq 'I',
　　4. ghiq 'yet', 5. a-kəmi 'to urinate']

　　kaḍla ghiq N-sari-a kurik. 'I'm just going to look for a match.'
　　　1　　2　　3　　　4
　　[1. kaḍla 'I', 2. ghiq 'yet', 3. N-sari 'to look for', 4. kurik
　　'match']

7) Conditional, wishes, possibility.

　　i-tappur-a kilap. 'May (I) be struck by lightning.' [1. i-tappur
　　　1　　2
　　'be struck', 2. kilap 'lightning']

　　R+sabbhan bhasa raza-a utaba kiniq-a. 'every language, big or
　　　1　　　　2　　3　　　4　　5
　　small.' [1. R+sabbhan 'every', 2. bhasa 'language', 3. raza

'big', 4. utaba 'or', 5. kiniq 'small']

pasira si uniŋ-a 'Who could possibly know?' [1. pasira 'who',
   1   2   3

  2. si 'rel. particle', 3. uniŋ 'to know']

baqna za.ria / ta-bhazhən ghallu si azhar-a. 'You're probably
  1   2   3   4   5   6

  studying too hard.' [1. baqna 'you', 2. za.ria 'that', 3. ta-
bhazhən 'too conscientious', 4. ghallu 'first, too', 5. si 'rel.
particle', 6. azhar 'to study']

mun taq ka-liru-a 'If I'm not mistaken' [1. mun 'if', 2. taq 'not',
  1 2   3

  3. ka-liru 'make a mistake']

8) Certain clause introducers are usually followed by verbal plus -a.
These are, among others: supaza 'in order to'; zhaq 'let's go and'; zhaq 'if
(contrary to fact)';[8] R+mugha, Rt+mugha, mandhar 'hopefully, let's hope that';
nazzhan, maski, maski-an-a, sumili, sumili-a, hatta-a 'even if, no matter how
much'; R+tadaq-na 'it's all because'; apa puli, maq puli 'how should, not to
speak of'; du 'how is it possible that'.

abaq-na N-suru supaza N-bhərsi-i-a miza. 'He ordered the table
  1   2   3   4   5

  cleaned.' [1. abaq-na, 'he', 2. N-suru 'to order', 3. supaza
  'in order to', 4. N-bhərsi-i 'to clean', 5. miza 'table']

majuq + zhaq N-puluŋ-a ñiur! 'Come on; let's gather coconuts.'
  1   2   3   4

  [1. majuq 'come on', 2. zhaq 'let's go and', 3. N-puluŋ 'to
  gather (fruit)', 4. ñiur 'coconut']

taŋ sakula-an /zhaq taq ulli-a bhantu-an ghuru, 'If my school
  1   2   3   4 5   6   7

  hadn't gotten teaching help,' [1. taŋ 'my', 2. sakula-an
  'school', 3. zhaq 'if', 4. taq 'not', 5. ulli 'to get',
  6. bhantu-an 'help', 7. ghuru 'teacher']

zhaq sinkuq dhaddhi-a baqna, 'If I were you,' [1. zhaq 'if',
  1   2   3   4

  2. sinkuq 'I', 3. dhaddhi 'to be, become', 4. baqna 'you']

The latter cooccurs with nouns and pronouns too, though this usage seems
to be on the borderline of grammaticality.

106

zhaq azam-a 'if it were a chicken' [1. azam 'chicken']
      1

R+mugha taq N-dhaddhi-aghi-a dhuka.ipun rama! 'May it not arouse
   1   2   3   4   5
   father's anger!' [1. R+mugha 'may', 2. taq 'not', 3. N-dhaddhi-
   aghi 'arouse', 4. dhuka.ipun 'his anger', 5. rama 'father']

sumili-a baqna N-ukir-a laŋŋiq sakali, 'Even if you could measure
   1   2   3   4   5
   the sky (i.e. no matter how smart you are)' [1. sumili-a 'even
   if', 2. baqna 'you', 3. N-ukir 'to measure', 4. laŋŋiq 'sky',
   sakali 'particle']

nazzhan muḍa-a sakali 'no matter how cheap it is' [1. nazzhan 'even
   1   2   3
   if, no matter how', 2. muḍa 'be cheap', 3. sakali 'particle']

apa puli aliq si tau-a + sinkuq dhibiq / ɪa ənzaq. 'How should
   1   2   3 4   5   6   7   8
   brother know; I myself don't?' [1. apa puli 'not to speak of',
   2. aliq 'younger sibling', 3. si 'rel. particle', 4. tau 'to
   know', 5. sinkuq 'I', 6. dhibiq 'self', 7. ɪa 'yes; particle',
   8. ənzaq 'no']

9) Negatives.

Some negative words and phrases are regularly followed by verbal plus -a.

taq a-ghinzhək sa-kuniq-a bhai. 'He didn't move even a little.'
   1   2   3   4
   [1. taq 'not', 2. a-ghinzhək 'to move', 3. sa-kuniq 'be a
   little', 4. bhai 'just']

si calakaq / N-pati kabbhi + taḍaq si uḍiq-a. 'Those in the accident
   1   2   3   4   5   1   6
   all died; not one lived.' [1. si 'rel. particle', 2. calakaq 'be
   in an accident', 3. N-pati 'to die', 4. kabbhi 'all', 5. taḍaq
   'there isn't', 6. uḍiq 'to live']

taq kira si taq uniŋ-a. 'There isn't anyone who doesn't know.'
   1   2   3 1   4
   [1. taq 'not', 2. kira 'think', 3. si 'rel. particle', 4. uniŋ
   'to know']

sinkuq ghəlaq taq N-bəli pau sittuŋ-a bhalakka. 'I didn't even buy
   1   2   3   4   5   6   7
   a single mango.' [1. sinkuq 'I', 2. ghəlaq 'past', 3. taq 'not',

107

4. N-bəli 'to buy', 5. pau 'manggo', 6. sittuŋ 'one', 7.

bhalakka 'even, merely']

10) -a also cooccurs with verbals in the following construction:

X / si X-a 'Did (ī) X?!'

    N-tinghu / si N-tinghu-a + antré karcés-na bhai / əla taq N-pilu.
      1   2   1   3   4   5   6   7   8

    'See it! I didn't even get a chance to stand on line for

    tickets.' [1. N-tinghu 'to see', 2. si 'rel. particle', 3.

    antré 'stand on line', 4. karcés-na 'its tickets', 5. bhai

    'just', 6. əla 'already', 7. taq 'not', 8. N-pilu 'to take

    part in']

    tuzuq / si tuzuq-a + si əla R+luŋu-an / sinkuq taq N-taŋali. 'Sit
     1   2   1   2   3   4   5   6   7

    down! I didn't even see it standing on tip-toe.' [1. tuzuq 'to

    sit', 2. si 'rel. particle', 3. əla 'already', 4. R+luŋu-an 'to

    stand on tip-toe', 5. sinkuq 'I', 6. taq 'not', 7. N-taŋali 'to

    see'

Reduplications

R

Rules for the generation of R (end reduplication) have been given on page
33f above. R is connected with the following morpheme by plus (+) juncture or,
in rapid speech, by dot (.) juncture. For example:

    R+apik → pèk+àpèk 'be careful'
    R.apik ,→ pèkkàpèk 'be careful'

Rules for placing R in relation to other prefixes will be given individually
in subsequent discussions.

1) The usual meanings associated with verbal R are those of repetition and
frequency of action or of action carried out over a period of time. For example:

    a-caca 'to talk'   a-R+caca 'to have a conversation'

    a-bənku 'to have a   a-R+bənku 'to have a household, to have
         house'   one's own house'

    aliq i-unzhaŋ. 'Brother was invited.'
     1   2

aliq i-R+unzhaŋ. 'Brother kept on being invited.' [1. aliq 'younger
    sibling', 2. i-unzhaŋ 'be invited']

sinkuq / əla abit / si R+N-antus baqna i ḍinnaq. 'I've been waiting
    1   2   3   4   5   6   7 8
    for you for a long time here.' [1. sinkuq 'I', 2. əla 'already',
    3. abit 'long (time)', 4. si 'rel. particle', 5. N-antus 'to wait',
    6. baqna 'you', 7. i 'in, at', 8. ḍinnaq 'here']

2) Negative commands with zhaq 'don't' of intransitive verbals often cooccur
with R indicating a prohibition over a period of time or meaning 'Don't be so,
don't be too'. For example:

    zhaq R+tuḍus! 'Don't be shy!' [1. tuḍus 'shy, embarrassed']
         1

    zhaq R+raza! 'Don't make it big!; It shouldn't be big!' [1. raza 'big']
         1

3) R cooccurs with a subclass of intransitive verbal predicates and indicates that the modified noun is plural and that all of the nouns possess the
quality, though not necessarily to the same degree. For example:

    saba-na / R+libar. 'His fields are broad.' [1. saba-na 'his wet rice
    1   2
    fields', 2. libar 'broad']

    pa-caca-na tamuj rua / R+banni. 'The guests talked about different
    1   2   3   4
    things.' [1. pa-caca-na 'the talking', 2. tamuj 'guest', 3. rua
    'that', 4. banni 'be different']

4) Cooccurring with transitive verbals R means action without any specified
object or goal. For example:

    ibhu si anḍiq-a ghabaj / mula-i sa-tia / əla R+N-pa-kunpul. 'Mother
    1   2 3   4   5   6   7   8
    who will give a feast beginning now has begun to get things to-
    gether.' [1. ibhu 'mother', 2. si 'rel. particle', 3. anḍiq-a
    'will have', 4. ghabaj 'a to-do, feast', 5. mula-i 'to begin',
    6. sa-tia 'now', 7. əla 'already', 8. N-pa-kunpul 'to gather,
    collect']

Compare the members of the following two pairs of sentences:

    aliq i-bəriq-i zhazhan 'Brother was given a snack.'
    1   2   3

109

aliq i-R+bəriq-i.   'Brother was given (things).'   [1. aliq 'younger
   sibling', 2. i-bəriq-i 'to be given', 3. zhazhan 'snack']

aliq i-suru intar ka pasar.   'Brother was told to go to the market.'
   1   2   3   4 5

aliq i-R+suru + intar ka pasar.   'Brother was given errands to do; he
   went to the market.'   [1. aliq 'younger sibling', 2. i-suru 'be
   ordered, be told', 3. intar 'to go', 4. ka 'to', 5. pasar 'market']

5) Some verbal R have specialized meanings.

   anɖiq 'to have, own'   R+anɖiq 'to have magic power'

Rt

Rules for the generation of Rt (total reduplication) have been given on
pages 34-35   above.   Except for a few special uses, Rt generally covers the same
semantic areas as R.   It is much more frequent in the western dialects than in
East Madurese.   In the latter it is regularly used only in combination with certain other affixes which will be discussed below (see page 158).

Rf

The rules for the generation of Rf (front reduplication) have been given on
page 34 above.   Rf derivatives are all intransitives.   Like R and Rt it is
joined to the following morpheme by plus or dot juncture, the latter in rapid
speech.   For example:

   Rf+N-zhual → a-Rf+zhual → àzházhũwál 'to trade'
   Rf.N-zhual → a-Rf.zhual → àzházzhũwál 'to trade'

The meanings of Rf are the same as those of R sections 1, 4, and 5 above.
For example:

   1) Repetition, frequency.

   maliŋ 'thief'   Rf+maliŋ 'to be a thief, go thieving'

   2) Without specific object.

   N-pukul 'to hit'   Rf+N-pukul 'to beat up, give a beating'

   3) Special.

   N-baca 'to read'   Rf+N-baca 'to sing (Madurese style)'

Rf most frequently cooccurs with other affixes and as such will be discussed in various places below.

Basic derivatives

There are three verbal derivatives which are frequent stems for further derivatives. These will be called the basic derivatives. The basic derivatives are null (intransitive), a- (intransitive), and N- (intransitive and transitive).[9] Verbal stems have one or two of the basic derivatives. For example:

one basic derivative	stem	derivative
null	ɖatəŋ	ɖatəŋ 'to come'
a-	taña	a-taña 'to ask'
N-	kalaq	N-kalaq 'to take'

two basic derivatives		
a-	kakan	a-kakan 'to hold (of brakes)'
N-	kakan	N-kakan 'to eat'
null	ka.lauq	ka.lauq 'to the south'
N-	ka.lauq	N-ka.lauq 'in the south'

Certain derivatives (both verbal and nominal) have the basic derivative as stem. This will be referred to below as being 'derived from the basic derivative.' The forms are as follows:

basic derivative	stem derived from the basic derivative
null	∅
a-	∅
N- (nasal)	N- → nasal
N- (a-)	N- → ∅

Examples using the nominal derivative pa- -na 'his -ing' follow:

basic derivative	derived from basic derivative
ɖatəŋ 'to come'	pa-daɬəŋ-na 'his coming'
a-taña 'to ask'	pa-taña-na 'his asking'
N-bəli 'to buy' → məli	pa-N-bəli-na → pa-məli-na 'his buying'
N-zhaiq 'to sew' → azhaiq	pa-N-zhaiq-na → pa-zhaiq-na 'his sewing'

Because there can be more than one basic derivative per root there are contrasts such as the following:

111

a-kakan 'to hold (of brakes)'   pa-kakan-na 'its holding'
N-kakan 'to eat'   pa-N-kakan-na 'his eating'
ka.lauq 'to the south'   pa-ka.lauq-na 'its going to the south'
N-ka.lauq 'in the south'   pa-N-ka.lauq-na 'its being in the south'

Null affix

Null affix verbals have no prefix. They are always intransitive and in
meaning are generally like English intransitive verbs or adjectives.

1) Verbs.

intar 'to go'
ɗatəŋ 'to come'
tiɗuŋ 'to sleep'
muli 'to go home'
masuq 'to enter'
ghagghar 'to fall'
baɗa 'there is'
taɗaq 'there isn't'
buru 'to run'

2) Adjectives.

raza 'be big'
kiniq 'be small'
cələŋ 'be black'
zhau 'be far'
baññaq 'be many'
ŋuɗa 'be young'
tutup 'be closed'
sughi 'be rich'

The first class rarely occurs reduplicated except in rather specialized
meanings. For example:

baɗa 'there is'
Rt+baɗa bhai 'there's always something going on'

Neither class cooccurs with Rf.

Other derivatives are used for both classes in the meaning of repeated
action: In this meaning verbs occur with R+ -an and adjectives occur with a-R+.
These will be discussed below.

112

As has been noted (page 109 above) the second class takes R in the meanings of plural subject and in negative commands.

a-

The prefix a- does not occur before roots beginning with the symbol a in any of their derivatives, except in a few cases where the extension -r- appears, e.g. a-r-apa 'how' (but *a-apa is impossible).

Thus verbs beginning with the symbol a such as:

> azhar 'to study'
> addhu 'to fight'
> anḍiq 'to possess'

are indistinguishable from the null prefix type beginning with a vowel, e.g. intar 'to go'. There is no way of separating them, i.e. of stating that some or all null-affix verbs beginning with the symbol a have a zero form of the a- prefix. Such verbals as the above three beginning with the symbol a will be considered null-affix derivatives.

Any statement below which places an a- prefix before a stem must take the above into consideration, i.e. |a-a... → |a... (also see page 89).

Verbal derivatives with a- are intransitive. The meanings are: 1. to perform the action indicated by the root, 2. to perform an action on oneself, 3. the action of the root is being performed or has been performed (impersonal; no agent), and 4. to own, have, or use the object indicated by the stem where the stem is a noun.

> 1) a-taña 'to ask'
>   a-ñaba 'to breathe'
>   a-ghəlaq 'to laugh'
>   a-cupa 'to spit'
>   a-zhalan 'to walk'
>   a-main 'to play'
>
> 2) a-cukur 'to shave (oneself)'
>   a-suddhuq 'to stab (oneself)'
>   a-bəgha 'to soak (oneself)'

113

3) a-uba 'to change'
   a-ubbhar 'to burn'
   a-issi 'be filled'

4) a-barna 'to have color, be colored'
   a-ciṭak 'have a head'
   a-bənku 'have a house'

No combinations with proclitics and a- alone occur in the corpus.

a- derivatives occur with all types of reduplication. Null affix adjectives generally have frequentative forms with a-R+. The ordering of prefixes is a-R+ stem.

a-tuluŋ 'to help'
a-Rf+tuluŋ 'to help (frequently)'
a-taña 'to ask'
a-R+taña keep on asking'
bhuŋa 'happy'
a-R+bhuŋa 'to be happy over a period of time'

Some verbals with a- and reduplication have the meaning of reciprocal action.

a-bhasa 'to use alus speech'
a-R+bhasa 'to use alus speech to each other'
a-bhidha 'to be different'
a-R+bhidha 'to be different from each other'

Specialized meanings are frequent.

bhərsi 'clean'
a-R+bhərsi 'to clean oneself (after menstruation)'
bəraq 'heavy'
a-Rf+bəraq 'to be pregnant'
a-labaŋ 'to have a door'
a-Rf+labaŋ 'to go from door to door'

For certain roots the difference between an a- derivative and an a-reduplication derivative is that the former means simply to have the object and the latter means to have it permanently, to cultivate it.

a-bənku 'to have a house'
a-R+bənku 'to have a household, one's own house'
a-zanguq 'to have a beard, be at an age where one's beard grows'

114

a-Rf+zanguq 'to grow, cultivate a beard, have a full growth'

N- (intransitive)[10]

These are derived from radical, extended and proclitic stems.

1) 'intransitive action, agentless action'

    N-pati 'to die'
    N-abbhər 'to fly'
    N-taŋis 'to weep'
    N-arti 'to understand'
    N-bukkaq 'to be open (of a store, museum)'
    N-sa.ari 'to spend a day' (proclitic stem)

2) 'reflexive action'

    N-panḍi 'to bathe'
    N-itək 'to hide'
    N-ciccir 'to stay behind'

3) 'be like, act like, do the job of'

sakiq 'sick'	N-sakiq 'act sick'
bəḍhi 'sand'	N-bəḍhi 'be gritty'
caciŋ 'worm'	N-caciŋ 'be scrawny'
tai 'faeces'	N-tai-n 'be rusty' (extended stem)
kulf 'coolie'	N-kulf 'work as a coolie'
timur 'east'	N-timur 'be the time of the east monsoon'

4) 'prepare (food)'

kupf 'coffee'	N-kupf 'to prepare coffee'

5) 'be in the location'

Derived from radical stems and proclitic stems with ka. 'to'.

baba 'down'	N-baba 'be under'
attas 'up'	N-attas 'be up, over'
buḍi 'back'	N-buḍi 'be back, behind'
kacir 'left'	N-kacir 'be to the left'
ka.ḍaza 'to the north'	N-ka.ḍaza 'be in the north'
pinghir 'side'	N-pinghir 'be to the side'

6) Special.

puti 'white'	N-puti 'eat nothing but rice'

The relative positions of N- and reduplication are: R+N-. When N- → a-, this a- appears before the reduplication. Also see page 88 for examples of this.

Reduplications occur in the meanings and environments given in the general discussion above (pages 108-110).

> N-tamuj 'to visit'
> R+N-tamuj, Rf+N-tamuj 'to visit different places or the same place
>   various times'
> N-kicuq 'to steal' (transitive)
> R+N-kicuq 'to steal (frequently, as a profession)'
> N-bəli 'to buy' (transitive)
> R+N-bəli 'to go shopping'
> N-pinghir 'on the side'
> zhaq R+N-pinghir! 'Don't (sit) on the side!' [1. zhaq 'don't']
>   1

Special cases:

> tanaŋ 'arm, hand'
> R+N-tanaŋ 'go unarmed, without weapon'
>
> N-panghaŋ 'to roast'
> azam R+N-panghaŋ 'roasting chicken' [1. azam 'chicken']
>   1

N- transitive

Transitive verbals have three forms: N-, i-, and ∅ (stem). The prefix i is connected to the following morpheme by dot juncture in fast speech, e.g. i.issi-i → èjèssèqè 'to be filled'.

The meanings are in general as follows: N- 'active' Examples are given below. N- is also used optionally in one type of imperative where the object is stressed. Compare the following pairs of sentences:

> zhaq ˊR+ghuli taŋ ghanbhar rua. 'Don't move my picture around.'
>   1   2   3   4   5
>   R-ghuli⎫
> zhaq R+N-ghuli⎰ taŋ ghanbhar ˊrua. 'Don't move my picture around.'
>   1   2   3   4   5
>   [1. zhaq 'don't', 2. R+ghuli 'move', 3. taŋ 'my', 4. ghanbhar
>   'picture', 5. rua 'that'].
>
> kalaq bukɗ za.ria + zhaq bəli. 'Take that book; don't buy it!'
>   1   2   3   4   5

kalaq
N-kalaq } bukú ´za.ria + zhaq si lain. 'Take <u>that</u> book, not the other!
1 2 3 4 6 7

[1. kalaq 'take', 2. bukú 'book', 3. za.ria 'that', 4. zhaq 'don't', 5. bəli 'buy', 6. si 'rel. particle', 7. lain 'other'].

i- 'passive' Examples are given below.

stem 'imperative' Examples are given above and below. Also certain other positions, e.g. the second of two passives:

paraq taq i-kəniŋ-a abas. 'Almost couldn't be seen' [1. paraq 'almost',
1 2 3 4

2. taq 'not', 3. i-kəniŋ-a 'able to be', 4. abas 'see'].

1) Transitive action.

N-kakan 'to eat'	i-kakan 'be eaten'	kakan 'eat (it)!'
N-tulis 'to write'	i-tulis 'be written'	tulis 'write (it)'
N-sari 'to look for'	i-sari 'be looked for'	sari 'look for (it)'
N-bəli 'to buy'	i-bəli 'be bought'	bəli 'buy (it)'

2) Where the stem is a noun, the derivative means 'to use that object in an action'.

pəḍhaŋ 'sword' N-pəḍhaŋ 'to strike with a sword'

All forms of these verbals except the stem form cooccur with the suffix -a.

The position of reduplication is as follows:

active:	R+N-
passive:	i-R+
stem:	R+

The meanings are those given in the general discussion above.

<u>-an</u>

Verbals with the suffix -an are intransitive.

1) Null affix verbals of the adjective type cooccur with -an, with or without (in free variation) the prefix a-, in a comparative meaning.

tua 'old'	tua-an	a-tua-an 'older'
baññaq 'much'	baññaq-an	a-baññaq-an 'more'
bhaghus 'good'	bhaghus-an	a-bhaghus-an 'better'
pintər 'clever'	pintər-an	a-pintər-an 'cleverer'

Cooccurring with locational intransitive N- (see page 115 above), -an also denotes 'further, more'.

> N-ka.ḍaləm 'to be inside, deep'
> N-ka.ḍaləm-an 'to be further inside, deeper'
> N-buḍi 'to be back'
> N-buḍi-an 'to be further back'

2) Derived from the proclitic stem with zhuŋ this derivative means 'superlative'.

> ghassaq 'swift'   zhuŋ ghassaq-an 'swiftest'
> bhaghus 'good'   zhuŋ bhaghus-an 'best'

A small group of stems indicating location also cooccur with zhuŋ -an. For example:

> buḍi 'back'   zhuŋ buḍi-an 'furthest back'

The comparative of such stems is formed with N- -an, e.g. N-buḍi-an 'further back' or with N-ka. -an (see above).

3) A frequentative is derived from the basic derivative by the suffixing of -an. Derivatives from null affix verbals optionally have a-.

> N-kəniŋ 'to hit'   N-kəniŋ-an 'frequently hit'
> N-amuk 'to run amok'   N-amuk-an 'run amok from time to time'
> N-antur 'to collide'   N-antur-an 'to keep colliding'
> a-bhutul 'to have a hole'   a-bhutul-an 'to be full of holes'
> a-ghazaq 'to joke'   a-ghazaq-an 'keep on joking around'
> ilaŋ 'to get lost'   ilaŋ-an, a-ilaŋ-an 'often get lost'

With reduplication:

> a-tuluŋ 'to help'   a-Rf+tuluŋ-an 'help frequently'
> N-kalaq 'to take'   R+N-kalaq-an 'take things often'
> N-zhual 'to sell'   R+N-zhual-an 'to trade'
> a-lazar 'to sail'   a-Rf+lazar-an 'go to sea, sail (for a living)'

4) Derived from some null-affix nouns, a- -an means 'to use regularly, to have (more or less) permanently'.

> a-uḍhəŋ 'to be wearing a head-cloth'

a-uḍhəŋ-an 'to wear a head-cloth (habitually)'

a-zanguq 'to have a beard'
a-zanguq-an 'to wear a beard'

5) -an with many null affix adjective stems means to have a quality over some length of time, as a personality trait, or to become that way easily.

ḍhusun 'impatient'
ḍhusun-an 'be an impatient person'

aləm 'praise'
aləm-an 'be pampered, spoiled'

baŋal 'brave'
baŋal-an 'be a brave person'

bhusən 'bored'
bhusən-an 'be bored easily'

cələp 'cold'
cələp-an 'get cold easily'

6) Cooccurring with some roots the -an derivative denotes a quality which has been applied,[11] e.g. kutur 'dirty', kutur-an 'dirtied'.

kutur 'dirty'	[aiŋ] kutur-an '[dish]water'	aiŋ 'water'
baba 'below'	[uriŋ] baba-an 'subordinate'	uriŋ 'person'
antré 'stand in line'	[bhəras] antré-an 'rationed [rice]'	bhəras 'rice'
ghabaj 'make'	ghabaj-an 'artificial'	
paku 'nail'	paku-an 'made with nails'	
tutu 'pound'	[bhəras] tutu-an 'pounded rice'	bhəras 'rice'

7) -an derived from null-affix adjectives denotes a collective quality of a specifically plural subject.

uriŋ zhaba-an 'Javanese (as a whole or a group of them)' [1. uriŋ
 1   2
   'person', 2. zhaba 'Java, Javanese']

zhukuq ghuriŋ-an 'fried foods' [1. zhukuq 'fish, meat food',
 1   2
   2. ghuriŋ 'fry']

si a-kunpul / madhura-an. 'Those who got together were Madurese.'
 1   2   3

119

[1. si 'rel. particle', 2. a-kunpul 'get together', 3. madhura 'Madura, Madurese']

8) Reciprocal meaning (very rare).

lain 'be different'　　　　lain-an 'be different from each other'

9) With units of time, -an means 'per, by the'.

ari 'day'　　　　　　　　ari-an 'daily'
bulan 'month'　　　　　　bulan-an 'monthly'

With the prefix a- these mean 'to do something by the'.

si N-bəli aiŋ / a-bulan-an. 'Those who buy water do it (pay)
1　 2　　3　　　　4
　　monthly.' [1. si 'rel. particle', 2. N-bəli 'to buy', 3.
　　aiŋ 'water', 4. a-bulan-an 'to do (it) monthly']

10) The use of -an with substitutes will be discussed below.

11) The use of -an with numbers will be discussed below.

-ən

There are few verbals with the suffix -ən. Only nine cases occur in the corpus. They cooccur with -a, but they do not reduplicate.

The meaning of this suffix is similar to that of -an 5 above, 'to have or to suffer from over a period of time'. It usually refers to diseases or other unhealthy conditions.

kuriŋ 'scabies'　　　　　　kuriŋ-ən 'to be scaby'
ghatəl 'itch'　　　　　　　ghatəl-ən 'to be itchy'
ɖuru 'wound'　　　　　　　ɖuru-ən 'be covered with wounds'
ɖara 'blood'　　　　　　　ɖara iluŋ-ən 'to have a nose-bleed'
iluŋ 'nose'

In some cases the connection is not clear:

kanciŋ 'button'　　　　　　kanciŋ-ən 'suffer from a disease (uniden-
　　　　　　　　　　　　　　　tified) in which one cannot close
　　　　　　　　　　　　　　　one's mouth; tetanus?'

pariŋ 'give'; [sakiq 'sick'] [sakiq] pariŋ-ən 'have smallpox'

In two cases the root does not occur elsewhere.

sighum-ən 'be sniffly'

p-al-iŋ+piŋ-ən 'be deafened'

-i (intransitive)

1) A small class of intransitive verbals derived from null-affix adjectives and nouns is formed with the N- prefix and -i suffix. The meaning is 'be like, act like (of people)' sometimes with the connotation of not actually being that way.

aghuŋ 'grand'	N-aghuŋ-i 'act like an important person'
anum 'young'	N-anum-i 'to look younger than one really is'
balandha 'Dutch'	N-balandha-i 'act like a Dutchman'
cina 'Chinese'	N-cina-i 'act like, look like a Chinese'
dhisa 'village'	N-dhisa-i 'act like, look like a villager'
kuʈʈa 'city'	N-kuʈʈa-i 'act like, look like a city person'

Some are derived from an extended stem in -n.

N-balandha-n-i 'act like a Dutchman'
N-dhisa-n-i 'act like a villager'

Reduplicated forms mostly occur as derivatives of reduplicated nouns.

R+k-anaq 'child'   R+N-k-anaq-i 'act childishly'

2) Some cases of Rf+N- -i occur in the meaning of plural action (cf. page 122 below).

N-pinta 'to request'	Rf+N-pinta-n-i 'to make all sorts of demands'
racun 'poison'	Rf+N-racun-i 'to poison (many objects often)'

3) Special

ɖua 'two'   N-par-ɖua-n-i 'to be doubtful, not do one thing or another definitely'

Three forms occur in the corpus which are intransitive -i derivatives but do not have N-. They are fixed expressions with non-literal meanings. Although grammatically they cooccur with -a, such a combination is highly unusual.

nasiq si əla kari sa-kuniq za.ria / pa-tutuk sakali + maq taq
 1   2   3   4   5   6   8   9 10
　　　R+bilis-i. 'Finish off the little remaining rice so the ants
　　　　11
　　　don't get it.' (i.e. so it doesn't go to waste) [1. nasiq 'cooked
　　　rice', 2. si 'rel. particle', 3. əla 'already', 4. kari 'be re-

maining', 5. sa-kuniq 'a little', 6. za.ria 'that', 7. pa-tutuk
'finish off!', 8. sakali 'completely', 9. maq 'so that', 10. taq
'not', 11. bilis 'ant']

zhukuq si sa-kuniq za.ria / cuma R+amis-i bhai. 'That little bit of
  1   2   3   4   5   6   7

meat is just enough for a smell (not enough to eat).' [1. zhukuq
'meat food', 2. si 'rel. particle', 3. sa-kuniq 'a little', 4.
za.ria 'that', 5. cuma 'only', 6. amis 'fish smell', 7. bhai
'just']

The latter sentence also occurs with R+anu-i in place of R+amis-i; the root
anu is the hesitation particle 'erh' or root which is a substitute for all other
roots.

-i (transitive)[12]

1) Transitive plural.

Transitives with -i denoting a repetition of the action on the same object
in an unbroken period of time or a performance of the action on a plurality of
objects are derived from transitive verbals without suffix. If the verb is
passive, it is the grammatical subject which is the goal of the action.

pəṭi ingha.panika / i-bhakta-i-a ghan R+sittuŋ. 'Those trunks
 1   2   3   4   5
will be carried one by one.' [1. pəṭi 'trunk', 2. ingha.panika
'that, those', 3. N-bhakta 'to carry', 4. ghan 'particle',
5. R+sittuŋ 'one by one']

ahmat / sa.ari bhəntiŋ / N-abas-i kulf si a-laku. 'Ahmat watched
 1   2   3   4   5 6 7
the working coolies for the whole day.' [1. ahmat 'Ahmat',
2. sa.ari 'a day', 3. bhəntiŋ 'whole', 4. N-abas 'to see',
5. kulf 'coolie', 6. si 'rel. particle', 7. a-laku 'to work']

sərina ka-sala-an-na əla i-aku-n-i, pɑlisf pas taq N-pukul-i puli.
   1   2   3   4   5   6   7   8   9
'Since his guilt was admitted, the police didn't beat him up any
more.' [1. sərina 'since', 2. ka-sala-an-na 'his guilt', 3.
əla 'already', 4. i-aku-n-i 'be admitted', 5. pɑlisf 'police',
6. pas 'then', 7. taq 'not', 8. N-pukul 'to hit', 9. puli 'again,
more']

N-anghiq-i R+taplaq-na miza. 'to embroider table-cloths'
   1   2   3

   [1. N-anghiq 'to embroider', 2. R+taplaq 'table-cloths', 3.
   miza 'table']

ghədhaŋ ghuriŋ za.ria / bəli-i tərus! 'Buy up the fried bananas!'
   1   2   3   4   5

   [1. ghədhaŋ 'banana', 2. ghuriŋ 'fried', 3. za.ria 'that,
   those', 4. N-bəli 'to buy', 5. tərus 'straight']

This derivative cooccurs with R and Rt reduplication in the meanings given
above on pages 108-110 . For example:

   rama si N-alli-a / mula-i R+N-bhakta-i bharaŋ-na. 'Father who will
    1   2   3   4   5   6

   move begins to carry his things.' [1. rama 'father', 2. si 'rel.
   particle', 3. N-alli-a 'will move', 4. mula-i 'to begin', 5.
   N-bhakta 'to carry', 6. bharaŋ-na 'his things']

   bhandhəŋ si i-zhəmur rua / i-R+bali-i. 'The drying bandeng kept
      1   2   3   4   5

   on being turned over.' [1. bhandhəŋ 'bandeng fish', 2. si 'rel.
   particle', 3. i-zhəmur 'be dried', 4. rua 'that', 5. N-bali 'to
   turn over']

   kacaŋ si i-kəla-a / əla i-R+bəgha-i. 'The peas to be cooked have
     1   2   3   4   5

   been soaked.' [1. kacaŋ 'pea', 2. si 'rel. particle', 3.
   i-kəla-a 'will be cooked', 4. əla 'already', 5. N-bəgha 'to soak']

2) Direct transitive.

Many intransitive verbals (null and N- types) have derived transitives with
the -i suffix. These have causative meaning.

   N-pati 'die, be dead'   N-pati-i 'to kill'
   zhagha 'wake up'   N-zhagha-i 'to wake (someone) up'
   bhərsi 'clean'   N-bhərsi-i 'to clean'

This derivative cooccurs with R reduplication.

3) Indirect transitive.

Many derivatives with -i have what can be called an indirect meaning, that
is in some way their objects are indirect objects (or subject when they are
passive).

a. Some are derived from nouns and mean 'to give or provide the object with that noun'.

  alɪ N-adhat-i uriŋ lain. 'Ali treats others properly.'
  1 2 3 4

   [1. alɪ 'Ali', 2. adhat 'customary law', 3. uriŋ 'person',
   4. lain 'other']

  tanbha 'medicine' N-tanbha-i 'to treat (someone)'

  mun baqna N-apuj-i nasiq za.ria, zhaq R+raza! 'When you put a
  1 2 3 4 5 6 7

   fire under that rice, don't make it big!' [1. mun 'when',
   2. baqna, 'you', 3. apuj 'fire', 4. nasiq 'rice', 5. za.ria
   'that', 6. zhaq 'don't', 7. raza 'big']

  pa-taña-na i-q-ɪa-i bhai. 'His question was just answered yes.'
  1   2   3

   [1. pa-taña-na 'his question', 2. ɪa 'yes', 3. bhai 'just']

  titi si əla tua za.ria / N-bhabhaza-n-i ɖaq uriŋ si libat.
  1 2 3 4 5   6   7 8 2 9

   'That old bridge is dangerous for passers-by.' [1. titi 'foot
   bridge', 2. si 'rel. particle', 3. əla 'already', 4. tua 'old',
   5. za.ria 'that', 6. bhabhaza 'danger', 7. ɖaq 'to', 8. uriŋ
   'person', 9. libat 'to pass by']

This type also cooccurs with reduplication or is derived from a reduplicated noun. The former often has a specialized meaning.

  asta 'hand'   R+N-asta-n-i 'to hold (a job)'

  b. Many are derived from basic derivative transitives (N-) taking direct objects or from intransitive verbals. The latter have some other derivative which takes a direct object. In the latter type, the passive is much more common in colloquial speech than the active. Instead of the active, the intransitive form plus a particle is usual, e.g. a-bəriq ɖaq 'to give to'; but passive: i-bəriq-i. The active form N-bəriq-i exists but is considered stilted and bookish.

  sinkuq i-bəriq-i rukuq. 'I am given cigarettes.' [1. sinkuq
  1   2   3

   'I', 2. a-bəriq 'to give', 3. rukuq 'cigaret']

124

sinkuq N-ankaq-i tamuj. 'I offer (food) to the guest.'
1   2   3

   [1. sinkuq 'I', 2. N-ankaq 'to lift up', 3. tamuj 'guest']

sərina R+k-anaq rua i-licik-i, mula-na pas N-taŋis. 'Since that
1   2   3   4   5   6   7

   child was lied to, he cried.' [1. sərina 'since', 2. R+k-anaq
   'child', 3. rua 'that', 4. licik 'to lie', 5. mula-na 'and so',
   6. pas 'then', 7. N-taŋis 'to cry']

sapa si N-bazar-i aliq baariq nəŋ pasar? 'Who paid for brother
1   2 3   4   5   6   7

   yesterday in the market?' [1. sapa 'who', 2. si 'rel. particle',
   3. N-bazar 'to pay (for something)', 4. aliq 'younger sibling',
   5. baariq 'yesterday', 6. nəŋ 'in', 7. pasar 'market']

With reduplication:

apuj 'fire'   R+N-apuj-i 'to egg on, bait'

kakaq mun R+baca-an / zhaq R+taña-i! 'When brother is reading,
1   2   3   4   5

   don't ask him a lot of questions!' [1. kakaq 'older brother',
   2. mun 'when', 3. R+baca-an 'be reading', 4. zhaq 'don't',
   5. a-taña 'to ask']

aliq i-R+bəriq-i. 'Brother was given things.' [1. aliq 'younger
1   2

   sibling', 2. a-bəriq 'to give']

aliq-na / zhaq R+azhar-i N-inum kupſ! 'Don't teach brother to
1   2   3   4   5

   drink coffee!' [1. aliq-na 'his brother', 2. zhaq 'don't',
   3. N-azhar 'to teach (something)', 4. N-inum 'to drink',
   5. kupſ 'coffee']

c. Closely connected with the preceding is the meaning involving

location, to or from a place.

saba / i-tamən-i paḍi. 'The field was planted with rice.'
1   2   3

   [1. saba 'wet rice field', 2. N-tamən 'to plant (something)',
   3. paḍi 'rice']

kənḍhi ghiq bəlun i.issi-i aiŋ. 'The jug has not yet been
1   2   3   4   5

   filled with water.' [1. kənḍhi 'jug', 2. ghiq 'yet',

125

3. bəlun 'not yet', 4. a-issi 'have content', 5. aiŋ 'water']

bənku si añar rua / i-alli-i su rama. 'The new house was moved
  1   2   3   4   5   6   7
into by father.' [1. bənku 'house', 2. si 'rel. particle',
3. añar 'new', 4. rua 'that', 5. N-alli 'to move', 6. su 'by',
7. rama 'father']

ɖatəŋ 'to come'   N-ɖatəŋ-i 'to come to (a place)'

N-singha 'to go away'   N-singha-i 'to go away from (a place,
                                        person)'

N-təŋa 'be in the   R+N-təŋa-i 'to intervene (in something)'
middle'

-aghi[13]

-aghi is connected with what precedes by normal (-), dot (.) or combination
(⁻) juncture. The first two are apparently in free variation and are far more
common than the latter.[14]   For juncture rules see Chapter II.

N-təraŋ-aghi → nə̀rrà̰ŋå̰ghí 'to explain'
N-təraŋ.aghi → nə̀rrà̰ŋŋàghí   "
N-təraŋ⁻aghi → nə̀rrà̰ŋŋàghí   "

N-bazhiq-aghi → à̰bá̰zhḭ́qá̰ghí 'to disgust'
N-bazhiq.aghi → à̰bá̰zhḭ́qà̰ghí   "
N-bazhiq⁻aghi → à̰bá̰zhḭ́qà̰ghí   "

i-licik-aghi → ḛ̀lḛ̀cḛ̀ghá̰ghí 'be considered a lie'
i-licik.aghi → ḛ̀lḛ̀cḛ̀kkà̰ghí   "
i-licik⁻aghi → ḛ̀lḛ̀cḛ̀gghá̰ghí   "

-aghi (intransitive)

There are extremely few intransitive verbals with -aghi. They cooccur with
N- or a-.

1) Two words meaning 'to rise' and 'to descend' are used for inanimate
subjects. Animate subjects take the null affix forms.

zhalan-na N-turun-aghi. 'The road descends.'
zhalan-na N-ungha-aghi. 'The road rises.'
[zhalan 'road', turun 'to descend', ungha 'to rise, go up']

2) A small number of intransitives in a- have derivatives with -aghi

with the meaning 'benefactive, to perform the action for someone else' (cf. page 130 below).

> a-tani-aghi saba-na paman. 'to work uncle's fields' [1. a-tani 'to
>   1   2   3
> farm', 2. saba-na 'his wet rice field', 3. paman 'uncle']

> a-ula-aghi zhazhan-na ibhu. 'to cook mother's snacks' [1. a-ula 'to
>   1   2   3
> cook', 2. zhazhan-na 'her snacks', 3. ibhu 'mother']

The transitive form N-ula-aghi also occurs.

> a-tanaq 'to cook (rice)'
> a-tanaq-aghi 'to cook (rice) for someone else'

Besides those given in the above examples only a few others occur.

-aghi (transitive)

1) A few transitive verbals referring to acts of the senses have derivatives with -aghi meaning 'to perform that act purposely'.

> N-abas 'to see'   N-abas-aghi 'to look at'
> N-iḍiŋ 'to hear'   N-iḍiŋ-aghi 'to listen to'

With reduplication:

> R+abas-aghi pula baḍa uriŋ N-ghiba təlur! 'Keep on looking; perhaps
>   1   2   3   4   5   6
> there's someone bringing eggs.' [1. N-abas 'to see', 2. pula
> 'perhaps', 3. baḍa 'there is', 4. uriŋ 'person', 5. N-ghiba 'to
> carry', 6. təlur 'egg']

2) A few verbals derived from null affix verbals and nouns mean 'to treat like, consider as'.

> mun a-main səhak, zhaq sanpiq N-bhuḍhu-aghi musu-na! 'When you play
> 1   2   3   4   5   6   7
> chess, don't underestimate your opponent.' [1. mun 'when',
> 2. a-main 'to play', 3. səhak 'chess', 4. zhaq 'don't', 5. sanpiq
> 'up to', 6. bhuḍhu 'stupid', 7. musu-na 'the opponent']

> taq maŋlu baqna su uriŋ rua si i-dhisa-aghi. 'It's only right that
> 1   2   3   4   5   6   7
> person treats you like a hick.' [1. taq maŋlu 'it's only right',
> 2. baqna 'you', 3. su 'by', 4. uriŋ 'person', 5. rua 'that',
> 6. si 'rel. particle', 7. dhisa 'village']

aliq N-licik.aghi apa si i-k-ucaq-aghi kakaq. 'Younger brother con-
1   2   3 4   5   6

siders what older brother said a lie.' [1. aliq 'younger sibling',

2. licik 'to lie', 3. apa 'what', 4. si 'rel. particle', 5.

i-k-ucaq-aghi 'it is said', 6. kakaq 'older brother']

With reduplication:

aliq i-R+zhubaq-aghi su kakaq ḍaq rama. 'Older brother keeps on
1   2   3   4   5   6

presenting younger brother as a bad person to father.' [1. aliq

'younger sibling', 2. zhubaq 'bad', 3. su 'by', 4. kakaq 'older

brother', 5. ḍaq 'to', 6. rama 'father']

3) Some derivatives with -aghi take direct objects and correspond to
those indirect transitives mentioned under -i 3b above which take indirect objects. The latter are in turn derived from intransitives.

a-taña 'to ask   N-taña-i 'to ask (some-   N-taña-aghi 'to ask (about
                                 one)'   something)'

uriŋ ria i-tular-i paŋ-sakit. 'This man was infected by a disease.'
1   2   3   4

tikus N-tular.aghi paŋ-sakit pis. 'Rats spread the plague.'
5   3   4   6

  [1. uriŋ 'person', 2. ria 'this', 3. N-tular 'be contagious',
  4. paŋ-sakit 'sickness', 5. tikus 'rat', 6. pis 'plague']

kənḍhi ghiq bəlun i.issi-i aiŋ. 'The jug has not yet been filled with
1   2   3   4   5

water.'

uriŋ rua N-issi-aghi bènsɪn ḍaq gənbrèŋ. 'The man puts gas into the
6   7   4   8   9   10

can.' [1. kənḍhi 'jug', 2. ghiq 'yet', 3. bəlun 'not yet',

4. a-issi 'to have content', 5. aiŋ 'water', 6. uriŋ 'person',

7. rua 'that', 8. bènsɪn 'gasoline', 9. ḍaq 'to', 10. gənbrèŋ

'can']

baqna i-pariŋ-i pau. 'You are given a mango.'
1   2   3

pau i-pariŋ.aghi ḍaq baqna. 'A mango is given to you.' [1. baqna
3   2   4   1

'you', 2. a-pariŋ 'to give' (intransitive), 3. pau 'mango',

4. ḍaq 'to']

In some cases the form in -i is rare, non-existent, or has a specialized meaning.

> N-k-ucaq 'to speak' (intransitive)
> i-k-ucaq-aghi 'it is talked about'

The form in -i (N-k-ucaq-i) does not seem to occur.

> a-carita 'to tell a story' (intransitive)
> N-carita-i 'to give a talking to, give a line to'
> N-carita-aghi 'to tell (a story), to narrate'
> a-bhazaŋ 'to pray'
> N-bhazaŋ.aghi 'to pray over (something)'
> N-bhazaŋ-i is rare.

4) Many suffixless transitive verbals have derivatives in -aghi meaning 'to use the object as an instrument'.

> pəɗhaŋ i-pəɗhaŋ.aghi ɖaq bhunka-na ghəɗhaŋ. 'The sword was struck
> 1   2   3   4   5
>> against the banana tree.' [1. pəɗhaŋ 'sword', 2. N-pəɗhaŋ 'to
>> strike with a sword', 3. ɖaq 'to', 4. bhunka-na 'its tree',
>> 5. ghəɗhaŋ 'banana']

> puqlut-na i-tulis.aghi ɖaq dhalubaŋ. 'The pencil was used for
> 1   2   3   4
>> writing on the paper.' [1. puqlut-na 'the pencil', 2.N-tulis
>> 'to write', 3. ɖaq 'to', 4. dhalubaŋ 'paper']

With reduplication:

> púlpin ria / zhaq R+tulis.aghi! 'Don't write with this pen!'
> 1   2   3   4
>> [1. púlpin 'pen', 2. ria 'this', 3. zhaq 'don't', 4. N-tulis
>> 'to write']

> mun tunkət-na baqna i-R+pukul.aghi kanţa za.ria, R+abit tantu
> 1   2   3   4   5   6   7   8
>> N-pa-luka ghəɗhuŋ. 'If you keep on hitting with your stick
>> 9   10
>> like that, you'll eventually make a hole in the wall.' [1. mun
>> 'if', 2. tunkət-na 'stick', 3. baqna 'you', 4. N-pukul 'to strike',
>> 5. kanţa 'like', 6. za.ria 'that', 7. R+abit 'finally', 8. tantu
>> 'sure', 9. N-pa-luka 'to wound', 10. ghəɗhuŋ 'masonry wall']

5) Derived from some suffixless intransitives and transitives -aghi

derivatives mean 'to make the object be or become or go do the action or root meaning'. When derived from an intransitive with a reflexive meaning, the -aghi derivative means to do that action to someone else.

    sərina aliq ghiq sakiq, ta-paksa sinkuq N-anghuj-aghi kalanbhi-na.
      1   2   3   4   5   6   7   8

       'Since brother is still sick, I had to put his shirt on (for him).'
       [1. sərina 'since', 2. aliq 'younger sibling', 3. ghiq 'still',
       4. sakiq 'sick', 5. ta-paksa 'be forced', 6. sinkuq 'I', 7.
       N-anghuj 'to wear, put on clothing', 8. kalanbhi-na 'his shirt']

    baqna zhaq səghut N-attas.aghi ka-pintər-an-na dhibiq bhai! 'Don't
      1   2   3   4   5   6   7

       keep on praising your own cleverness.' [1. baqna 'you', 2. zhaq
       'don't', 3. səghut 'often', 4. N-attas 'be on top', 5. ka-pintər-
       an-na 'his cleverness', 6. dhibiq 'self', 7. bhai 'just']

    kiai pratanu N-pakun ɖaq kiai bagənu supaza N-éslam.aghi-a raqjàt.ipun
      1   2   3   4   1   5   6   7   8

           'Kijai Pratano ordered Kijai Bageno to islamize his
       people.' [1. kiai 'Moslem title', 2. pratanu 'proper name',
       3. N-pakun 'to order', 4. ɖaq 'to', 5. bagənu 'proper name',
       6. supaza 'in order to', 7. éslam 'Moslem', 8. raqjàt.ipun 'his
       people']

    ghuru rua / i-bhantu-aghi ɖaq sakula-an SMP. 'That teacher was sent
      1   2   3   4   5   6

       to help at the SMP school.' [1. ghuru 'teacher', 2. rua 'that',
       3. a-bhantu 'to help', 4. ɖaq 'to', 5. sakula-an 'school, 6. SMP
       [ês+êm+pé] 'junior high school']

    a-sari 'to sleep'   N-sari-aghi 'to put to sleep'
    təraŋ 'clear'   N-təraŋ-aghi 'to explain'

6) Certain intransitive verbals indicating motion have transitive derivatives with -aghi meaning 'to perform the action with (the object)'.[15]

    a-laŋŋuj 'to swim'   N-laŋŋuj-aghi 'to swim away with'

7) All suffixless transitive verbals have a derivative in -aghi meaning 'to perform the action for someone else, on an object belonging to someone else'. This will be called the 'benefactive' use. When the subject of the sentence is the recipient of the benefactive action, the passive retains the N-. The N- is

130

also retained in the imperative when the person for whom the action is done is the goal of the action. In cases where N- → a-, the N- → Ø in the benefactive passive and imperative. For example:

i-N-bəli-aghí → èmèllèjàghí 'be bought for'

i-N-zhaiq-aghí → èzháɾqághí 'be sewed for'

N-bəli-aghí → mèllèjàghí 'buy for'

N-zhaiq-aghí → zháɾqághí 'sew for'

Compare the following two passive sentences:

sinkuq i-N-bəli-aghi rukuq. 'I was bought cigarettes.'
1   2   3

rukuq i-bəli-aghi ka-anghuj sinkuq. 'Cigarettes were bought for me.'
3   2   4   1

  [1. sinkuq 'I', 2. N-bəli 'to buy', 3. rukuq 'cigaret',

  4. ka-anghuj 'for']

Compare the following two imperative sentences:

bəli-aghi rukuq za.ria! 'Buy those cigarettes (for somebody)!'
1   2   3

N-bəli-aghi sinkuq + rukuq za.ria! 'Buy me those cigarettes!'
1   4   2   3

  [1. N-bəli 'to buy', 2. rukuq 'cigaret', 3. za.ria 'that, those',

  4. sinkuq 'I']

Examples of benefactive -aghi follow:

rama N-bhakta-aghi punapa ɖaq ibhu? 'What did father bring to
1   2   3   4   5

  mother?' [1. rama 'father', 2. N-bhakta 'to carry', 3. punapa

  'what', 4. ɖaq 'to', 5. ibhu 'mother']

paman N-bazar-aghi siwà-na bənku + margha sinkuq sakiq. 'Uncle payed
1   2   3   4   5   6   7

  the rent, because I'm sick.' [1. paman 'uncle', 2. N-bazar 'to

  pay', 3. siwà-na 'its rent', 4. bənku 'house', 5. margha 'because',

  6. sinkuq 'I', 7. sakiq 'sick']

ibhu əla i-N-bəgha-aghi bhəras si bhakal i-ka-ghabaj-a təpuŋ. 'Rice
1   2   3   4   5   6   7   8

  which will be made into flour has been soaked (by someone) for

  mother.' [1. ibhu 'mother', 2. əla 'already', 3. N-bəgha 'to

  soak', 4. bhəras 'rice', 5. si 'rel. particle', 6. bhakal 'will',

7. i-ka-ghabaj-a 'will be made into', 8. təpuŋ 'flour']

ənbhuk i-N-sikut.aghi kalanbhi.   '(Someone) cut a blouse for sister.'
  1   2   3

   [1. ənbhuk 'older sister', 2. N-sikut 'to cut', 3. kalanbhi
   'upper garment']

aliq i-sanghup-i i-N-bəli-aghi-a sapiɖa.   'Brother was promised (to
  1   2   3   4

   be bought) a bike.'   [1. aliq 'younger sibling', 2. i-sanghup-i
   'be promised', 3. N-bəli 'to buy', 4. sapiɖa 'bicycle']

Note that the i- of the second passive is retained if it is benefactive.

Since the -aghi benefactive cannot be added to a derivative which already
has a suffix, there can be ambiguity.[16]

   N-kutəp 'to throw (at something)'
   N-kutəp-aghi 'to throw (something) [instrumental -aghi] or 'to throw
      (at something) for someone else'

   aliq N-kutəp-aghi pau ka-anghuj kakaq.   'Younger brother throws a
    1   2   3   4   5

     mango for older brother.' or 'Younger brother throws (something)
     at a mango for older brother.'   [1. aliq 'younger sibling',
     2. N-kutəp 'to throw at', N-kutəp-aghi 'to throw', 3. pau 'mango',
     4. ka-anghuj 'for', 5. kakaq 'older brother']

The 'benefactive' also cooccurs with R or Rt.

   mun i-R+N-bəli-aghi uriŋ, baqna kudhu N-k-ucaq sa-ka-lankuŋ.   'When
    1   2   3   4   5   6   7

     people buy things for you, you must say thank you.'   [1. mun
     'when', 2. N-bəli 'to buy', 3. uriŋ 'people', 4. baqna 'you',
     5. kudhu 'must', 6. N-k-ucaq 'to say', 7. sa-ka-lankuŋ 'thank you]

ta-

Intransitive verbals with the prefix ta- are derived from the root. They
are generally passive in meaning.

   1) 'to do unintentionally, accidentally; to happen accidentally, unintentionally, suddenly, or without any specifically mentioned agent.'

     tiɖuŋ 'to sleep'   ta-tiɖuŋ 'to fall asleep'
     a-ubbhar 'to burn'   ta-ubbhar 'to get burned down'

uriŋ tani si a-laku nəŋ saba rua / ta-bhəɗhil.   'The farmer working
1   2   3   4   5   6   7   8

   in that field got shot accidentally.' [1. uriŋ 'person', 2. tani
   'farm', 3. si 'rel. particle', 4. a-laku 'to work', 5. nəŋ 'in',
   6. saba 'wet rice field', 7. rua 'that', 8. bhəɗhil 'shoot']

baktu-na ɗókar rua ta-antur-a ɗaq mutur, kósér-na N-pa-bhiluk
1   2   3   4   5   6   7   8

   zharan-na ka kacir.   'When the dogcart was about to collide with
   9   10 11

   the automobile, the driver turned his horse to the left.'
   [1. baktu-na 'when', 2. ɗókar 'dog-cart', 3. rua 'that', 4. antur
   collide', 5. ɗaq 'to', 6. mutur 'automobile', 7. kósér-na 'its
   driver', 8. N-pa-bhiluk 'to turn', 9. zharan-na 'his horse',
   10. ka 'to', 11. kacir 'left']

labaŋ-na / supaza taq ta-bukkaq-a bhai, pasaŋ-i batu! 'Put a stone
1   2   3   4   5   6   7

   (there) so the door won't come open.' [1. labaŋ-na 'the door',
   2. supaza 'in order to', 3. taq 'not', 4. bukkaq 'to open',
   5. bhai 'just', 6. pasaŋ-i 'install', 7. batu 'stone']

N- is retained in derivatives from intransitive verbals with N-.

pissi-na aliq ta-N-turuq ta-ka-balanzha. 'Brother's money got spent
1   2   3   4

   too (accidentally).' [1. pissi-na 'his money', 2. aliq 'younger
   sibling', 3. N-turuq 'go along in doing something', 4. N-ka-
   balanzha 'spend (money)']

Less frequent are ta- derivatives with active meaning. Some derived from
N- transitives always retain the N-; others optionally retain N-.

sinkuq ta-N-abas ɗaq paman. 'I (accidentally) saw uncle.'
1   2   3   4

   [1. sinkuq 'I', 2. N-abas 'to see', 3. ɗaq 'to', 4. paman 'uncle']
aliq {ta-kakan racun. 'Brother (accidentally) ate poison.' [1. aliq
     {ta-N-kakan
1   2   3

   'younger sibling', 2. N-kakan 'to eat', 3. racun 'poison']

Reduplication precedes ta-.

baktu musim uŋsi-an baññaq uriŋ si R+ta-ankuq R+bharaŋ-na ka.baraq
1   2   3   4   5   6 7   8   9

   ka.timur. 'During the evacuation time, many people's possessions
   10

133

got carried back and forth.' [1. baktu 'during', 2. musim
'season', 3. uŋsi-an 'evacuation', 4. baññaq 'many', 5. uriŋ
'person', 6. si 'rel. particle', 7. ankuq 'transport', 8.
R+bharaŋ-na 'their things', 9. ka.baraq 'to the west', 10.
ka.timur 'to the east']

R+laun-na baqna si a-zhalan + maq sanpiq R+ta-antur ɖaq miza.
1   2   3   4   5   6   7 8
'Walk slowly or you'll keep smashing into the table.' [1.
R+laun-na 'slowly', 2. baqna 'you', 3. si 'rel. particle',
4. a-zhalan 'to walk', 5. maq sanpiq 'or else', 6. antur
'collide', 7. ɖaq 'to', 8. miza 'table']

2) Derived from null-affix verbals with adjective meaning and certain
other intransitive verbals in N-, the ta- derivation means 'too much, very
much'. The verbal is often followed by the word ghallu.

kupiqan rua / i-anbhat a-margha takuq ta-tinghi ghallu. 'The kite
1   2   3   4   5   6   7
was pulled because it was feared it (would go) too high.'
[1. kupiqan 'kite', 2. rua 'that', 3. i-anbhat 'be pulled',
4. a-margha 'because', 5. takuq 'be afraid', 6. tinghi 'high',
7. ghallu 'first, before']

baqna si N-siram tana za.ria / ta-bassa ghallu. 'You who watered
1   2   3   4   5   6   7
the ground (made it) too wet.' [1. baqna 'you', 2. si 'rel.
particle', 3. N-siram 'to water', 4. tana 'ground', 5. za.ria
'that', 6. bassa 'wet', 7. ghallu 'first']

baqna si tuzuq / ta-buɖi ghallu. 'You're sitting too far back.'
1   2   3   4   5
[1. baqna 'you', 2. si 'rel. particle', 3. tuzuq 'sit', 4. buɖi
'back', 5. ghallu 'first']

This sentence can also occur with ta-N-buɖi 'be too far back'.

Such derivatives also cooccur with proclitic stems in ka. or affixal N-ka.
stems.

ɖaləm 'deep'   ta-ɖaləm ta-ka.ɖaləm ta-N-ka.ɖaləm 'too deep'
ɖaza 'north'   ta-ka.ɖaza ta-N-ka.ɖaza 'too much to the
                                              north'

3) Very rarely, ta- denotes the ability to perform the action, generally

134

preceded by taq 'not' or, if positive, followed by kia 'anyway'.

> miza tulis si raza rua / sumili-a i-ka-ɖua-i, taq ta-ankaq
> 1   2   3 4   5   6   7   8   9
>
> > sa-kuniq-a bhakalla. 'Even though that big desk was handled
> > 10   11
> >
> > by two men, it couldn't even be lifted a little.' [1. miza
> > 'table', 2. tulis 'write', 3. si 'rel. particle', 4. raza 'big',
> > 5. rua 'that', 6. sumili-a 'even though', 7. i-ka-ɖua-i 'be done
> > by two', 8. taq 'not', 9. ankaq 'lift up', 10. sa-kuniq-a 'a
> > little', 11. bhakalla 'merely']

ta- cooccurs with other affixes which have been discussed up to this
point. The meanings are combined. These are rare in everyday speech.

ta- -i

> 1) Locational.

> > R+k-anaq si libat i baba rua / ta-cupa-i. 'The child passing below
> > 1   2   3 4 5   6   7
> >
> > got spit on.' [1. R+k-anaq 'child', 2. si 'rel. particle',
> > 3. libat 'to pass by', 4. i 'at', 5. baba 'below', 6. rua
> > 'that', 7. N-cupa-i 'to spit on']

> 2) Plural.

> > R+bəli-n-na kaɗla ta-bazar-i paman. 'My purchases got payed for by
> > 1   2   3   4
> >
> > uncle.' [1. R+bəli-n-na 'purchases of', 2. kaɗla 'I', 3.
> > N-bazar-i 'to pay for (pl.)', 4. paman 'uncle']

ta- -an

> ta-tanɖuŋ 'to stumble'   ta-tanɖuŋ-an 'keep on stumbling'

pa-

In very rapid speech N-pa-ma... → ma.ma..., e.g. N-pa-mabuq → ma.mabuq →
mammabúq 'make drunk'. For reduplicated order see page 138.

pa- (intransitive)

1) N-pa- intransitive verbals derived from some intransitive verbals and
some nouns mean 'to act in such and such a way, to make oneself do such and such
a thing purposely.'

> bui 'dumb, unable to speak'   N-pa-bui 'to keep silent'

bunkul 'round'	N-pa-bunkul 'to appear round'
ilaŋ 'to get lost'	N-pa-ilaŋ 'to disappear'
tamuj 'guest'	N-pa-tamuj 'to go visiting'
bunkuq 'bent over'	N-pa-bunkuq '(walk) bent over'

With reduplication in the order R+N-pa- :

ilaŋ 'to get lost'	R+N-pa-ilaŋ 'keep coming and going'

2) Derivatives with R+N-pa- or N-pa-Rt+ from intransitive verbals and some nouns mean 'to pretend, to appear to be'. They cannot be reduplicated.

> taŋ kanca rua / pintər N-pa-Rt+anum. 'That friend of mine
> 1   2   3   4   5
> knows how to look young(er than he is).' [1. taŋ 'my', 2.
> kanca 'friend', 3. rua 'that', 4. pintər 'clever', 5. anum
> 'young']

> R+k-anaq za.ria / cuma R+N-pa-bhudhu bhai. 'That child is only pre-
> 1   2   3   4
> tending to be stupid.' [1. R+k-anaq 'child', 2. za.ria 'that',
> 3. cuma 'only', 4. bhudhu 'stupid', 5. bhai 'just']

Rf+bini-q 'woman'	R+N-pa-Rf+bini-q 'act like a woman'

This derivative also cooccurs with proclitic stems with taq 'not' in the order R+N-pa-taq. 'pretend not to'.

> sudhaghar rua /baktu i-datəŋ-i tukaŋ pazhək, R+N-pa-taq.andiq.
> 1   2   3   4   5   6   7
> 'When that merchant was visited by the tax man, he pretended not
> to own anything.' [1. sudhaghar 'merchant', 2. rua 'that',
> 3. baktu 'when', 4. i-datəŋ-i 'be visited', 5. tukaŋ 'person who',
> 6. pazhək 'tax', 7. andiq 'to possess']

tau 'to know'	R+N-pa-taq.tau 'to pretend not to know'

3) Derived from a very small number of roots describing noises, derivatives with salaŋ pa- mean 'to perform an action several times in a short, unbroken space of time'.

> pa-N-inum-na / salaŋ pa-cəlgək. 'He kept gulping down his drink.'
>   1   2   3
> [1. pa-N-inum-na 'his drinking', 2. salaŋ 'mutual', 3. cəlgək
> 'gulp']

136

ñiur-na si ghagghar / salaŋ pa-talbhuk. 'The coconuts fell with
  1   2   3   4   5

    thumps.' [1. ñiur-na 'the coconuts', 2. si 'rel. particle',

    3. ghagghar 'to fall', 4. salaŋ 'mutual', 5. talbhuk 'thump']

4) There are a few derivatives with a-pa- meaning 'to have (over some

period of time)'.[17] The stem is a noun.

    sərina sinkuq a-pa-bhala R+k-anaq, dhaddhi taŋ anpir kutur bhai.
     1   2   3   4   5   6   7   8   9

    'Since I have children in my family, my porch is dirty.'

    [1. sərina 'since', 2. sinkuq 'I', 3. bhala 'family', 4.

    R+k-anaq 'child', 5. dhaddhi 'so', 6. taŋ 'my', 7. anpir

    'porch', 8. kutur 'dirty', 9. bhai 'just']

    sapiɖa za.ria / a-pa-argha baranpa? 'What's the value of that bike?'
     1   2   3   4

    [1. sapiɖa 'bike', 2. za.ria 'that', 3. argha 'price', 4.

    baranpa 'how much']

    a-bənku 'to have a house'   a-pa-bənku 'to have a household'

5) There are a few derivatives in pa- derived from basic derivatives

which mean 'to be a person who often does or does well at (the action)'.

    a-ghazaq 'to joke'   pa-ghazaq 'to be a jokester'

    a-laŋŋuj 'to swim'   pa-laŋŋuj 'to be a good swimmer'

    N-buaŋ 'to throw away'   pa-N-buaŋ 'to be a spendthrift'

Special

    ituŋ 'count'   R+pa-r-ituŋ   }
                                       'to be calculating'
                     R+pa-r-ituŋ-an   }

    ruba 'shape, form'   pa-ruba 'to be what sex?'

                        pa-ruba-an 'to be what sexes (plural)?'

pa- -an
pa- -ən   (intransitive)

There are a few derivatives with these circumfixes meaning 'to be such and

such a way as a personality trait'. They are derived from the basic derivative

and some nouns.

    a-caca 'to talk'   pa-caca-ən 'to be talkative'

    a-carita 'to narrate'   pa-carita-ən 'to give excuses for
                                         oneself'

zhalan 'road'	pa-zhalan-an 'to be a traveller'
zikar 'bullock-cart'	[sapi] pa-zikar-an 'draught [cow]'
luppa 'to forget'	pa-luppa-ən 'to be forgetful'
ati 'liver'; R+ati 'be careful'	pa-r-ati-n 'be (a) cautious (person)'

<u>taq.pa-</u> occurs with a very limited number of stems (basic derivatives and nouns) in the meaning 'not do that action, not be that way in general'.

a-main 'to play'	taq.pa-main 'not to gamble'
ibhu 'mother'	taq.pa-ibhu 'to be motherless'
bənku 'house'	taq.pa-bənku 'to be homeless'
a-ghazaq 'to joke'	taq.pa-ghazaq 'to be a serious person'
N-inum 'to drink'	taq.pa-N-inum 'to be a non-drinker'
N-kakan 'to eat'	taq.pa-N-kakan 'to be a fussy eater'
tiɖuŋ 'to sleep'	taq.pa-tiɖuŋ 'to have difficulty sleeping' or 'to need little sleep'

pa- (transitive)

Derivatives with pa- can most generally be described as 'causative'. The form of the stem depends on the basic derivative and on the syntax of the sentence, as will be shown below.

Reduplication order of pa-

The following formulae show all possible orderings of inflected pa- and reduplications. These are apparently in free variation. Orderings in square brackets are rarely used in East Madurese.[18]

	<u>R+</u>	<u>Rt+</u>
active:	R+N-pa-(N-) N-pa-R+(N-)	N-pa-Rt+(N-)
passive:	i-R+pa-(N-) i-pa-R+(N-) [R+i-pa-(N-)]	i-pa-Rt+(N-)
stem:	R+pa-(N-) [pa-R+(N-)]	pa-Rt+(N-)

For example, the following are derived from N-pa-kunpul 'to gather'.

active:	R+N-pa-kunpul N-pa-R+kunpul	N-pa-Rt+kunpul
passive:	i-R+pa-kunpul i-pa-R+kunpul [R+i-pa-kunpul]	i-pa-Rt+kunpul
stem:	R+pa-kunpul [pa-R+kunpul]	pa-Rt+kunpul

Derivational history

1) Derived from intransitive verbals:

```
active:    N-pa-(N-)

passive:   i-pa-(N-)

stem:      pa-(N-)
```

If the underlying stem has an adjectival meaning, the derivative means 'to make (the object) be or become that'. These often have reflexive meaning 'to make (oneself) be or become that', and in these cases either active or passive forms are used interchangeably. If the underlying stem has a verbal meaning, the derivative means 'to make, allow, permit (the object) to perform that action'.

sapa si N-pa-rusak? 'Who broke it?' [1. sapa 'who', 2. si 'rel.
1   2   3
   particle', 3. rusak 'broken']

apuj rua / i-pa-tirəp. 'The fire was extinguished.' [1. apuj 'fire',
1   2   3
   2. rua 'that', 3. tirəp 'be extinguished']

R+apa si i-ghiba-a / pa-sadia! 'Prepare whatever will be brought!'
1   2   3   4
   [1. R+apa 'whatever', 2. si 'rel. particle', 3. i-ghiba-a 'will be
   brought', 4. sadia 'prepared']

abaq-na N-pa-ka.luar pissi dari kantuŋ-na. 'He took money out of his
1   2   3   4   5
   pocket.' [1. abaq-na 'he', 2. ka.luar 'to go out', 3. pissi
   'money', 4. dari 'from', 5. kantuŋ-na 'his pocket']

ghuru ciq pintər-na N-pa-N-arti R+k-anaq si bhudhu. 'Teacher is clever
1   2   3   4   5   6 7
   at making dumb children understand.' [1. ghuru 'teacher', 2. ciq
   'very', 3. pintər-na 'clever', 4. N-arti 'to understand', 5.
   R+k-anaq 'child', 6. si 'rel. particle', 7. bhudhu 'stupid']

sinkuq ghəlaq əla N-pa-bali sapida-na baqna. 'I've returned your
1   2   3   4   5   6
   bike.' [1. sinkuq 'I', 2. ghəlaq 'earlier', 3. əla 'already',
   4. a-bali 'to go back', 5. sapida-na 'bike of', 6. baqna 'you']

mun baqna N-pa-N-anghur uriŋ malas, tantu pas sazani malas. 'If you
1   2   3   4   5   6   7   8   5
   fire lazy people they surely become lazier.' [1. mun 'if',
   2. baqna 'you', 3. N-anghur 'to be out of work', 4. uriŋ 'person',
   5. malas 'lazy', 6. tantu 'sure', 7. pas 'then', 8. sazini
```
```

'increasingly']

bhunka-na pau-na / i-pa-bua ghallu + pas i-tuttu. 'His mango tree
   1   2   3   4   5   6

was allowed to bear fruit first, and then it was pruned.' [1.
bhunka-na 'tree of', 2. pau-na 'his mango', 3. a-bua 'to bear
fruit', 4. ghallu 'first', 5. pas 'then', 6. i-tuttu 'he pruned']

R+k-anaq i-pa-N-taŋis su ənbhuk. 'Sister made the child cry.'
   1   2   3 4
[1. R+k-anaq 'child', 2. N-taŋis 'to cry', 3. su 'by', 4. ənbhuk
'older sister']

With reduplication

R+pa-barna ra! 'Make them different colors!' [1. a-barna 'to have
    1   2
color', 2. ra 'emphatic particle']

ibhu /zhaq R+pa-imut ɖaq putra-na si mankat a-pəraŋ! 'Don't remind
 1 2   3   4   5   6 7   8
mother of her son who went to war.' [1. ibhu 'mother', 2. zhaq
'don't', 3. imut 'to remember', 4. ɖaq 'to', 5. putra-na 'her son',
6. si 'rel. particle', 7. mankat 'to go', 8. a-pəraŋ 'to make war']

R+lazu-an-na / sa-əla-na i-R+pa-kunpul, pas i-zhual ɖaq lazu-an.
   1   2   3   4   5   6   7
'After the old clothes were gathered together they were sold to the
old-clothes dealer'. [1. R+lazu-an-na 'the old clothes', 2.
sa-əla-na 'after', 3. a-kunpul 'to get together', 4. pas 'then',
5. i-zhual 'be sold', 6. ɖaq 'to', 7. lazu-an 'old clothes dealer']

This sentence could also have had: i-pa-R+kunpul or R+i-pa-kunpul. The
latter would be the least likely.

R+anɖiq-na /⎰ i-R+pa-tau. 'His possessions were showed off.'
  1   i-pa-R+tau.
            [R+i-pa-tau].
            i-pa-Rt+tau.
              2

[1. R+anɖiq-na 'his possessions', 2. tau 'to know']

pa- derivatives from stems with Rf+ are themselves intransitive.

a-Rf+zhual 'to trade' (intransitive)
N-pa-Rf+zhual 'to make (someone) trade' (intransitive)

Examples with reflexive meaning follow:

mun baqna təru sughi-a, kudhu dhaddhi si N-pa-barikkiŋ. 'If you want
　1　　2　　3　　　4　　　　5　　　6　　7　　　8

　　　to be rich, you must be stingy.' [1. mun 'if', 2. baqna 'you',

　　　3. təru 'want', 4. sughi-a 'will be rich', 5. kudhu 'must',

　　　6. dhaddhi 'be, become', 7. si 'rel. particle', 8. barikkiŋ

　　　'stingy']

　　si azhar / N-pa-bhazhən. 'He studied hard.' [1. si 'rel. particle',
　　1　2　　　3

　　　2. azhar 'to study', 3. bhazhən 'conscientious']

Compare the preceding active sentence with the following passive.

　　si a-laku / i-pa-bhazhən. 'He worked hard.' [1. a-laku 'to work']
　　　　1

　　mun baqna tiɗuŋ-a, pa-N-kantuk ghallu! 'When you want to go to sleep,
　　1　　2　　3　　　　4　　　　5

　　　let yourself get sleepy first.' [1. mun 'when', 2. baqna 'you',

　　　3. tiɗuŋ-a 'will sleep', 4. N-kantuk 'to be sleepy', 5. ghallu

　　　'first']

With reduplication

　　si ɗatəŋ / R+N-pa-maləm. 'He made himself come late.' [1. si 'rel.
　　1　2　　　　3

　　　particle', 2. ɗatəŋ 'to come', 3. maləm 'night, late']

　2) Derived from transitive verbals.

pa- derivatives from N-transitives form the following classes:[19]

A.	Active:	1. N-pa-N-	'to have, make (the object) do the action'
		2. N-pa-	'to have the action done (to the object)' or 'to give (the object) to someone to do'
B.	Passive:	1. i-pa-N-	'(subject) is made to do the action'
		2. i-pa-	'(subject) is had that action done to it' or '(subject) is given (to someone) to have that action done to it'
C.	Stem:	1. pa-N-	'make (object) do that action'
		2. pa-	'make (object) have that action done to it' or 'give (object) (to someone) to do'

As can be seen, the difference between 1 and 2 in all cases is the presence

or absence of N-. When N- → a- these two types fall together at the phonetic

level. For the rules which handle this see pages 89 and 111 above. For example:

　　N-bhantu → a-bhantu 'to help'. Therefore N-pa-N-bhantu →

N-pa-a-bhantu → N-pa-bhantu → ma-bhantu 'to have (object) help'
and N-pa-bhantu → ma-bhantu 'to have (object) helped' or 'to give
(object) to someone to help'.

A1. N-pa-N-

paman N-pa-N-anbaq anaq-na nəŋ aḍaq-an. 'Uncle has his child go and
  1   2   3   4   5
wait in front (of the house).' [1. paman 'uncle', 2. N-anbaq 'go
and wait for', 3. anaq-na 'his child', 4. nəŋ 'in', 5. aḍaq-an
'front']

ibhu N-pa-N-bhantu aliq a-laku nəŋ ḍapur. 'Mother has brother help by
  1   2   3   4   5   6
working in the kitchen.' [1. ibhu 'mother', 2. N-bhantu 'to help',
3. aliq 'younger sibling', 4. a-laku 'to work', 5. nəŋ 'in',
6. ḍapur 'kitchen']

A2. N-pa-

ibhu N-pa-añi paḍi-na ḍaq uriŋ baññaq. 'Mother has her rice harvested
  1   2   3   4   5   6
by many people.' [1. ibhu 'mother', 2. N-añi 'to harvest', 3.
paḍi-na 'her rice', 4. ḍaq 'to', 5. uriŋ 'person', 6. baññaq
'many']

rama N-pa-bhakta-a aliq ḍaq surbhaza. 'Father will have brother taken
  1   2   3   4   5
to Surabaja.' [1. rama 'father', 2. N-bhakta 'to carry', 3. aliq
'younger sibling', 4. ḍaq 'to', 5. surbhaza 'Surabaja']

R+N-pa-ghiba apa kakaq ḍaq baqna? 'What did brother give you to
     1   2   3   4   5
carry?' [1. N-ghiba 'to carry', 2. apa 'what', 3. kakaq 'older
brother', 4. ḍaq 'to', 5. baqna 'you']

B1. i-pa-N-

anaq-na i-pa-N-anbaq bēcaq nəŋ aḍaq-an. 'His child was made to go and
  1   2   3   4   5
wait for a trishaw in front (of the house).' [1. anaq-na 'his
child', 2. N-anbaq 'go and wait for', 3. bēcaq 'trishaw',
4. nəŋ 'in', 5. aḍaq-an 'front']

aliq i-pa-N-kakan ghallu. 'Brother was fed first.' [1. aliq
  1   2   3
'younger sibling', 2. N-kakan 'to eat', 3. ghallu 'first']

142

aliq i-pa-N-kəla ghədhaŋ. 'Sister was made to cook bananas.'
  1   2   3

   [1. aliq 'younger sibling', 2. N-kəla 'to cook', 3. ghədhaŋ
   'banana']

B2. i-pa-

taŋ paḍi i-pa-añi ḍaq Rf+bini-q rua. 'My rice was given to that
1   2   3   4   5   6

   woman to harvest.' [1. taŋ 'my', 2. paḍi 'rice', 3. N-añi 'to
   harvest', 4. ḍaq 'to', 5. Rf+bini-q 'woman', 6. rua 'that']

kupiqan si pəghaq tali-na / i-pa-anbhat ḍaq sinkuq. 'I was made to
1   2   3   4   5   6   7

   pull the kite whose rope was broken.' [1. kupiqan'kite', 2. si
   'rel. particle', 3. pəghaq 'broken', 4. tali-na 'its rope',
   5. N-anbhat 'to pull', 6. ḍaq 'to', 7. sinkuq 'I']

zhazhan i-pa-kakan ḍaq aliq. 'The snack was fed to brother.'
1   2   3 4

   [1. zhazhan 'snack', 2. N-kakan 'to eat', 3. ḍaq 'to', 4. aliq
   'younger sibling']

ghədhaŋ i-pa-kəla ḍaq aliq. 'The banana was given to sister to cook.'
1   2   3 4

   [1. ghədhaŋ 'banana', 2. N-kəla 'to cook', 3. ḍaq 'to', 4. aliq
   'younger sibling']

Compare the preceding two sentences with the last two of section B1 above.

C1. pa-N-

aliq / pa-N-cuntu tulis-an-na baqna! 'Have brother imitate your
1   2   3   4

   writing.' [1. aliq 'younger sibling', 2. N-cuntu 'to imitate',
   3. tulis-an-na 'writing of', 4. baqna 'you']

uriŋ ria / pa-N-tabur zhaghuŋ! 'Have this man sow corn!' [1. uriŋ
1 2   3   4

   'person', 2. ria 'this', 3. N-tabur 'to sow', 4. zhaghuŋ 'corn']

C2. pa-

tulis-an-na baqna / pa-cuntu ḍaq aliq! 'Have your writing imitated
1   2   3   4 5

   by brother.' [1. tulis-an-na 'writing of', 2. baqna 'you',
   3. N-cuntu 'to imitate', 4. ḍaq 'to', 5. aliq 'younger sibling']

zhaghuŋ ria / pa-tabur ḍaq uriŋ ria! 'Have this corn sown by this
1   2   3   4 5 2

man.' [1. zhaghuη 'corn', 2. ria 'this', 3. N-tabur 'to sow',
4. ɖaq 'to', uriη 'person']

Compare the preceding two with the two sentences of section C1 above.

pa- also cooccurs with proclitic stems with taq 'not' and salaη 'mutual'.
These stems are derived from null affix intransitives, and are not common.

taq abit 'not long (time)'   i-pa-taq.abit 'made not long'
taq baηal 'not brave'   i-pa-taq.baηal 'made not brave'

Reduplication order

active: N-pa-R+taq.
passive: i-pa-R+taq.   [i-pa-taq.R+]
stem: pa-R+taq.

pa- -an

Derived from intransitive verbals with -an, derivatives with pa- combine
the meanings of both (causative plus -an meanings).

1) Frequency.

pitəna ria / N-pa-cagghik-an uriη. 'Slander makes people quarrel.'
  1   2   3   4

   [1.pitəna 'slander', 2. ria 'this', 3. a-cagghik 'to quarrel',
   4. uriη 'person']

pɪɖató-na si taq səmaηat / tantu N-pa-N-kantuk-an uriη. 'His listless
  1   2 3   4   5   6   7
   speeches sure make people sleepy.' [1. pɪɖató-na 'his speech',
   2. si 'rel. particle', 3. taq 'not', 4. səmaηat 'spirited',
   5. tantu 'sure', 6. N-kantuk 'be sleepy', 7. uriη 'person']

2) Comparative

zhalan-na / pa-cupiq-an sa-kuniq! 'Make the road a little narrower!'
  1   2   3

   [1. zhalan-na 'the road', 2. cupiq 'narrow', 3. sa-kuniq 'a little']

lamaq-na i-pa-masuq-an sa-kuniq. 'The mat was inserted a little.'
  1   2   3

   [1. lamaq-na 'the mat', 2. masuq 'enter', 3. sa-kuniq 'a little']

pa-ta-

Derived from verbals with ta- this derivative combines the meanings of
both prefixes.

nasiq-na / i-pa-ta-kakan ɖaq kuciŋ.   'The rice was accidentally fed to
     1   2   3   4

     the cat.' [1. nasiq-na 'the rice', 2. ta-kakan 'got eaten',

     3. ɖaq 'to', 4. kuciŋ 'cat']

i-pa-ta-attas ghallu.   'Made too high' [1. ta-attas ghallu 'too high']
     1

si a-kalanbhi / i-pa-ta-baliq.   'He put his shirt on inside out.'
1   2   3

     [1. si 'rel. particle', 2. a-kalanbhi 'to have, wear a shirt',

     3. ta-baliq 'reversed']

pa- -i

1) Derived from certain null affix intransitives -i here has the meaning

'more, further' (cf. -an in pa- -an above).

     zhuraŋ-na / i-pa-ɖaləm-i sa-kuniq.   'The ditch was deepened a little.'
        1   2   3

          [1. zhuraŋ-na 'the ditch', 2. ɖaləm 'deep', 3. sa-kuniq 'a little']

     baqna / mun ɖatəŋ, pa-maləm-i sa-kuniq.   'Come a little later.'
        1   2   3   4   5

          [1. baqna 'you', 2. mun 'when', 3. ɖatəŋ 'come', 4. maləm 'be late',

          5. sa-kuniq 'a little']

2) Derived from derived transitive verbals the meanings of the two

affixes are combined (plural, location, etc.).

These follow the rules given above on page 141.

     N-pa-bhakta-i punapa panzhənəŋan ɖaq rama? 'What (things) did you
        1   2   3   4   5

          give to father to carry?' [1. N-bhakta-i 'carry', 2. punapa 'what',

          3. panzhənəŋan 'you', 4. ɖaq 'to', 5. rama 'father']

     ghədhuŋ / i-pa-luncaq-i ɖaq aliq. 'Brother was made to jump over the
        1   2   3   4

          wall.' [1. ghədhuŋ 'wall', 2. N-luncaq-i 'jump over', 3. ɖaq 'to',

          4. aliq 'younger sibling']

     aliq i-pa-N-kura-i piriŋ. 'Brother was given the dishes to wash.'
        1   2   3

     piriŋ / i-pa-kura-i ɖaq aliq. 'The dishes were given to brother to
        3   2   4   1

          wash.' [1. aliq 'younger sibling', 2. N-kura-i 'to wash', 3.piriŋ

          'dish', 4. ɖaq 'to']

With reduplication

ibhu R+N-pa-bali-i R+inzham-an-na. 'Mother returns what she borrowed.'
1   2   3

[1. ibhu 'mother', 2. N-pa-bali 'to give back', 3. R+inzham-an-na

'what she borrowed']

cina i-R+pa-ghaḍhi-i səluq. 'The ring was pawned again and again to
1   2   3

the Chinese.' [1. cina 'Chinese', 2. N-pa-ghaḍhi 'to pawn',

3. səluq 'ring']

3) Special

anaq 'child   N-pa-r-anaq-i 'to deliver a woman of (a
                                             child)'

bini 'wife'   N-pa-bini-i 'to marry off'

4) Frequently the combination pa- -i means 'to use something as the place

for performing the action'. In the corpus it only occurs in the passive:

i-pa-N- -i.

pənaj si i-pa-N-baḍḍa-i zhukuq / kudhu sabun ghallu. 'The pot which
1   2   3   4   5   6   7

is used for fish must be soaped (and washed) first.' [1. pənaj

'pot', 2. si 'rel. particle', 3. N-baḍḍha-i 'put in a place',

4. zhukuq 'fish', 5. kudhu 'must', 6. sabun 'soap', 7. ghallu

'first']

kamar-na aliq / i-pa-N-simpən-i nanka su sinkuq. 'I use brother's
1   2   3   4   5 6

room for storing jack-fruit.' [1. kamar-na 'his room', 2. aliq

'younger sibling', 3. N-simpən 'to store', 4. nanka 'jack-fruit',

5. su 'by', 6. sinkuq 'I']

tumaŋ si i-pa-N-tunu-i zhaghuŋ / marḍa-na əla N-pati. 'The coals of
1   2   3   4   5   6   7

the hearth used for roasting corn are dead.' [1. tumaŋ 'hearth',

2. si 'rel, particle', 3. N-tunu 'to roast', 4. zhaghuŋ 'corn',

5. marḍa-na 'its coals', 6. əla 'already', 7. N-pati 'dead']

With reduplication

aiŋ i-pa-R+N-kura-i piriŋ. 'Water was used for washing dishes.'
1   2   3

[1. aiŋ 'water', 2. N-kura-i 'to wash', 3. piriŋ 'dish']

<u>pa- -aghi</u>

1) The combination of pa- and -aghi often combines the meaning of these two, causative plus benefactive. These cases follow the rules given above on page 141 ; -aghi is merely suffixed to the stem.

    a. derived from intransitive basic derivatives.

ghuru N-pa-N-arti-aghi zhalan-na ituŋ-an za.ria. 'Teacher explains
  1   2   3   4   5
    the method of (solving) that problem.' [1. ghuru 'teacher',
    2. N-arti 'to understand', 3. zhalan-na 'its way', 4. ituŋ-an
    'calculation', 5. za.ria 'that']

lubaŋ-na i-pa-ɗaləm-aghi. 'The hole is deepened (for someone).'
  1   2
    [1. lubaŋ-na 'the hole', 2. ɗaləm 'deep']

si N-tutu zhamu / pa-alus-aghi! 'The person grinding medicine should
 1   2   3   4
    make it fine.' [1. si 'rel. particle', 2. N-tutu 'to grind',
    3. zhamu 'native medicine', 4. alus 'be fine']

    b. derived from transitive basic derivatives.

ibhu N-pa-baca-aghi surat za.ria ɗaq sinkuq. 'Mother has me read that
 1   2   3   4   5   6
    letter (for, to her).' [1. ibhu 'mother', 2. N-baca 'to read',
    3. surat 'letter', 4. za.ria 'that', 5. ɗaq 'to', 6. sinkuq 'I']

kazu-na i-pa-ukur-aghi ɗaq sinkuq. 'The wood was given to me to
  1   2   3   4
    measure.'

sinkuq i-pa-N-ukur-aghi kazu-na. 'I was given the wood to measure.'
  4   2   1
    [1. kazu-na 'the wood', 2. N-ukur 'to measure', 3. ɗaq 'to',
    4. sinkuq 'I']

2) Often, however, the combination of pa- and -aghi has no causative meaning and just seems to be equivalent to a benefactive derivative with -aghi.[20]

    a. derived from intransitive basic derivatives.

active: N-pa-(N-)   -aghi

passive: i-pa-(N-)   -aghi

stem: pa-(N-)   -aghi

ibhu N-pa-balanzha-aghi ənbhuk si sakiq. 'Mother shops for sister
1   2   3   4 5

    who is sick.' [1. ibhu 'mother', 2. a-balanzha 'to go shopping',

      3. ənbhuk 'older sister', 4. si 'rel. particle', 5. sakiq 'sick']

b. derived from transitives. N- is always present in the stem.

active: N-pa-N-   -aghi

passive: i-pa-N-   -aghi[21]

stem: pa-N-   -aghi

ibhu N-pa-N-bəli-aghi rukuq + ka-anghuj sinkuq. 'Mother buys
1   2   3   4

    cigarettes for me.'

ibhu N-pa-N-bəli-aghi sinkuq + rukuq. [1. ibhu 'mother', 2. N-bəli
1   2   5   3

    'to buy', 3. rukuq 'cigarette', 4. ka-anghuj 'for', 5. sinkuq 'I']

sinkuq i-pa-N-bəli-aghi rukuq. 'I am bought cigarettes.'

rukuq za.ria / i-pa-N-bəli-aghi ibhu. 'Those cigarettes were bought
    (for me) by mother.'

Ambiguity arises where these forms fall together with the forms which in-
clude the meaning of 'causative'. For example:

    paman / i-pa-N-uan.aghi sapi-na. 'Uncle's cows were raised (by some-
    1   2   3

      body for him).' or 'Uncle was given his cows to raise.' [1. paman
      'uncle', 2. N-uan 'to raise', 3. sapi-na 'his cow']

pa-ka.

A small number of roots form a special subcategory because of the derivatives
they form with pa- and proclitic ka. The meaning of this derivative is 'put (the
object) in the, to the, towards the (root meaning)'. These derivatives combine
with -an and -i 'more', -i 'plural', and -aghi 'benefactive'. There also occur
such derivatives from intransitive N-ka. stems with locative meaning.

Reduplication order

	R+			Rt+
active:	N-pa-R+ka.	R+N-pa-ka.	[N-pa-ka.R+]	N-pa-Rt+ka.
passive:	i-pa-R+ka.	i-R+pa-ka.	i-pa-ka.R+	i-pa-Rt+ka.

148

R+   Rt+

stem: pa-R+ka.   R+pa-ka.   pa-ka.R+   pa-Rt+ka.

> aliq N-pa-ka.buḍi sapiḍa-na tamuj.   'Brother moves the guest's bike
> 1   2   3   4
>
> back.' [1. aliq 'younger sibling', 2. ka.buḍi 'to the back',
>
> 3. sapiḍa-na 'his bike', 4. tamuj 'guest']

> mutur-na za.ria / pa-ka.buḍi-an sa-kuniq!   'Move that car further back
> 1   2   3   4
>
> a little.' [1. mutur-na 'his car', 2. za.ria 'that', 3. ka.buḍi
>
> 'to the back', 4. sa-kuniq 'a little']

> tuzuq-na baqna / abak pa-N-ka.ḍaləm!   'Sit way inside!' [1. tuzuq-na
> 1   2   3   4
>
> 'sitting of', 2. baqna 'you', 3. abak 'rather', 4. ka.ḍaləm
>
> 'to the inside'; N-ka.ḍaləm 'on the inside']

> sinkuq N-pa-ka.aiŋ zhukuq za.ria supaza taq N-pati-a.   'I put that
> 1   2   3   4   5   6   7
>
> fish in water so it wouldn't die.' [1. sinkuq 'I', 2. ka.aiŋ 'to
>
> the water', 3. zhukuq 'fish', 4. za.ria 'that', 5. supaza 'so that',
>
> 6. taq 'not', 7. N-pati-a 'will die']

Some of the roots in the above category also have the suffix -na either directly following the root or following the suffix -an. Such derivatives with -na cannot take the future suffix -a. They are thus not verbals by our definition but rather a unique verbalized noun stem. For example:

> ka.iriŋ-na miza }   'to the side of the table'
> ka.iriŋ-an-na miza }

> i-pa-ka.iriŋ-na miza } 'put to the side of the table'
> i-pa-ka.iriŋ-an-na miza }

These derivatives usually occur in the passive or imperative, and the meaning is 'to put (the object) in the, to the (root meaning) of some other object'.

> kursf za.ria /   i-pa-ka.iriŋ-na   } miza.   'That chair was placed
>   i-pa-ka.iriŋ-an-na }
> 1   2   3   4
>
> next to the table.' [1. kursf 'chair', 2. za.ria 'that',
>
> 3. ka.iriŋ 'to the side', 4. miza 'table']

> sapi-na /   i-pa-ka.ḍaza-na   } suŋaj.   'The cow was put north of the
>   i-pa-ka.ḍaza-an-na }
> 1   2   3

149

river.' [1. sapi-na 'the cow', 2. ka.ɖaza 'to the north', 3. suŋaj 'river']

aliq i-pa-ka.təŋa-na ⎫lincak. 'Brother was placed in the middle of
i-pa-ka.təŋa-an-na⎭
 1   2   3

the couch.' [1. aliq 'younger sibling', 2. ka.təŋa 'to the middle', 3. lincak 'bamboo couch']

The first or second object need not be overtly present in the sentence.

aliq i-pa-ka.təŋa-na. ⎫ 'Brother was placed in the middle (of it).'
i-pa-ka.təŋa-an-na.⎭

si N-buaŋ / i-pa-ka.zhau-an-na. 'He threw it far (from him).' [1. si
 1   2   3

'rel. particle', 2. N-buaŋ 'to throw away', 3. zhau 'far']

With some roots the 'other object' is usually assumed known.

i-pa-ka.panas-na ⎫ 'it was put in the heat (of the sun)'
i-pa-ka.panas-an-na ⎭

i-pa-ka.nauŋ-na ⎫ 'it was put in the shade (of the tree,
i-pa-ka.nauŋ-an-na ⎭ house, etc.)'

There are several roots for which the notion of 'other object' has no meaning.

i-pa-ka.uzhan-na ⎫ 'it was put in the rain'
i-pa-ka.uzhan-an-na ⎭

i-pa-ka.zhalan-na   'it was put on the road'

ka- (intransitive)

The meaning of these derivatives is generally passive. The reduplication order is R+ka-

1) The root does not occur elsewhere.

ka-sanbuq 'be surprised'
ka-unaŋ 'be well-known'

2) The root never occurs alone, but other derivatives without ka- do occur.

ka-ləlǝp 'to go under (water)'
ka-liru 'to make a mistake, be mistaken'

3) Derived from the radical stem of transitive and intransitive basic derivatives.

150

si ka-ḍua / ka-ghanzhar buta. 'The two were struck blind.' [1. si
1   2   3   4
'rel. particle', 2. ka-ḍua 'the two', 3. N-ghanzhar 'to strike',

4. buta 'blind']

hal si ka-səbhut. 'The above mentioned fact.' [1. hal 'matter',
1   2   3

2. si 'rel. particle', 3. N-səbhut 'to mention']

taŋ paman ka-ituŋ uriŋ sughi. 'My uncle is in the class of rich
1   2   3   4   5

people.' [1. taŋ 'my', 2. paman 'uncle', 3. N-ituŋ 'to count',

4. uriŋ 'person', 5. sughi 'rich']

ka-rassa ba-ramma baqna ghəlaq si i-cacar? 'How did you feel when you
1   2   3   4   5 6

got vaccinated?' [1. a-rassa 'to feel', 2. ba-ramma 'how',

3. baqna 'you', 4. ghəlaq 'before', 5. si 'rel. particle',

6. i-cacar 'be vaccinated']

4) For some roots there is the additional meaning of 'ability'.

tulis-an rua / taq ka-baca. 'That writing was unreadable.' [1. tulis
1   2   3   4

-an 'writing', 2. rua 'that', 3. taq 'not', 4. N-baca 'to read']

kursí si baññaq rua / mun i-pa-atur-an, tantu ka-buaq kabbhi. 'If all
1   2   3   4   5   6   7   8   9

those many chairs are put in order, they certainly all can be

loaded.' [1. kursí 'chair', 2. si 'rel. particle', 3. baññaq

many', 4. rua 'that', 5. mun 'if', 6. i-pa-atur-an 'be put in

order', 7. tantu 'sure', 8. N-buaq 'to fit, contain', 9. kabbhi

'all']

pa-N-tənbhaŋ-na paman ka-pirəŋ ḍaq lauq suŋaj. 'Uncle's singing could
1   2   3   4   5   6

be heard south of the river.' [1. pa-N-tənbhaŋ-na 'his singing',

2. paman 'uncle', 3. N-pirəŋ 'to hear', 4. ḍaq 'to', 5. lauq

'south', 6. suŋaj 'river']

5) Special

ḍatəŋ 'to come'   R+ka-ḍatəŋ 'to be moody, act differently
                                        from one time to the next'

N-abiq 'to finish up'   R+taq.ka-abiq 'it couldn't be finished,
                                           used up'

Two fixed expressions occur with ka- -a. They are ka-ucaq-a (less commonly

151

with the root variant ucap), and ka-catur-a 'it is said that, once upon a time'.

ka- -i

One root, luppa 'forget', regularly occurs with ka- -i.

> R+bhundhuq-an-na / ka-luppa-i nəŋ ranghun ɗissa. 'His bundles were
> 1   2   3   4   5
>
> forgotten in that field-house.' [1. R+bhundhuq-an-na 'his bundles',
> 2. luppa 'to forget', 3. nəŋ 'in', 4. ranghun 'field-house',
> 5. ɗissa 'over there']

This derivative also occurs with active meaning, as does luppa.

> sinkuq ka-luppa-i + taq N-sanbi taŋ tas. 'I forgot to bring my bag.'
> 1   2   3   4   5
>
> [1. sinkuq 'I', 2. taq 'not', 3. N-sanbi 'bring along', 4. taŋ
> 'my', 5. tas 'bag']

This derivative never occurs with N- and rarely occurs with passive i-. It also occurs as base for the following:

> N-pa-ka-luppa-i   'to put something out of one's mind'
> ta-ka-luppa-i   'it was forgotten'

ka- -an (intransitive)

No reduplicated cases occur in the corpus.

1) Derived from radical stems the meaning is 'to be affected by (the root meaning), often in some adverse way'.

> abaq-na / ka-pati-an anaq buŋsu-na. 'His youngest child died.'
> 1   2   3   4
>
> [1. abaq-na 'he', 2. pati 'die', 3. anaq 'child', 4. buŋsu-na
> 'his oldest']

> sinkuq ka-maliŋ-an pissi. 'I had my money stolen.' [1. sinkuq 'I',
> 1   2   3
>
> 2. maliŋ 'thief', 3. pissi 'money']

> baqna mun əla ka-bagi-an, azzhaq antré puli! 'When you've gotten
> 1   2   3   4   5   6   7
>
> your share, don't line up again.' [1. baqna 'you', 2. mun 'when',
> 3. əla 'already', 4. bagi 'distribute', 5. azzhaq 'don't',
> 6. antré 'to line up', 7. puli 'again']

> uzhan 'to rain'   ka-uzhan-an 'to be caught in the rain'

ilaŋ 'to be lost'   ka-ilaŋ-an 'to suffer the loss (of something)'

Some of these derivatives have the complementary extension -n.

    bənku rua / ka-tunu-n. 'That house burned down.' [1. bənku 'house',
     1   2   3

      2. rua 'that', 3. tunu 'burn']

    əla ka-bhukti-n. 'It has been proved.' [1. əla 'already', 2. bhukti
     1   2

      'prove']

For this root ka-bhukti-an also occurs.

    si əla ka-laku-n 'What has already happened' [1. a-laku 'to work, do']
             1

At least one root, saksi, cooccurs with three forms: ka- -an, ka- -n, ka-

-n-an: ka-saksi-an, ka-saksi-n, ka-saksi-n-an 'witnessed'.

In West Madurese this affix also appears as k- -an before a root beginning

with a vowel.

    2) Derived from adjective type null affix verbals this derivative means

'very, too'; in this meaning it is sometimes followed by the word ghallu.

    bhakal-na / ka-tua-an ghallu. 'His fiancee is too old.' [1. bhakal-na
     1   2

      'his fiancee', 2. tua 'old']

    si N-issi-i aiŋ / ka-ləbi-an. 'He filled it with too much water.'
    1   2   3

      [1. si 'rel. particle', 2. N-issi-i 'to fill', 3.aiŋ 'water',

      4. ləbi 'more']

    za.ria / ka-alus-an ghallu. 'That is very fine.' [1. za.ria 'that',
     1   2

      2. alus 'fine']

    3) Derived from nouns meaning kinship terms, this derivative means 'to be

in that relation to'.

    ahmat ka-aliq-an baɖu. 'Ahmat is younger brother to Badu.' [1. aliq
          1

      'younger sibling']

    4) Special.

    utaŋ 'debt'   ka-pa-r-utaŋ-an 'to be indebted'

ka- -ən (intransitive)

As for ka- -an above, these derivatives do not occur reduplicated. They are derived from null-affix verbals.

1) 'be very, too'

ghaŋan-na / ka-cia-ən. 'The soup is too bland.' [1. ghaŋan-na 'the
   1   2

(kind of) soup', 2. cia 'bland']

si N-ghula-i ti / ka-manis-ən. 'He made the tea too sweet.' [1. si
1   2   3   4

'rel. particle', 2. N-ghula-i 'to sugar', 3. ti 'tea', 4. manis
'sweet']

As for ka- -an above, this derivative is often followed by ghallu in this
meaning.

2) '(the subject) feels (too or very)'

R+k-anaq za.ria / sapuq-i pa-təpaq + maq taq ka-cələp-ən! 'Wrap up
  1   2   3   4   5 6   7

that child well so he's not too cold.' [1. R+k-anaq 'child',
2. za.ria 'that', 3. sapuq-i 'wrap up!', 4. pa-təpaq 'make (it)
exact!', 5. maq 'particle', 6. taq 'not', 7. cələp 'cold']

si N-kakan / ka-dhuzan-ən + sa.tuplis i-pa-abiq. 'He got his full of
1   2   3   4   5

eating; a jarful was finished.' [1. si 'rel. particle', 2. N-kakan
'to eat', 3. dhuzan 'like, enjoy', 4. sa.tuplis 'a jarful',
5. i-pa-abiq 'be finished off']

si N-pinta su si a-bəriq / ka-paɖa-ən. 'The asker and the giver were
1   2   3 1   4   5

of the same mind (i.e. agreed).' [1. si 'rel. particle', 2. N-pinta
'to request', 3. su 'and', 4. a-bəriq 'to give', 5. paɖa 'same']

Compare the following sentences containing ka-kuraŋ-an and ka-kuraŋ-ən. The
sentence with ka- -ən describes how the subject feels about something, while that
with ka- -an states a fact.

si N-kakan ghəɖhaŋ rua / ka-kuraŋ-ən. 'He didn't have enough bananas
1   2   3   4   5

to eat.' [1. si 'rel. particle', 2. N-kakan 'to eat', 3. ghəɖhaŋ
'banana', 4. rua 'that', 5. kuraŋ 'less, not enough']

si N-dhuum ghəɖhaŋ / ka-kuraŋ-an + taq cukup. 'He distributed too few
1   2   3   4   5 6

bananas; there weren't enough.' [1. si 'rel. particle', 2. N-dhuum

'to distribute', 3. ghədhaŋ 'banana', 4. kuraŋ 'less, not enough',
5. taq 'not', 6. cukup 'enough']

3) Special.

ɗaq rusia za.ria / aliq / əla ka-tau-ən.   'Brother is in the know on
1   2   3   4   5   6
    that secret.' [1. ɗaq 'to', 2. rusia 'secret', 3. za.ria 'that',
    4. aliq 'younger sibling', 5. əla 'already', 6. tau 'to know']

N-ka- (intransitive)

No reduplicated examples occur.

Derived from color terms this derivative means 'to become that color', 'to
be ...ish'.

kuniŋ 'yellow'	N-ka-kuniŋ	'to turn yellow, be yellowish'
puti 'white'	N-ka-puti	'become white, be whitish'
cələŋ 'black'	N-ka-cələŋ	'turn black, be blackish'

ka- (transitive)

Reduplication order

		R+		Rt+
active:	N-ka-R+			N-ka-Rt+
passive:	i-ka-R+	i-R+ka-		i-ka-Rt+
stem:	ka-R+	R+ka-		ka-Rt+

1) Derived from nouns this derivative means 'to have, use (object) as
root meaning), or (object) becomes (root meaning)'.

bhunka-na ghədhaŋ rua / i-ka-batəs antara taŋ təghal musu təgal-na.
1   2   3   4   5   6   7   8   9
    'That banana tree forms the boundary between my field and his
    field.' [1. bhunka-na 'its tree', 2. ghədhaŋ 'banana', 3. rua
    'that', 4. batəs 'boundary', 5. antara 'between', 6. taŋ 'my',
    7. təghal 'dry field', 8. musu 'with, and', 9. təghal-na 'his
    dry field']

ka-laku-an si i-ka-bhabhaza za.ria / ghiq baññaq bhai + uriŋ si
1   2   3   4   5   6   7   8   2
    a-lamar. 'There were still many people who applied for that
    9
    dangerous work.' [1. ka-laku-an 'work', 2. si 'rel. particle',
    3. bhabhaza 'danger', 4. za.ria 'that', 5. ghiq 'still', 6.

155

bañ̃aq 'many', 7. bhai 'just', 8. uriŋ 'person', 9. a-lamar 'to apply']

sinkuq N-idiŋ kabhar caq-na baqna əla N-ka-bhakal putra-na paq
1   2   3   4   5   6   7   8   9

badhana. 'I've heard that you've become engaged to the son of the
10

wedana.' [1. sinkuq 'I', 2. N-idiŋ 'to hear', 3. kabhar 'news',
4. caq-na 'they say', 5. baqna 'you', 6. əla 'already', 7. bhakal
'future, fiance', 8. putra-na 'son of', 9. paq 'father', 10.
badhana 'wedana (local official)']

sərina taq N-təmu bhantal, dhaddhi saŋ ətas ſa i-ka-bhantal kia.
1   2   3   4   5   6 7 8   4   8
'Since I couldn't find a pillow, my purse served as one.'
[1. sərina 'since', 2. taq 'not', 3. N-təmu 'to find', 4. bhantal
'pillow', 5. dhaddhi 'so', 6. saŋ 'my', 7. ətas 'purse', 8. ſa...
kia 'anyway, just the same']

ibhu N-pa-N-accin.aghi təlur si i-ka-saŋu-a. 'Mother salts the eggs
1   2   3   4   5
which will be the provisions.' [1. ibhu 'mother', 2. N-pa-N-
accin.aghi 'to salt (benefactive)', 3. təlur 'egg', 4. si 'rel.
particle', 5. saŋu 'supplies, provisions']

Somewhat special is:

anaq 'child'   i-ka-r-anaq 'to be raised (by someone not one's
mother)'

2) Derived from null affix intransitives, this derivative means 'to become
(root meaning); (subj. of passive) is the cause of becoming (root meaning)';
'become (root meaning) about'.

caq-na uriŋ tua / zhamu ria / i-ka-baras. 'Old people say this medi-
1   2   3   4   5   6
cine cures you.' [1. caq-na 'they say', 2. uriŋ 'person', 3.
tua 'old', 4. zhamu 'native medicine', 5. ria 'this', 6. baras
'cured, healthy']

mun zhankrik i-pakan-i cabbhi, caq-na i-ka-baŋal. 'They say if
1   2   3   4   5   6
crickets are fed hot peppers, they become brave.' [1. mun 'if',
2. zhankrik 'cricket', 3. i-pakan-i 'be fed', 4. cabbhi 'hot
pepper', 5. caq-na 'they say', 6. baŋal 'brave']

N-ka-bhuŋa apa baqna?   'What's making you happy?' [1. bhuŋa 'happy',
1   2   3

2. apa 'what', 3. baqna 'you']

aliq-na / zhaq R+azhar-i N-inum kupf + kiḍiq i-ka-R+biasa.   'Don't
1   2   3   4   4   6   7

teach brother to drink coffee; he'll become used to it.' [1.

aliq-na 'brother of', 2. zhaq 'don't', 3. R+azhar-i 'teach to!',

4. N-inum 'to drink', 5. kupf 'coffee', 6. kiḍiq 'later', 7.

biasa 'accustomed']

3) Derived from the radical stem of affixed intransitives, the derivative
means 'use (the object) to perform the action, have (the object) as the cause of
the action'.

aiŋ i pǝnaj za.ria / ka-baccu ghan R+sa-kuniq! 'Wash with the water
1 2 3   4   5   6   7

in that jug little by little!' [1. aiŋ 'water', 2. i 'in', 3.

pǝnaj 'jug', 4. za.ria 'that', 5. a-baccu 'to wash', 6. ghan

'particle', 7. R+sa-kuniq 'little by little']

hal za.ria / sǝghut kali i-ka-R+minpi su sinkuq. 'I often dream
1   2   3   4   5   6 7

about that.' [1. hal 'matter', 2. za.ria 'that', 3. sǝghut

'often', 4. kali 'time', 5. a-minpi 'to dream', 6. su 'by',

7. sinkuq 'I']

4) Derived from the radical stem of transitive verbals, this derivative
means 'to use (the object) to perform the action; turn (the object) into something by performing the action; (subject of passive) is the cause, origin or
instrument of the action'.

pǝṭi ria / i-ka-ghabaj ḍari kazu. 'This trunk is made of wood.'
1   2   3   4   5

[1. pǝṭi 'trunk', 2. ria 'this', 3. N-ghabaj 'to make', 4. ḍari

'from', 5. kazu 'wood']

pissi i attas-na lamari za.ria / ka-bazar sakula-an-na baqna! 'Use
1   2 3   4   5   6   7   8

the money on top of the wardrobe for paying for your school!'

[1. pissi 'money', 2. i 'on', 3. attas-na 'its top', 4. lamari

'wardrobe', 5. za.ria 'that', 6. N-bazar 'to pay', 7. sakula-an-na

'school of', 8. baqna 'you']

i-ka-bəli apa bhai + taŋ pissi si sa.pulu rupia za.ria?   'Just what
1   2   3   4   5   6 7   8   9

did my ten rupiahs buy?' [1. N-bəli 'to buy', 2. apa 'what',

3. bhai 'just', 4. taŋ 'my', 5. pissi 'money', 6. si 'rel.

particle', 7. sa.pulu 'ten', 8. rupia 'rupiah', 9. za.ria 'that']

dhalubaŋ za.ria / ka-bhundhuq bukɗ-na baqna si əla kutur!   'Wrap your
1   2   3   4   5   6 7   8

dirty book with that paper!' [1. dhalubaŋ 'paper', 2. za.ria

'that', 3. N-bhundhuq 'to wrap', 4. bukɗ-na 'book of', 5. baqna

'you', 6. si 'rel. particle', 7. əla 'already', 8. kutur 'dirty']

5) With reduplication (R or Rt) the derivative sometimes means 'to

consider, to treat (the object) as (root meaning)'.

uriŋ rua / i-ka-Rt+maliŋ su ibhu.   'Mother thinks that man's a thief.'
1   2   3   4 5

[1. uriŋ 'person', 2. rua 'that', 3. maliŋ 'thief', 4. su 'by',

5. ibhu 'mother']

aliq si R+N-bəli / su ibhu / i-ka-R+laraŋ.   'Mother thought brother
1   2   3   4 5   6

spent too much shopping.' [1. aliq 'younger sibling', 2. si 'rel.

particle', 3. R+N-bəli 'to shop', 4. su 'by', 5. ibhu 'mother',

6. laraŋ 'expensive']

ka- -aghi

This combination occurs so rarely that no generalizations can safely be

made about it.

baññaq uriŋ taq N-arti apa si i-ka-ɗhabu-aghi paq bupati rua.   'Many
1   2   3   4   5   6 7   8   9   10

people didn't understand what the bupati talked about.' [1.

baññaq 'many', 2. uriŋ 'person', 3. taq 'not', 4. N-arti 'to

understand', 5. apa 'what', 6. si 'rel. particle', 7. a-ɗhabu 'to

speak', 8. paq 'father', 9. bupati 'local official', 10. rua

'that']

taŋ ghanbhar za.ria / ka-main.aghi!   'Play with my picture!' [1. taŋ
1   2   3   4

'my', 2. ghanbhar 'picture', 3. za.ria 'that', 4. a-main 'to play']

tau 'to know'   N-ka-tau-aghi 'to show appreciation' (intransi-
                                   tive??); 'to take care of (someone
                                   else's things)'

158

<u>ka- -i</u>

1) Makes transitive equivalents to some null affix intransitives.

    hal za.ria / taq i-ka-tau-i. 'That is not known.' [1. hal 'matter',
     1   2   3   4

       2. za.ria 'that', 3. taq 'not', 4. tau 'to know']

    bukū si kəma + i-ka-təru-i? 'Which book is wanted?' [1. bukū 'book',
     1   2 3   4

       2. si 'rel. particle', 3. kəma 'which', 4. təru 'to want']

    baqna si i-pukul baariq rua / ka-iŋaq-i! 'Remember you got hit yester-
     1   2   3   4   5   6

       day.' [1. baqna 'you', 2. si 'rel. particle', 3. i-pukul 'be hit',

       4. baariq 'yesterday', 5. rua 'that', 6. iŋaq 'to remember']

    ləbi 'be more'   N-ka-ləbi-i 'to exceed'

Several such derivatives have the complementary extension k-.

    ənɖaq 'to wish, want'   i-k-ənɖaq-i 'be wanted, wished for'

    ənəŋ 'to stay, live'   i-k-ənəŋ-i 'be lived in, stayed at'

2) Special

    anaq 'child'   N-ka-r-anaq-i 'to deliver (a woman of a child)'

As a sub-category of the above, this derivative in ka- -i is frequently
made from null affix intransitives denoting feelings. The derivative (used
mostly in the passive) means 'the subject (of the passive) causes or is the
source of that feeling'.

    alf lancaŋ tanaŋ + mula-na i-ka-bazhiq-i R+tatangha-na. 'Ali likes
     1   2   3   4   5   6

       to steal, and so he's disliked by his neighbors.' [1. Alf (proper

       name), 2,3. lancaŋ tanaŋ 'be lightfingered, thievish', 4. mula-na

       'and so', 5. bazhiq 'to dislike, feel disgusted', 6. R+tatangha-na

       'his neighbors']

    ka-baŋal-an-na R+k-anaq za.ria / i-ka-mənaq-i uriŋ bańñaq. 'That
     1   2   3   4   5   6

       child's bravery was surprising to many.' [1. ka-baŋal-an-na 'his

       bravery', 2. R+k-anaq 'child', 3. za.ria 'that', 4. mənaq 'be

       surprised', 5. uriŋ 'person', 6. bańñaq 'many']

    baqna za.ria / mun N-pikkir-i abaq-na dhibiq bhai, tantu taq
     1   2   3   4   5   6   7   8   9

i-ka-sənəŋ-i uriŋ. 'If you just think about yourself, people
  10

won't be happy with you.' [1. baqna 'you', 2. za.ria 'that',

3. mun 'if', 4. N-pikkir-i 'to think of', 5. abaq-na 'body of',

6. dhibiq 'self', 7. bhai 'just', 8. tantu 'certain', 9. taq 'not',

10. sənəŋ 'happy, content']

    3) Some derivatives with this meaning are derived from proclitic stems in

taq 'not, un-'.

      uriŋ si s-um-əŋit i-ka-taq.libur-i uriŋ. 'People dislike a sullen
       1 2   3   4   1

      person.' [1. uriŋ 'person', 2. si 'rel. particle', 3. s-um-əŋit

      'sullen', 4. taq libur 'not enjoy']

      pûlisf ghəlaq intar ḍaq k-ənəŋ-an pa-N-uba-an-na sapiḍa + karana
       1   2   3   4 5   6   7   8

      baḍa si i-ka-taq.parcaza-i. 'The police went to the bicycle repair
       9 10   11

      shop because there was something suspicious.' [1. pûlisf 'police',

      2. ghəlaq 'before', 3. intar 'to go', 4. ḍaq 'to', 5. k-ənəŋ-an

      'place', 6. pa-N-uba-an-na 'changing of', 7. sapiḍa 'bicycle',

      8. karana 'because', 9. baḍa 'there is', 10. si 'rel. particle',

      11. taq parcaza 'not to believe']

ta-ka-

An extremely rare combination, combining 'accidental' and 'use' meanings.

      pissi-na aliq / ta-N-turuq ta-ka-balanzha. 'Brother's money got spent
       1   2   3   4

      too.' [1. pissa-na 'his money', 2. aliq 'younger sibling', 3.

      ta-N-ṭuruq 'went along', 4. N-balanzha 'to go shopping';

      N-ka-balanzha 'to spend (while shopping)']

R+ -an

This derivative is intransitive.

    1) Derived from the radical stems of both transitives and intransitives

meaning 'to perform the action over some period of time (often without specific

goal); to be engrossed in, to be in the middle of the action while something else

is happening'.

        a-zhalan 'to walk'   R+zhalan-an 'to go for a walk, take a
                                       walk'

aliq si a-zhalan / sərina R+abas-an ɖaq lain k-ənəŋ-an, mula-na
  1   2   3   4   5   6 7   8   9

    ta-tanɖuŋ. 'Because brother was looking elsewhere when walking, he
    10

    stumbled.' [1. aliq 'younger sibling', 2. si 'rel. particle',

    3. a-zhalan 'to walk', 4. sərina 'since', 5. N-abas 'to look, see',

    6. ɖaq 'to', 7. lain 'different', 8. k-ənəŋ-an 'place', 9. mula-na

    'and so', 10. ta-tanɖuŋ 'to stumble']

mun baqna R+azhar-an, kudhu si bhrəntəŋ. 'When you study, you must be
  1   2   3   4   5   6

    serious.' [1. mun 'when', 2. baqna 'you', 3. azhar 'to study',

    4. kudhu 'must', 5. si 'rel. particle', 6. bhrəntəŋ 'serious,

    conscientious']

baqna zhaq R+naiq-an nəŋ paghar! 'Don't climb around on the fence!'
  1   2   3   4   5

    [1. baqna 'you', 2. zhaq 'don't', 3. naiq 'to climb, go up',

    4. nəŋ 'on', 5. paghar 'fence']

kakaq mun R+baca-an, zhaq R+taña-i! 'When brother is reading, don't
  1 2   3   4   5

    question him!' [1. kakaq 'older brother', 2. mun 'when', 3.

    N-baca 'to read', 4. zhaq 'don't', 5. R+taña-i 'question (him)!']

uriŋ si anɖiq / ñaman bhai R+bəli-an kain. 'People with money usually
  1   2   3   4   5   6   7

    buy cloth.' [1. uriŋ 'person', 2. si 'rel. particle', 3. anɖiq

    'to have', 4. ñaman 'pleasant', 5. bhai 'just', 6. N-bəli 'to buy',

    7. kain 'cloth']

2) 'reciprocal action', derived from the radical stems of intransitive

verbals.

    R+k-anaq si tuzuq i anpir rua / R+aɖaq-an. 'The children sit on the
      1   2   3 4 5   6   7

    porch facing each other.' [1. R+k-anaq 'child, children,' 2. si

    'rel. particle', 3. tuzuq 'to sit', 4. i 'on', 5. anpir 'porch',

    6. rua 'that', 7. aɖaq 'in front']

    taŋ aliq su kanca-na / paɖa R+bhasa-an inghi bhuntən. 'My brother and
     1 2   3   4   5   6   7

    his friends use alus language to each other.' [1. taŋ 'my', 2.

    aliq 'younger sibling', 3. su 'and', 4. kanca-na 'his friends',

    5. paɖa 'all', 6,7. a-bhasa inghi bhuntən 'to use alus language']

The above two categories more rarely follow the basic derivative.

R+ -an derivative

usual	rare	basic derivative
R+bəli-an	R+N-bəli-an 'to shop'	N-bəli 'to buy'
R+musu-an	a-R+musu-an 'to oppose each other'	a-musu 'to be hostile'

3) Derived from the radical stems of verbals in the meaning 'play at the action, act like, make believe to do the action'.

kakaq pintər unghu a-tinka R+balandha-an. 'Brother is really clever
　　1　　2　　　3　　　4　　　5
at acting Dutch-like.' [1. kakaq 'older brother', 2. pintər
'clever', 3. unghu 'really', 4. a-tinka 'to act, behave, 5.
balandha 'Dutch']

aliq si R+zhual-an / N-ghabaj R+baruŋ-an. 'Brother who plays at sell-
1　2　　3　　　　4　　　5
ing makes a toy food-stand.' [1. aliq 'younger sibling', 2. si
'rel. particle', 3. N-zhual 'to sell', 4. N-ghabaj 'to make',
5. R+baruŋ-an 'toy food stand']

R+k-anaq si R+pəraŋ-an rua / pintər R+bhədhil-an.'The children who play
　　1　　　2　　　3　　　4　　5　　　6
at war are good at play shooting.' [1. R+k-anaq 'child, children',
2. si 'rel. particle', 3. a-pəraŋ 'to make war', 5. pintər 'clever',
5. N-bhədhil 'to shoot']

4) From a small number of roots (among them kinship terms) this derivative means 'to keep on saying that word'.

ajuq 'let's go'	R+ajuq-an 'keep on saying 'let's go''
aliq 'younger sibling'	R+aliq-an 'keep on calling 'younger sibling!''
adu 'groaning noise'	R+adu-an 'keep on groaning'

5) Derived from null affix or N- intransitives this derivative means 'superlative, high degree'. This is frequently followed by the word ka-dhibiq 'oneself, alone'. Those derived from N- intransitives optionally retain the N- in the derivative.

N-attas 'to be on top'　　R+attas-an　⎫
　　　　　　　　　　　　R+N-attas-an⎬'to be the highest'
　　　　　　　　　　　　　　　　　　⎭

baktu ka-uzhan-an, sinkuq si R+bassa-an + karana taq a-pazuŋ. 'When
1   2   3   4   5   6   7   8

> caught in the rain, I got very wet, because I didn't have an
> umbrella.' [1. baktu 'when', 2. ka-uzhan-an 'caught in the rain',
> 3. sinkuq 'I', 4. si 'rel. particle', 5. bassa 'wet', 6. karana
> 'because', 7. taq 'not', 8. a-pazuŋ 'to have an umbrella']

In some cases the stem for such a derivative is a noun.

> baraq 'west'   R+baraq-an 'the most westerly'

6) Some derivatives in R+ -an are also used attributively. As such, they
cannot cooccur with -a 'future'.

> kunpul-an R+maus-an 'reading club' [1. kunpul-an 'association, club',
> 1   2
>
> 2. maus 'to read']

> zhalan R+ungha-an 'rising road' [1. zhalan 'road', 2. ungha 'to go up']
> 1   2

> musim R+uzhan-an 'rainy season' [1. musim 'season', 2. uzhan 'to rain']
> 1   2

> anghuj R+ari-n 'everyday clothes' (with complementary extension)
> 1   2
>
> [1. anghuj 'clothes', 2. ari 'day']

> anaq R+aku-n 'adopted child', (with complementary extension) [1. anaq
> 1   2
>
> 'child', 2. N-aku 'to acknowledge, admit']

7) Derived from names of time periods this derivative means 'for ...s and
...s'. It occurs with or without a- in free variation.

bulan 'month'	R+bulan-an a-R+bulan-an	'for months and months'
taun 'year'	R+taun-an a-R+taun-an	'for years and years'
ari 'day'	R+ari-an	'for days and days'

Compare the latter with R+ari-n 'everyday, daily'.

Rf+ -an

Extremely few cases are recorded.

> kazu Rf+bhiru-n 'green wood, soft wood' [1. kazu 'wood', 2. bhiru
> 1   2
>
> 'green']

<u>R+ -ən</u>

This derivative is intransitive.

1) Same as R+ -an 5 above 'superlative', as well as 'quickly, easily, frequently, completely, keep on being ...'. Often rather specialized meanings.

bhusən 'bored'	R+bhusən-ən 'easily bored, very bored'
bara 'swollen'	R+bara-ən 'swollen all over'
təru 'to want'	R+təru-ən 'have insatiable desire(s)'
bini 'wife'	R+bini-ən 'get married over and over again'
N-pati 'to die'	R+N-pati-ən 'keep on going out (of fire)'
upa 'pay'	R+upa-ən 'always expect to get paid, won't do something for nothing'

2) Various.

añar 'new'	R+añar-ən 'begin something with enthusiasm which quickly dies down'
bənku 'house'	R+bənku-ən 'do well on one's home ground but badly away from it'
ghila 'crazy'	R+ghila-ən 'act like a madman'
caciŋ 'worm'	R+caciŋ-ən 'be wormy (with intestinal worms)'
dhuñña 'world, worldly goods'	R+dhuñña-ən 'be a fair weather friend'
pissi 'money'	R+pissi-ən 'be interested only in money'
N-iḍiŋ 'to hear'	R+N-iḍiŋ-ən 'to hear things (imaginary)'

Minor affixes

The following affixes (prefixes and infixes) are non-productive in Madurese. Their use is extremely limited. All are intransitive.

<u>Prefixes</u>

kuma-	lancaŋ 'ahead of time (in pejorative sense), out of turn'
	kuma-lancaŋ atur 'to speak out of turn'
kami-	purun 'to want'
	kami-purun 'to pretend to want'
par- -an	təŋa 'middle, half', N-təŋa 'be in middle'
	anaq par-N-təŋa-an 'middle child'

Infixes

-um-	lanpa 'walk'	a-l-um-anpa 'to walk'
	səŋit 'sullen'	s-um-əŋit 'sullen'
	təka 'grant'	t-um-əka 'be granted'
	rasa 'feel'	a-r-um-asa 'to realize'
	ghilir 'turn'	R+gh-um-ilir 'to take turns'
	turun 'descend'	R+t-um-urun 'to go from generation to generation'
	ghantuŋ 'hang'	gh-um-antuŋ 'to depend'
-in-	tuluŋ 'help'	R+t-in-uluŋ 'to help each other'
-al-	zhimət 'sit quietly'	zh-al-imət 'be a quiet person'
	burik 'spotted black and white'	b-al-urik 'id'
-im-	turun 'descend'	R+t-im-urun 'to go from generation to generation'
-ar-	kətək 'heart beat'	k-ar-ətək 'to think about'
	R+kədhəp 'lightning'	N-k-ar-ədhəp 'to sparkle'

NOUNS

A noun is a stem which can cooccur with the suffix -na or .ipun 'definite, third person'.[22]

Null affix

Many nouns are equivalent to the root in shape. For example:

mata 'eye'
tanaŋ 'hand'
iluŋ 'nose'
culuq 'mouth'
zhila 'tongue'
aiŋ 'water'
uzhan 'rain'
daun 'leaf'
zhaba 'Java'
surbhaza 'Surabaja'

Occasionally null affix nouns are also the same in shape as null affix verbals. For example:

165

suara talbhuk-an za.ria / su ahmat i-sanka ghagghar-na ñiur. 'Ahmat
　　1　　　2　　　　　3　　　　4　5　　6　　　　7　　　　　8
thought the thumping sound was the falling of the coconut.'
[1. suara 'sound', 2. talbhuk-an 'thump', 3. za.ria 'that', 4.
su 'by', 5. ahmat 'Ahmat', 6. i-sanka 'be thought', 7. ghagghar
'fall, falling', 8. ñiur 'coconut']

taq bəciq dhaddhi-na. 'The result is not good.' [1. taq 'not', 2.
　1　　2　　　3
bəciq 'good', 3. dhaddhi 'become, becoming, result']

baḍa-na sinkuq nəŋ kantur 'my being in the office' [1. baḍa 'being',
　1　　　2　　3　　4
there is', 2. sinkuq 'I', 3. nəŋ 'in', 4. kantur 'office']

R+N-arəp ḍatəŋ-na sapa baqna? 'Whose arrival are you expecting?'
　1　　　　2　　　3　　4
[1. R+N-arəp 'to expect', 2. ḍatəŋ 'arrival, to come', 3. sapa
'who', 4. baqna 'you']

Much less frequent, and probably in imitation of a similar construction in
Indonesian, is the nominalization of verbals which are transitives or derived
verbals with prefixes. Such nominalizations are more frequent in formal con-
texts such as speeches, lectures, written articles.

N-dhaddhi-aghi a-R+bhida-na cara paŋ-urip-an-na 'Causes the differen-
　　1　　　　　2　　　　3　　　4
tiation of their way of life' [1. N-dhaddhi-aghi 'to cause', 2.
a-R+bhidha 'differentiation, to differ from each other', 3. cara
'manner', 4. paŋ-urip-an 'life']

a-margha ta-pisa-na utaba raŋ+raŋ-na ta-panghi-na 'Because of their
　1　　　　2　　　3　　　4　　　　5
separation or the rareness of their meeting' [1. a-margha 'because',
2. ta-pisa 'separation, be separated', 3. utaba 'or', 4. raŋ+raŋ-na
'rareness of', 5. ta-panghi 'meeting, to meet']

Reduplications

As with verbals, the reduplication affix forms of nouns are connected to
what follows by plus or dot juncture, the latter in rapid speech.

R

1) Reduplication with R of null affix nouns and some types of derived
nouns has a plural meaning. 'Plural' in Madurese, means 'a group of objects

166

viewed as consisting of different individuals'.

2) Certain nouns only occur reduplicated. The root does not occur alone.

R+alun 'town square'
R+saap 'nightmare'

3) Derived from radical and extended stems R+ derivatives mean 'that which is, that which is ...en'.

anghuj 'wear'	R+anghuj 'clothing'
ankaq 'serve'	R+ankaq 'food served'
bəriq 'give'	R+bəriq 'gift'
baḍa 'there is'	R+baḍa 'what there is'
bhakta 'carry'	R+bhakta-n 'gift' (extended stem)

4) Many derivatives with R+ have rather special meanings which are similar in some way to the meanings of the null affix nouns from which they are derived.

anaq 'offspring'	R+k-anaq 'child (young human being)' (extended stem)
abu 'dust'	R+abu 'medicine used to rub down woman who has just given birth'
azhin 'seller's price'	R+azhin 'real value'
baktu 'time'	R+baktu 'particular time - about 6 in the evening'
bini 'wife'	R+bini 'seed rice'
biraŋ 'shy'	R+biraŋ 'kind of caterpillar'
ciṭak 'head'	R+ciṭak scarecrow'
lagghu 'morning'	R+lagghu 'early morning'
tunbu 'growth'	R+tunbu 'part of a plow'

5) Derived from the radical stems of transitive verbals this derivative means 'an instrument used to perform that action, though not necessarily one specifically designed for that purpose.'

N-añi 'to harvest'	R+añi 'small knife for harvesting rice'
N-zhuzzhu 'to prod'	R+zhuzzhu 'a prod'
N-təbha 'to sweep'	R+təbha 'broom, anything used for sweeping'
N-taḍa-i 'catch from'	R+taḍa 'anything used for collecting something dripping from above'

6) Derived from the radical stems of certain null affix and N- intransi-

tives this derivative means 'the place where'.

baba 'below'   R+baba 'bottom'
pətəŋ 'be dark'   R+pətəŋ 'the dark, dark place'
N-təŋa 'be in the center'   R+təŋa 'center'

7) Derived from certain other intransitives this derivative means 'the state of the verbal meaning'.

buccuq 'rotten'   R+buccuq 'the rottenness'
ɖatəŋ 'to come'   R+ɖatəŋ 'the coming'
kiniq 'small'   R+kiniq 'the smallness'

<u>Rf+</u>

1) Some nouns occur both with null affix and with Rf+ with no apparent difference in meaning.

bhaziq   Rf+bhaziq 'infant'
bhaʈaŋ   Rf+bhaʈaŋ 'corpse'
batək   Rf+batək 'personality, character'

2) Some nouns occur only with Rf+, i.e. the root does not occur alone.

Rf+pati 'vizier'
Rf+pisu 'curse'
Rf+ghaman 'sharp weapon'

These nouns usually take Rt+ rather than R+ for the plural meaning.

3) Same as R+ 3 above 'that which is, that which has been'.

bəriq 'give'   Rf+bəriq 'gift'
təŋər 'sign'   Rf+təŋər 'sign, mark'

4) Special.

pətəŋ 'dark'   Rf+pətəŋ 'magic to make self invisible'
asi 'love'   Rf+k-asi 'sweetheart' (extended stem)

<u>Rtw+</u>

Same as R+ 1 above 'plural' for all null affix nouns and some types of derived noun such as Rf+ and compound nouns:

Rf+bhaza 'danger'   Rtw+Rf+bhaza 'dangers'
bhala-pəraŋ 'army'   Rtw+bhala-pəraŋ 'armies'

pa-

Derived from the basic derivative and from all other intransitives these
derivatives are mostly action nouns 'the ...ing'. [23]

Reduplication order

pa-R+(N-)   pa-Rtm+(N-)

1) Derived from intransitives this derivative is only followed by a subjective genitive.

    buru 'to run'   pa-buru-na 'his running'

    pa-ciccir-na bharaŋ kaq-ɖissa / paman taq N-ka-tau-i. 'Uncle didn't
          1   2   3   4   5   6
    know about that thing's getting left behind.' [1. ciccir 'get
    left behind', 2. bharaŋ 'thing', 3. kaq-ɖissa 'that there', 4.
    paman 'uncle', 5. taq 'not', 6. N-ka-tau-i 'to know about']

    pa-N-ciccir-na aliq .si a-zhalan / ciq tanbhan-na. 'Brother let him-
          1   2   3 4   5   6
    self get far behind when walking. [1. N-ciccir 'to stay behind',
    2. aliq 'younger sibling', 3. si 'rel. particle', 4. a-zhalan
    'to walk', 5. ciq 'very', 6. tanbhan-na 'its farness']

    bənku-na baqna / pa-N-ka.ɖaləm-na baranpa mitir ɖari luruŋ raza?
      1   2   3   4   5   6   7   8
    'How many meters in is your house from the main road?' [1.
    bənku-na 'house of', 2. baqna 'you', 3. N-ka.ɖaləm 'be inside',
    4. baranpa 'how much', 5. mitir 'meter', 6. ɖari 'from', 7. luruŋ
    'road, street', 8. raza 'big']

Certain other derivatives with this affix, where the stem is a derived intransitive or a proclitic stem, are grammatically possible but rarely used.

    R+N-pa-sakiq 'to pretend to be sick'
    pa-R+N-pa-sakiq-na 'his pretending to be sick'
    taq sənəŋ 'unhappy'
    pa-taq.sənəŋ-na 'his being unhappy'

2) Intransitives with transitive equivalents in N-ka- -i (see page 159)
have nominal derivatives with pa-N-ka- as well as with pa-.

    təru 'to want'   i-ka-təru-i 'wanted'   pa-N-ka-təru-na 'his wanting'
    tau 'to know'   i-ka-tau-i 'known'   pa-N-ka-tau-na 'his knowing'

3) Derived from suffixless transitives this derivative is followed by a subjective or an objective genitive.[24]

> kakaq / pa-N-anbhat-na tali / cəpət unghu-an. 'Brother's pulling of
>   1   2   3   4   5
>
>   the rope was really swift.' [1. kakaq 'older brother', 2. N-anbhat
>   'to pull', 3. tali 'rope', 4. cəpət 'swift', 5. unghu-an 'really']

> uriŋ miskin rua / pa-N-kakan-na / a-səla ari. 'That poor man eats
> 1   2   3   4   5   6
>
>   (only) every other day.' [1. uriŋ 'person', 2. miskin 'poor',
>   3. rua 'that', 4. N-kakan 'to eat', 5. a-səla 'to skip one', 6.
>   ari 'day']

> pa-N-pa-lain-na ibhu / cuma sa-kuniq. 'Mother only puts aside a
>   1   2   3   4
>
>   little.' [1. N-pa-lain 'to put aside', 2. ibhu 'mother', 3. cuma
>   'only', 4. sa-kuniq 'a little']

With reduplication

N-k-ucaq 'to speak'	pa-R+N-k-ucaq-na 'his constant talking'
N-kira 'to estimate'	pa-R+N-kira-na 'his calculating'
	pa-Rtm+N-kira-na 'his calculating'

-an

1) Derived from radical stems of basic derivatives this derivative has such meanings as 'result of the action, product of the action, that which is affected by the action, location of the action'.

N-kakan 'to eat'	kakan-an 'food'
a-pikkir 'to think'	pikkir-an 'thought'
N-bazar 'to pay'	bazar-an 'payment'
a-sakula 'go to school'	sakula-an 'school'
N-inum 'to drink'	inum-an 'drink'
zhau 'far'	zhau-an 'distance'
lucu 'funny'	lucu-n 'joke' (complementary extension)

2) 'Something which in some way is similar to the root meaning or has the quality of the root meaning, or in some less direct way than section 1 is the product of the root meaning.'

asta 'hand'	asta-an 'letter, handle, work'
kuniŋ 'yellow'	kuniŋ-an 'brass'

170

lanciŋ 'young man'   lanciŋ-an 'short pants'

kazu 'wood'   kazu-an 'tree'

bəkas 'trace, remnant'   bəkas-an 'result'

3) Derived from names of units of money this derivative means 'a bill or coin worth that amount'.

rupia 'rupiah'   rupia-an 'one rupiah bill'

4) A few of these derivatives, derived from the radical stem of transitive verbals, have a passive meaning 'its being ...'.

miññaq-na / manabi anpun a-baḍḍha kadhi ingha.panika, tantu pas
        1   2   3   4   5   6   7   8

ghanpaŋ tanbiq-an-na. 'If the oil has been put in a place like
      9   10

that, carrying it is surely easy.' [1. miññaq-na 'the oil', 2. manabi 'if', 3. anpun 'already', 4. a-baḍḍha 'to have a place', 5. kadhi 'like', 6. ingha.panika 'that', 7. tantu 'sure', 8. pas 'then', 9. ghanpaŋ 'easy', 10. N-tanbiq 'to carry']

5) Derivatives from radical or extended stems with the meanings 'person who, person connected with' and 'collective plural' (cf. verbals on page 119) are infrequent.

lazu 'worn out'   lazu-an 'old clothes dealer'

əmas 'gold'   k-əmas-an 'gold smith' (extended stem)

bini-q 'female'   bini-q-an 'women'

laki-q 'male'   laki-q-an 'men'

ka- -an

Derived from null affix verbals and nouns.

1) Abstract nouns.

baḍa 'there is'   ka-baḍa-an 'situation'

bhaghus 'good'   ka-bhaghus-an 'goodness'

parcaza 'believe'   ka-parcaza-an 'belief'

aman 'safe'   ka-aman-an 'safety, security'

parzugha 'dashing'   ka-parzugha-an 'dashingness'

2) Locational.

ənəŋ 'stay'   k-ənəŋ-an 'place' (complementary extension)

171

malu 'ashamed'   ka-malu-an 'genitals'
tiɖuŋ 'sleep'   ka-tiɖuŋ-an 'bed'
bəli 'buy'   ka-bəli-an 'place, time for buying'
badhana 'wedana (adminis-   ka-badhana-n 'area covered by such an
        trative office)'   office or the office itself'
                                      (complementary extension)

   3) Special.

   a-laku 'to do, act, work'   ka-laku-an 'work, behavior'
   sala 'wrong, mistake'   ka-sala-an 'guilt'
   iɖiŋ 'hear'   ka-iɖiŋ-an 'what something sounds like'
   bəraq 'heavy'   ka-bəraq-an 'faeces'
   lagghu 'morning'   ka-lagghu-an 'the next day'

Plurals of nouns in ka- -an are usually formed with Rtwɬ.

Grammatically possible, but rarely used are nouns derived from null-affix

stems by means of ka-taq.ka- -an or taq.ka- -an. These are usually preceded by

the word hal 'thing, matter'.

   ghunbhira 'joyful'   (hal) ka-taq.ka-ghunbhira-an 'joylessness'
   dhaddhi 'to become'   (hal) ka-taq.ka-dhaddhi-an 'failure (to
                                              do something)'

pa- -an

Derived from the basic derivative,[25] and from some null-affix nouns these de-

rivatives have a variety of meanings.

   1) Locational.

   N-ɖhaar 'to eat'   pa-ɖhaar-an 'stomach, mouth'
   ghəlaŋ 'bracelet'   pa-ghəlaŋ-an 'wrist'
   bhaku 'tobacco'   pa-bhaku-an 'tobacco store, stand'
   a-bhazaŋ 'to pray'   pa-bhazaŋ-an 'prayer house'
   N-buaq 'to be loaded'   pa-N-buaq-an 'place for loading'
   cina 'Chinese'   pa-cina-n 'Chinese quarter' (complemen-
                                      tary extension)
   ghunuŋ 'mountain'   pa-ghunuŋ-an 'the mountains'
   a-Rɬtəmu-n 'to meet'   pa-Rɬtəmu-n-an 'meeting place' (extended
                                      stem)

   2) Agent.

   a. person (often preceded by uriŋ 'person')

aiŋ 'water'	pa-aiŋ-an 'water seller'	
bhaku 'tobacco'	pa-bhaku-an 'tobacconist'	
N-anghur 'be out of work'	pa-N-anghur-an 'unemployed person'	

b. instrument (often preceded by some other noun)

biddhaŋ 'hot water'	pa-biddhaŋ-an 'pot'	
N-cukur 'to shave'	[laddhiŋ] pa-N-cukur-an 'razor'	laddhiŋ 'knife'
a-nanghala 'to plow'	[sapi] pa-nanghala-an 'plow cow'	sapi 'cow'
N-usap 'to wipe'	pa-N-usap-an 'eraser'	
N-timur 'dry seasonal'	[zhaghuŋ] pa-N-timur-an 'corn planted in the dry season'	zhaghuŋ 'corn'

3) Special.

təḍha 'eat'	pa-təḍha-n 'left over food'
	cf. pa-N-təḍha-an 'eating place'

Reduplication order

R+pa- -an   Rtw+pa- -an

    pa-N-cukur-an 'razor'   R+pa-N-cukur-an 'razors'

                                                    Rtw+pa-N-cukur-an 'razors'

paŋ-

The morphophonemics of paŋ- have been given above. The derivatives are from the radical stem.

1) Agent

a. personal.

aḍaq 'front'	paŋ-aḍaq 'important person'
bhighal 'rob'	paŋ-bhighal 'robber'
uan 'herd'	paŋ-uan 'shephard'
zaga 'guard'	paŋ-zaga 'guard'
zhaiq 'sew'	paŋ-zhaiq 'tailor'
ladhin 'serve'	paŋ-ladhin 'servant'

b. instrumental.

anbhuŋ 'kiss, smell'	paŋ-anbhuŋ 'nose'
bazar 'pay'	paŋ-bazar 'payment'
asi 'love'	paŋ-asi 'love magic, potion'

zhaiq 'sew'	paŋ-zhaiq 'sewing instruments, materials'
təbha 'sweep'	paŋ-təbha 'broom'
tulak 'reject'	paŋ-tulak 'means by which one wards off evil'

2) Wide variety of meanings: 'result of the action, thing connected with the action, etc.'.

rasa 'feel'	paŋ-rasa 'feeling'
arəp 'hope'	paŋ-arəp 'hope'
istu 'true'	paŋ-istu 'sincerity'
nisər 'love, pity'	paŋ-nisər 'love-gift'
zhual 'sell'	paŋ-zhual 'capital'

3) Special.

bhurus 'dog'	paŋ-bhurus 'dog'
sirəp 'be quiet'	paŋ-sirəp → pàŋsèrəp 'sleeping potion'

Reduplication order

R+paŋ-   Rtw+paŋ-

paŋ-cukur 'razor'	R+paŋ-cukur 'razors'
	Rtw+paŋ-cukur 'razors'

Compare this with the Rtm+ derivatives of page 173.

Rtw+paŋ-cukur-na → pàñòkòr-pàñòkòrrà 'his razors'

pa-Rtm+N-cukur-na → pàñòkòr+ñòkòrrà 'his constant shaving'

paŋ- -an

Derived from the root, many of these are recent loans from Indonesian. Some are partly or wholly Madurized.

1) Instrumental.

ulat 'see'	paŋ-ulat-an 'mirror, eye-glasses'
takut 'fear'	paŋ-takut-an 'scarecrow'

2) Various, mostly taken from or based on the Indonesian model pəN- -an.

ghabaj 'do'	paŋ- ghabaj-an 'work'
ankuq 'transport'	paŋ-ankuq-an 'transportation'
abas 'see'	paŋ-abas-an 'appearance'
arti 'understand'	paŋ-arti-an 'understanding'
bagi 'distribute'	paŋ-bagi-an 'distribution'

174

buaŋ 'throw away'	paŋ-buaŋ-an 'place of exile'
asil 'origin'	paŋ-asil-an 'result'
parinta 'order'	paŋ-parinta-an 'government'

Reduplication order

R+paŋ- -an   Rtw+paŋ- -an

R+ -an

1) 'collective plural', derived from some null affix nouns.

bua 'fruit'	R+bua-an 'fruits'
taritan 'sibling'	R+taritan-an 'siblings, all relatives of the same generation'
kazu 'wood'	R+kazu-an 'trees'
kənbhaŋ 'flower'	R+kənbhaŋ-an 'flowers'

2) 'similar to, imitation of'.

tunkul 'bud'	R+tunkul-an 'heart (organ)'
laŋŋiq 'sky'	R+laŋŋiq-an 'palate'
anaq 'child'	R+ənaq-an 'doll'
bənku 'house'	R+bənku-an 'toy house'
bintaŋ 'star'	R+bintaŋ-an 'fireworks'
mira 'red'	R+mira-an 'egg yolk'

3) 'that which is..., that which is to be...'

alli 'move'	R+alli-an 'decal'
asta 'hand'	R+asta-an 'favorite thing'
bali 'go back'	R+bali-n 'change (money)' (complementary extension)
bəla 'split'	R+bəla-an 'shards'
bəli 'buy'	R+bəli-n 'purchases' (complementary extension)
dhina 'leave'	R+dhina-n 'heirlooms' (complementary extension)
ubu 'raise, bring up'	R+ubu-an 'pet'

4) 'place where'.

anbu 'stop'	R+anbu-an 'stopping place'
bhiluk 'curve'	R+bhiluk-an 'curved place (in road, etc.)'
sarpa 'garbage'	R+sarpa-an 'garbage heap'

Rtm+ -an

Same as R+ -an section 1.

175

bua 'fruit'   Rtm+bua-an 'fruits'

<u>Rf+ -an</u>

Few cases of this derivative occur.

　1) Collective plural.

　　ɖaun 'leaf'   Rf+ɖaun-an 'leaves'

　2) Various.

　　buruk 'instruct'   Rf+buruk-an 'advice, lessons'
　　lucu 'funny'   Rf+lucu-n 'joke' (complementary extension)
　　tai 'faeces'   Rf+tai-n-an 'rust' (extended stem)
　　cali 'blame, criticize' Rf+cali-n 'person criticized' (comple-
                                   mentary extension)
　　laku 'do, act'   Rf+laku-n 'work' (complementary extension)

<u>Rf+ -ən</u>

Very few cases occur.

　　sunpa 'oath, swear'   Rf+sunpa-ən 'thing about which an oath
                                   is made'

<u>sa-</u>

　1) Usually derived from the basic derivative this means 'whatever is ...,
all of ...'.

　　sa-bhutu-na aliq si a-sakula / i-tanghuŋ paman. 'All of brother's
　　1   2   3 4   5   6
　　needs at school were taken care of by uncle.' [1. a-bhutu 'to
　　need', 2. aliq 'younger sibling', 3. si 'rel. particle', 4.
　　a-sakula 'to go to school', 5. i-tanghuŋ 'be taken care of',
　　6. paman 'uncle']

　　sa-N-tudhiŋ-na aliq / i-N-bəli-aghi. 'Whatever brother pointed at
　　1   2   3
　　was bought (for him).' [1. N-tudhiŋ 'to point at', 2. aliq
　　'younger sibling', 3. i-N-bəli-aghi 'be bought for']

　　baqna kudhu N-tarima apa sa-dhuum-na. 'You should accept whatever is
　　1   2   3   4   5
　　distributed.' [1. baqna 'you', 2. kudhu 'must', 3. N-tarima 'to
　　receive', 4. apa 'what', 5. N-dhuum 'to distribute']

　　sa-issi-na bənku rua / sakiq kabbhi. 'Everyone in that house is
　　1   2   3   4   5

176

sick.' [1. a-issi 'to have constant', 2. bənku 'house', 3.
rua 'that', 4. sakiq 'sick', 5. kabbhi 'all']

Reduplication order

R+sa-

    R+sa-karəp 'whatever (I) want'

  2) Special.

ruba 'shape'	sa-ruba-n 'whatever there is'
kubhəŋ 'around'	sa-kubhəŋ 'vicinity'
ka-liŋ+liŋ 'around'	sa-ka-liŋ+liŋ 'in the vicinity'
zhalan 'road, go'	sa-zhalan 'along the length'

sa-pa-

The meaning of this derivative is the same as sa- 1 above.

N-iḍiŋ 'to hear'	sa-pa-N-iḍiŋ-na 'whatever he hears, has heard'
uniŋ 'to know'	sa-pa-uniŋ-na 'whatever he knows'
N-zawap 'to answer'	sa-pa-zawap-na 'everything he answered'
a-zhalan 'to walk'	sa-pa-zhalan-na 'wherever he goes'
a-pariŋ 'to give'	sa-pa-pariŋ-na 'whatever (one) can give'

Intransitive verbals with corresponding transitives in N-ka- -i optionally
retain N-ka- in this derivative.

tau 'to know'	sa-pa-N-ka-tau-na, sa-tau-na, sa-pa-tau-na 'whatever he knows'
təru 'to want'	sa-pa-N-ka-təru-na 'whatever he wants'

sa-pa- -an

  1) Same as the preceding sa-pa- above.

tau 'to know'	sa-pa-N-ka-tau-an-na 'whatever he knows'

  2) Derived from the basic derivative this means 'the distance (of the
root meaning)'.

N-bhəḍhil 'to shoot'	sa-pa-N-bhəḍhil-an 'shooting distance'
a-iraq 'to shout'	sa-pa-iraq-an 'shouting distance'
a-luncaq 'to jump'	sa-pa-luncaq-an 'jumping distance'
manzhəŋ 'to stand'	sa-pa-manzhəŋ-an 'height of something standing'

sa-pa- -ən

Same meaning as sa-pa -an 2 above, but many fewer cases.

N-uluk 'to call'   sa-pa-N-uluk-ən 'calling distance'

Minor nominal affixes

par-, par- -an, pari- -an

Some of these words are borrowed from Indonesian.

tinka 'step'		par-tinka 'behavior, theory'
mula 'begin'		par-mula-an 'beginning'
zhalan 'road'		par-zhalan-an 'trip'
zhanzhi 'promise'		par-zhanzhi-an 'agreement, appointment'
taña 'ask'		par-taña-an 'question'
tapa 'seclude'		par-tapa-an 'hermitage, place of seclusion'
		par-tapa-n 'id'
bhasa 'language'		par-bhasa-n 'proverb'
		pari-bhasa-n 'id'
kami-	tua 'old'	kami-tua 'village elder'
-al-	buntuq 'tail'	b-al-untuq 'tail hair' ??
-ar-	kəɖhəp 'lightning'	k-ar-əɖhəp 'sparkle'
-an-	sulap 'dazzled'	s-an-ulap-an 'sleight of hand'
ka-	bəli 'buy'	ka-bəli 'purchase price'
-q	laki 'husband'	laki-q, Rf+laki-q 'man, male'
	bini 'wife'	bini-q, Rf+bini-q 'woman, female'
pi-	utaŋ 'debt'	pi-utaŋ 'what is owed to one'
	taña 'ask'	pi-taña 'question'
	tuluŋ 'help'	pi-tuluŋ 'help'
	tudhu 'point'	pi-tudhu 'advice'
pi- -an	atur 'regulate'	pi-atur-an 'regulations'
sa-par-	kiɖhəp 'wink'	sa-par-N-kiɖhəp 'an instant, moment'

OTHER VERBALS

The following derivatives are on the borderline of being verbals. Although grammatically they cooccur with the suffix -a, this sounds somewhat strange to Madurese. The syntactic positions of the following derivations also differ from other verbals.

sa- -an

1) 'to be enough for one ...; to be only, just; to be passing, momentary'.
These are derived from the basic derivative and from nouns. They are intransitive.

bhadhan 'body'	sa-bhadhan-an 'to be just body size'
a-balanzha 'to shop'	sa-balanzha-an 'to be enough for a shopping trip (of money)'
bibir 'lip'	sa-bibir-an 'to be superficial'
dhamar 'lamp'	sa-dhamar-an 'to be a lampful'
uniŋ 'to know'	sa-uniŋ-an 'just to know (something, and not act on it)'
təru 'to want'	sa-təru-an 'to be a passing desire'

2) Special.

N-ulat-i 'to see'	sa-ulat-an, sa-N-ulat-an 'to get a glimpse, to be just a glimpse'
ruba 'shape, form'	R+sa-ruba-n 'to do something any old way, carelessly'
abaq 'body, person'	R+sa-abaq, abaq+sa-abaq 'all alone'

sa-pa- -an, sa-pa- -ən

1) Same meaning as sa- -an 1 above.

N-ulat-i 'to see'	sa-pa-N-ulat-an, sa-pa-N-ulat-ən 'to get only a glimpse'

2) Special.

N-panghaŋ 'to roast'	sa-pa-N-panghaŋ-ən 'to be grown enough for roasting (of chickens)'

PARTICLES

In the following section all non-predicators will be discussed. A more detailed analysis depending on syntactic function will not be made. Most of the affixes employed, however, are the same in shape as those already described for verbals and nouns.

Shortening (S)

The rules for deriving shortening have already been given on page 30f and 82f. Meanings are as follows:

1) Vocatives of some personal names and kinship terms.

    S+aliq 'younger sibling!'

    S+paman 'uncle!, old man!'

    S+ibhu 'mother!'

    S+əpaq 'father!'

    S+ahmat 'Ahmat!'

punapa ibhu anpun N-təḍha + S+aliq? 'Has mother eaten, brother?'
  1   2   3   4

[1. punapa 'question particle', 2. ibhu 'mother', 3. anpun 'already', 4. N-təḍha 'to eat']

S+əpaq and S+ibhu are also used before proper names and some nouns indicating office or title. These show respect and are used in address or in reference.

    S+əpaq ghuru 'teacher'

    S+əpaq sallim 'Mr. Salim'

2) The kasar and təŋa words (see Fn. 22) for 'yes', ɩa and ənghi respectively, also occur with S+ in sentence final position with question intonation. The meaning is a question expecting a yes answer or a suggestion or softened command.

tərus ka bənku + S+ɩa? 'Straight home, OK?' [1. tərus 'straight',
 1 2   3
2. ka 'to', 3. bənku 'house']

The alus form inghi 'yes' does not have such a shortened form.

3) The numbers from 1 to 10 have shortened forms which are used in rapid counting. The q set of numbers is used (see below under numbers).

1. S+sittuŋ	6. S+ənəm
2. S+ḍua-q	7. S+pittu-q
3. S+təlu-q	8. S+ballu-q
4. S+ənpa-q	9. S+saŋa-q
5. S+lima-q	10. S+sa.pulu

The result is as follows phonetically: [tŏŋ, wáq, lŏq, páq, mãq, nə̃m, tŏq, lúq, ŋãq, lŏ]

4) A few words have shortened forms which are more common in colloquial

speech than the long forms.[26]

musu 'with, by'	su
azzhaq 'don't'	zhaq
labiq 'by means of'	biq
lamun 'if, when'	mun

R+

Often derived from null affix intransitives with adverbial meaning.

A fair number of special types occur. Connections are not always clear.

abit 'long (time)'	R+abit 'finally'
tau 'to know'	R+tau 'suddenly'
taḍaq 'there isn't'	R+taḍaq-na 'it's all because'
kaḍhaŋ kala 'sometimes'	R+kaḍhaŋ 'sometimes'
baariq 'yesterday'	R+baariq-na 'in the recent past'
mula 'begin'	R+mula-n-na 'at first' (extended stem)

Rt+ special shapes:

abit 'long (time)'	abit-na+abit 'at long last'
unghu 'true'	unghu-an+unghu 'really and truly'

-a

A number of fixed expressions occur with -a:

 təka-a '(not) even (a single)'

mandhaq-a 'how (___ it is)!' e.g. mandhaq-a raza-na! 'How big it is!'

ucaq 'say'   ka-ucaq-a 'it is said, once upon a time'

Various words meaning 'no matter how, even if' have -a:

sumili-a, maski-an-a, nazzhan-a

-an

unghu 'real'	unghu-an 'really, truly'
talbhuk 'thump'	talbhuk-an 'with a thump'
dhulit 'touch with finger tip'	[i-unzhaŋ] dhulit-an '[invited] in an informal way'

-i

abit 'long (time)'	N-abit-i 'starting from'

181

<u>pa- -i</u>

Preceded by the particle la (from əla 'already'?) and derived from null affix adjective type intransitives this derivative means 'no matter how'.

     la pa-pintər-i baqna / mun a-musu su ghuru, tantu taq kira ungha.
         1   2   3   4   5 6   7   8   9   10

     'No matter how smart you are, if you oppose the teacher, you won't be promoted.' [1. pintər 'smart', 2. baqna 'you', 3. mun 'if', 4. a-musu 'to oppose', 5. su 'with', 6. ghuru 'teacher', 7. tantu 'certain', 8. taq 'not', 9. kira 'think, believe', 10. ungha 'go up, be promoted']

     la pa-muɖa-i R+zhual-na baqna / sinkuq taq N-bəli-a. 'No matter how
      1   2   3   4   5   6

     cheap your goods are, I won't buy.' [1. muɖa 'cheap', 2. R+zhual-na 'what is sold of', 3. baqna 'you', 4. sinkuq 'I', 5. taq 'not', 6. N-bəli-a 'will buy']

<u>ka-</u>

     anghuj 'use'   ka-anghuj 'for, in order to' (also:
                                      k-anghuj)

     suun 'request'   ka-suun 'thank you'

<u>ka- -an</u>

     bhəndər 'true'   ka-bhəndər-an 'by chance'

     ɖu. 'two'

     maləm 'night'   ka-ɖu.maləm-an-na 'day before yesterday'

The latter also occurs as: ka-ɖu.maləm-na and ɖu.maləm-na with the same meaning.

<u>tar-, tur-</u>

Only occurs in tar-kaɖhaŋ, tur-kaɖhaŋ 'sometimes' and in tar-unghu 'serious', but the latter is probably a verbal.

<u>par-</u> Only occurs in the following doubtful cases:

     cuma 'only'   par-cuma 'gratis'

     mila-na 'and so'   par-mila 'because of'

<u>-na</u>

Particle derivatives with -na occur in a large number of fixed expressions.

     maləm 'night'   maləm-na 'last night'

lagghu 'morning'	lagghu-na 'tomorrow'
biasa 'usual'	biasa-na 'usually'
ruba 'shape'	ruba-na 'apparently'
ənzaq 'no'	ənzaq-na 'or not' (in alternative questions)
buḍi 'back'	R+buḍi-na 'at last, finally'

sa-

1) Various.

sa-tia, sa-N-tuntu, sa-mankin 'now'
sa-kəzhaq 'for a while'

nalika, natkala 'when'	sa-nalika, sa-natkala 'at that moment'
ḍu.maləm 'two nights'	sa-ḍu.maləm 'the day after tomorrow'
lagghiq 'almost'	sa-lagghiq 'as long as'
mula 'begin'	sa-mula-i 'since (the time that)'
banni 'be different'	sa-banni 'some, various'

2) 'together with'. These show some features of nouns.

baqna si intar ḍaq ghunuŋ / sa-kanca R+baranpa-an? 'You're going to
1   2   3   4 5   6   7
the mountains with how many friends?' [1. baqna 'you', 2. si 'rel.
particle', 3. intar 'to go', 4. ḍaq 'to', 5. ghunuŋ 'mountain',
6. kanca 'friend', 7. R+baranpa-an 'how many in the group']

sinkuq sa-bhala / ballu-ŋ.uriŋ kabbhi. 'I and my family are 8 in all.'
1   2   3   4   5
[1. sinkuq 'I', 2. bhala 'family', 3. ballu-ŋ. 'eight', 4. uriŋ
'person', 5. kabbhi 'all']

tana kaq-ɪssa / i-zhual sa-cunpuq-na. 'That land is sold with its
1   2   3   4
house.' [1. tana 'land', 2. kaq-ɪssa 'that there', 3. i-zhual 'be
sold', 4. cunpuq 'house']

3) 'the same'. These show some features of verbals.

naghara 'country'	[uriŋ] sa-naghara 'fellow countryman'
rənbhak 'consult'	sa-rənbhak 'be of the same opinion'

4) 'the whole, entire'.

kulɪ rua / buḍḍhak cəlut sa-bhadhan. 'The worker is covered with mud
1   2   3   4   5
all over his body.' [1. kulɪ 'coolie', 2. rua 'that', 3. buḍḍhak
'be covered, has something spread around', 4. cəlut 'mud', 5.

bhadhan 'body']

uriŋ sa-dhisa / i-pa-kunpul Ŕf+kabbhi.   'The whole village was
1   2   3   4
gathered together.' [1. uriŋ 'person', 2. dhisa 'village', 3.
i-pa-kunpul 'be gathered together', 4. Ŕf+kabbhi 'all']

R+sa-

Derived from names of time periods this derivative means 'every'.

ari 'day'	R+sa-ari 'every day'
maləm 'night'	R+sa-maləm 'every night, night after night'

R+sa- -na

Derived from names of time periods this derivative means '... after ...'

ari 'day'	R+sa-ari-na 'day after day, day in day out'
bulan 'month'	R+sa-bulan-na 'month after month, month in month out'

sa- -na

1) Various.

əla 'already'	sa-əla-na, sa-q-əla-na 'after'
bəlun 'not yet'	sa-bəlun-na 'before'
istu 'true'	sa-istu-na 'in fact, actually'
kabbhi 'all'	sa-kabbhi-na 'all kinds of'
ñaman 'tasty, comfortable'	sa-ñaman-na '(do) just as (you) like'
ka.buɖi 'to the back'	sa-ka.buɖi-na 'in future'

2) Derived from the basic derivative this derivative means 'when, after'.

sa-ghubhar-na ibhu / aliq pas N-taŋis.   'When mother went home,
1   2   3   4   5
brother wept.' [1. ghubhar 'to go home', 2. ibhu 'mother', 3.
aliq 'younger sibling', 4. pas 'then', 5. N-taŋis 'to weep']

sa-N-capuq-na baqna si N-tabaŋ mutur rua / pas tura-i pukul
1   2   3   4   5   6   7   8   9
baɣanpa!   'When you catch up to the car you're chasing, note down
10
the time.' [1. N-capuq 'to catch up to', 2. baqna 'you', 3. si
'rel. particle', 4. N-tabaŋ 'to chase after', 5. mutur 'automobile', 6. rua 'that', 7. pas 'then', 8. tura-i 'note down!',
9. pukul 'hour, o'clock', 10. baranpa 'how much']

sa-N-ʈaʈʈaŋ-na labaŋ / tamuj pas masuq. 'When he opened the door, the
1   2   3   4   5
guest came in.' [1. N-ʈaʈʈaŋ 'to open wide', 2. labaŋ 'door',
3. tamuj 'guest', 4. pas 'then', 5. masuq 'to enter']

sa-N-inum-na aiŋ / pas sakiq tabuq. 'After he drank the water, he
1   2   3   4   5
got sick to his stomach.' [1. N-inum 'to drink', 2. aiŋ 'water',
3. pas 'then', 4. sakiq 'sick', 5. tabuq 'stomach']

Grammatically possible though rarely used are such derivatives based on
proclitic stems with taq. 'not'.

sa-taq.N-bukkaq-na tuku / sinkuq a-paləsér. 'When ⎰Since⎱ the store wasn't
1   2   3   4
open, I went for a walk.' [1. taq N-bukkaq 'not to be open',
2. tuku 'store', 3. sinkuq 'I', 4. a-paləsér 'take a walk around']

3) Derived from names of time periods this derivative means 'each, every'.

si a-langhan-an aiŋ / sa-bulan-na / lima.bəlas rupia. 'Those who
1 2   3   4   5   6
subscribe to water (pay) 15 rupiahs a month.' [1. si 'rel.
particle', 2. a-langhan-an 'to be a subscriber', 3. aiŋ 'water',
4. bulan 'month', 5. lima.bəlas 'fifteen', 6. rupia 'rupiah']

rama N-balanzha-i ibhu sa-ari-na + s.atus rupia. 'Father gives mother
1   2   3   4   5   6
100 rupiahs shopping money every day.' [1. rama 'father', 2.
N-balanzha-i 'to provide with shopping money', 3. ibhu 'mother',
4. ari 'day', 5. s.atus 'one hundred', 6. rupia 'rupiah']

sa-R+ -na, sa-Rtm+ -na (in free variation)

Derived from the basic derivative, this derivative means 'as ... as possible', 'no matter how'.

pissi za.ria / ka-balanzha ⎰ sa-R+cukup-na!   'Spend as much of that
1   2   3   ⎱ sa-Rtm+cukup-na!
                                      4
money as is sufficient for shopping.' [1. pissi 'money', 2. za.ria
'that, 3. ka-balanzha 'spend in shopping!', 4. cukup 'sufficient']

a-zhalan sa-R+N-ɖapaq-na 'to walk as far as one can' [1. a-zhalan
1   2
'to walk', 2. N-ɖapaq 'to arrive at']

sa-R+maləm-na baqna + su sinkuq / i-antus-a. 'No matter how late you
  1   2   3   4   5

are, I'll wait.' [1. maləm 'late, night', 2. baqna 'you', 3. su
'by', 4. sinkuq 'I', 5. i-antus-a 'will be waited for']

sa- -an

Derived from the basic derivatives and from nouns this derivative means
'each time'.

tamuj-na / sa-ɗatəŋ-an / sa.pulu.uriŋ. 'The guests came ten at a
   1   2   3

time.' [1. tamuj-na 'the guest', 2. ɗatəŋ 'to come', 3.
sa.pulu.uriŋ '10 persons']

sa-mius-an / sa.mingu + abit-na. 'He goes away for a week at a time.'
  1   2   3

[1. mius 'to go', 2. sa.mingu 'a week', 3. abit-na 'the time']

ghuru mun a-dhuŋŋiŋ, ciq lanzhaŋ-na + sa-dhuŋŋiŋ-an / təlu zham.
  1   2   3   4   5   3   6   7
'When teacher tells a story, it lasts long; each telling is three
hours.' [1. ghuru 'teacher', 2. mun 'when', 3. a-dhuŋŋiŋ 'tell a
story', 4. ciq 'very', 5. lanzhaŋ-na 'the length', 6. təlu 'three',
7. zham 'hour']

sa-pa- -na

Derived from the basic derivative this derivative means the same as sa- -na
2 above, 'when, after'.

sa-pa-carita-na uriŋ rua / i-iɗiŋ.aghi tərus. 'When he narrated, he
      1   2   3   4   5
was listened to straight through.' [1. a-carita 'to tell a story',
2. uriŋ 'person', 3. rua 'that', 4. i-iɗiŋ.aghi 'be listened to',
5. tərus 'straight']

The derivative in the preceding example, however, could be considered a
noun, 'whatever he narrated'.

sa-pa-ɗapaq-na paman / pas a-taña + 'When uncle arrived, he asked...'
     1   2   3   4
[1. ɗapaq 'to arrive', 2. paman 'uncle', 3. pas 'then', 4. a-taña
'to ask']

Included in this section are all substitutes of morphological interest: demonstrative, locational, interrogative, as well as others which show similar derivatives. For the sake of completeness personal pronouns, which have neither internal morphology nor derivatives, are given in an appendix below.

Although many of the substitutes show similar partials, the relationship between these partials is usually not clear cut, for example: (for levels see fn. 22).

kasar	təŋa	alus
apa	napi	punapa 'what'
sapa	sira	pasira 'who'

Only where a partial extends through a large part or all of a paradigm will cuts be made, for example:

kasar	təŋa	alus
kannaq	kuq-kantu	kaq-kantu 'hither'
kassa	kuq-kassa	kaq-kassa 'thither'

Reduced forms

Reduced forms of substitutes occur in rapid, colloquial speech. Reduced forms are one symbol or one syllable shorter than ordinary forms according to the following rules:

1) |pu and |pa become zero. For example:

punapa	→ napa 'what A'
pasira	→ sira 'who A'
sa-punapa	→ sa-napa 'how much A'
gha.panika	→ gha.nika 'that A'

2) $\left.\begin{array}{l} -k \\ -\text{d} \end{array}\right\}$ become zero, but the following vowel remains the same alternant as in the ordinary form.[27]

kaq-dintu	→ kaq-íntu 'here A'
kuq-dissa	→ kuq-íssa 'there T'
kaq-kanza	→ kaq-anza 'hither A'
kuq-kassa	→ kuq-assa 'thither T'

3) ɖaq$|_{r}^{k}$} become ɖaq by loss of the following consonant. The alternant

of the next vowel is determined in the usual manner (J- and P-Rules) according to

the intervening juncture, for example:

  ɖaq-kannaq → ɖaq-annaq → ɖáqánnàq 'hither K'

  ɖaq kannaq → ɖaq annaq → ɖáqànnàq 'hither K'

  ɖaq-kassa → ɖaq-assa → ɖáqássà 'thither K'

  ɖaq kassa → ɖaq assa → ɖáqàssà 'thither K'

  ɖaq-ria   → ɖaqia   → ɖáqíjá 'this way K'

  ɖaq-rintu → ɖaqintu   → ɖáqíntò 'this way T'

Substitutes will be presented in paradigmatic sets according to level (K,

T, and A). Where more than one form is given, both or all occur in the standard

dialect.

Demonstratives

K	T	A
1. ria	niku	panika
aria	aniku	
2. za.ria	gha.niku	gha.panika
		ingha.panika
		angha.panika
3. rua	gha.rua	ingha.rua
arua		angha.rua
za.rua		

1) The forms in row one indicate objects near the speaker or that the

associated noun is a class term. Thus zharan ria means 'this horse' or 'horses'.

Another example follows:

    pitəna ria biasa-na N-pa-cagghik-an uriŋ. 'Slander usually makes
      1   2   3   4   5

    people quarrel.' [1. pitəna 'slander', 2. ria 'this', 3. biasa-na

    'usually', 4. N-pa-cagghik-an 'to make quarrel often', 5. uriŋ

    'person']

2) The forms in row two indicate objects near the person spoken to or

objects just mentioned, known in the context, and the like. Thus zharan za.ria

means 'that horse (near you and not near me)' or 'the horse we were just talking about, just mentioned, which somehow you know about'. More rarely than those in row one it is associated with nouns as class terms. For example:

> rəbhuŋ za.ria i-ka-ghatəl ɖaq kuliq. 'Bamboo shoots make the skin
> 1   2   3   4   5
>
>   itch.' [1. rəbhuŋ 'bamboo shoots', 2. za.ria 'that', 3.
>   i-ka-ghatəl 'is the cause of itching', 4. ɖaq 'to', 5. kuliq
>   'skin']

3) The forms in row three indicate objects far from both speaker and addressee.

Forms used to cover AT situations are taken from the locational set to be discussed below.

Some other dialect forms follow:

West Madurese: zè   for za.ria

                punika for panika

Kangean: rinna   for ria

                əntu   for rua

Derivatives

The above forms occur with -q in a strengthened meaning 'here you are, here it is, etc.'.

> ria-q + bukɗ-na aliq / pa-rinkəs! 'Here you are; put brother's books
> 1   2   3   4
>
>   away.' [1. ria 'this', 2. bukɗ-na 'book of', 3. aliq 'younger
>   sibling', 4. pa-rinkəs 'put away']

> rua-q + zhu taq taŋ bukɗ? 'Isn't <u>that</u> my book?' [1. rua 'that',
> 1   2   3 4 5
>
>   2. zhu 'particle', 3. taq 'not', 4. taŋ 'my', 5. bukɗ 'book']

> bukɗ-na sanpian + panika-q. 'Your book is <u>that</u> one.' [1. bukɗ-na
> 1   2   3
>
>   'book of', 2. sanpian 'you', 3. panika 'that']

Locationals

The forms given here occur preceded by i 'at' (West Madurese: laq 'at'), ghan 'up to', nəŋ 'in, on, at', or by a noun.

<u>'here'</u>[28]

	K	T	A
1.	ɖinnaq	ɖintu	kaq-ɖintu
		kuq-ɖintu	kaq-əntu
		kuq-əntu	
2.	ɖia	kuq-ɖia	kaq-ɖia

<u>'there'</u>

	K	T	A
1.	za.ɖia	gha.ɖia	ingha.ɖia
			angha.ɖia
2.	ɖissa	kuq-ɖissa	kaq-ɖissa

The alus forms, kaq-ɖintu and kaq-ɖissa, are also used for alus tinghi demonstratives.

'here': The difference between rows one and two is not entirely clear. Those in row one seem to mean 'near the speaker; right near by; the latter' while those in row two seem to mean 'further away from the speaker, in the vicinity, around here (thus also including the area covered by the words in row one)'.

'there': Those in row one mean 'near the addressee, previously mentioned, already known'. Those in row two mean 'far from the speaker and addressee'.

> sa-əla-na ləsu tuzuq i ɖinnaq, sinkuq intar ka.aɖaq-an. 'After
>   1   2   3   4   5   6   7   8
> getting tired of sitting here, I went up front.' [1. sa-əla-na
> 'after', 2. ləsu 'tired', 3. tuzuq 'to sit', 4. i 'in', 5. ɖinnaq
> 'here', 6. sinkuq 'I', 7. intar 'to go', 8. ka.adaq-an 'to the
> front']

> taŋ təghal a-batəs ghan ɖinnaq. 'My field goes up to here.' [1. taŋ
> 1   2   3   4   5
> 'my', 2. təghal 'dry field', 3. a-batəs 'to have a boundary',
> 4. ghan 'up to', 5. ɖinnaq 'here']

> kaq-ɖintu taɖaq arti-na. 'The latter has no meaning.' [1. kaq-ɖintu
>   1   2   3
> 'the latter', 2. taɖaq 'there is not', 3. arti-na 'its meaning']

> adhuni i kaq-ɖintu saus + pas ɖhaar i kaq-ɩa sakali! 'Prepare it
> 1   2   3   4   5 6   2   7   8

190

right here and then drink it here (on the premises).' [1. adhuni 'prepare', 2. i 'in', 3. kaq-ɖintu 'here', 4. saus 'just', 5. pas 'then', 6. ɖhaar 'drink', 7. kaq-ɟa 'here', 8. sakali 'just, just go ahead and']

bañ̃aq maliŋ i kuʈʈa ɖia. 'There are many thieves here in the city.'
1   2   3   4   5
[1. bañ̃aq 'many', 2. maliŋ 'thief', 3. i 'in', 4. kuʈʈa 'city', 5. ɖia 'here']

zhaq manzhəŋ i za.ɖia! 'Don't stand there!' [1. zhaq 'don't', 2.
1   2   3   4
manzhəŋ 'to stand', 3. i 'in, at', 4. za.ɖia 'there']

nəŋ sanpaŋ baɖa k-ənəŋ-an i-ñama-i pabhabharan + caq-na i za.ɖia
1   2   3   4   5   6   7   8 9
k-ənəŋ-an-na paŋiran trŭnuzòjò bhabhar. 'In Sampang there is a
4   10   11   12
place named Pabhabharan; they say there is where Prince Trunodjojo was born.' [1. nəŋ 'in', 2. sanpaŋ 'Sampang', 3. baɖa 'there is', 4. k-ənəŋ-an 'place', 5. i-ñama-i 'be named', 6. pabhabharan 'Pabhabharan', 7. caq-na 'they say', 8. i 'in', 9. za.ɖia 'there', 10. paŋiran 'prince', 11. trŭnuzòjo 'Trunodjojo', 12. bhabhar 'to be born']

nəŋ kamar ɖissa rua 'in that room' [1. nəŋ 'in', 2. kamar 'room', 3.
1   2   3   4
ɖissa 'there', 4. rua 'that']

<u>Dialect forms</u>

West Madurese: ghi-kaq-ɖia and gha-kaq-ɖia for ingha.ɖia.

<u>Directionals</u>[29]

The following also occur preceded by ɖaq., ɖaq-, or ɖaq 'to'.

<u>'hither'</u>

	<u>K</u>	<u>T</u>	<u>A</u>
1.	kannaq	kuq-kantu	kaq-kantu
	əntu	kuq-əntu	kaq-əntu
2.	kanza	kuq-kanza	kaq-kanza

Rows one and two correspond to one and two of locationals 'here' respectively.

'thither'

<u>K</u>   <u>T</u>   <u>A</u>

kassa   kuq-kassa   kaq-kassa

əsa   kuq-əsa   kaq-əsa

Locationals preceded by ɗaq or ɗaq. 'to' also occur in the meanings of
directionals, e.g. ɗaq ɗia 'hither', ɗaq ɗissa 'thither'.

pa-cupa-an za.ria / kura-i + pas ghiba kannaq! 'Clean up that sputum
1   2   3   4   5   6
    and carry it over here.' [1. pa-cupa-an 'sputum', 2. za.ria 'that',
    3. kura-i 'clean up', 4. pas 'then', 5. ghiba 'carry', 6. kannaq
    'hither']

i-atur-i rabu kaq-kantu! 'Please come here.' [1. i-atur-i 'please',
1   2   3
    2. rabu 'to come', 3. kaq-kantu 'hither']

kaɗla takuq si intar-a kaq-kassa. 'I'm afraid to go there.' [1.
1   2   3   4   5
    kaɗla 'I', 2. takuq 'be afraid', 3. si 'rel. particle', 4. intar-a
    'will go', 5. kaq-kassa 'thither']

mula-na baññaq uriŋ N-cabis ɗaq kassa. 'and so many people visited
1   2   3   4   5   6
    there.' [1. mula-na 'and so', 2. baññaq 'many', 3. uriŋ 'person',
    4. N-cabis 'to visit (a superior)', 5. ɗaq 'to', 6. kassa 'there']

Derivatives

<u>R+ -an</u> 'plural actor'

sərina i kaq-ɗintu anpun səla, i-atur-i sadhaza R+kaq-kassa-an.
1   2   3   4   5   6   7   8
    'Since it's crowded here, please all move over there.' [1. sərina
    'since', 2. i 'in', 3. kaq-ɗintu 'here', 4. anpun 'already', 5.
    səla 'crowded', 6. i-atur-i 'please', 7. sadhaza 'all', 8. kaq-
    kassa 'thither']

<u>-an</u> 'a little'

ɗaq kanza-an 'over here a little'
kassa-an 'over there a little'

Special

R+kassa-n.aghi 'do something everywhere', for example:

sumili-a si N-sari / əla R+kassa-n.aghi, ꭍa ghiq taq i-təmu kia.
  1   2   3   4   5   6   7 8 9   6

'Although he looked for it all over, it still couldn't be found.'
[1. sumili-a 'even though', 2. si 'rel. particle', 3. N-sari 'to
look for', 4. əla 'already', 5. kassa 'thither', 6. ꭍa...kia 'anyway', 7. ghiq 'still', 8. taq 'not', 9. i-təmu 'be found']

Interrogatives: locational and directional

'where' (locational)[30]

K	T	A
ɖimma	kuq-ɖimma	kaq-ɖimma

'whither' (directional)

kamma	kuq-kamma	kaq-kamma
kəma	kuq-kəma	kaq-kəma

The locationals preceded by ɖaq, ɖaq-, or ɖaq. 'to' also have directional
meaning.

ɖimma bisa N-bəli? 'Where can one buy it?' [1. ɖimma 'where', 2.
  1   2   3

bisa 'be able', 3. N-bəli 'to buy']

uriŋ ɖimma si dhuzan N-kakan-an ular? 'People from where like to eat
  1   2   3 4   5   6

snake?' [1. uriŋ 'person', 2. ɖimma 'where', 3. si 'rel.
particle', 4. dhuzan 'to like to', 5. N-kakan-an 'to eat often',
6. ular 'snake']

i ɖimma-na tapsꭍồn bənku-na baqna? 'Where's your house from the
1 2   3   4   5

station?' [1. i 'in, at', 2. ɖimma-na 'where of', 3. tapsꭍồn
'station', 4. bənku-na 'house of', 5. baqna 'you']

intar-a kamma maq masi kabhuru? 'Where are you going in such a
1   2   3 4   5

hurry?' [1. intar-a 'to be going', 2. kamma 'whither', 3. maq
'particle', 4. masi 'appear', 5. kabhuru 'hurried']

aŋin sa-tia ara-na ɖaq kamma? 'Which way is the wind blowing now?'
1   2   3   4 5

[1. aŋin 'wind', 2. sa-tia 'now', 3. ara-na 'its direction',
4. ɖaq 'to', 5. kamma 'whither']

193

Derivatives

-an 'plurality (of place)'

> R+tamuj-na baqna baariq ɖari kamma-an?   'Where did your guests come
> 1   2   3   4   5
>> from yesterday?' [1. R+tamuj-na 'guests of', 2. baqna 'you',
>>
>> 3. baariq 'yesterday', 4. ɖari 'from', 5. kamma 'whither']

> likər-na aliq si ilaŋ i-təmu i ɖimma-an?   'Brother's lost marbles were
> 1   2   3   4   5   6 7
>> found where?' [1. likər-na 'marbles of', 2. aliq 'younger sibling',
>>
>> 3. si 'rel. particle', 4. ilaŋ 'be lost', 5. i-təmu 'be found',
>>
>> 6. i 'in, at', 7. ɖimma 'where']

-a bhai K, -a saus A '---ever'

> i dhisa ɖimma-a bhai, mun nəŋ madhura, masʈi baɖa langhar.   'In what-
> 1 2   3   4   5   6   7   8   9   10
>> ever village in Madura, there must be a prayer-house.' [1. i 'in',
>>
>> 2. dhisa 'village', 3. ɖimma 'where', 4. bhai 'just', 5. mun 'if',
>>
>> 6. nəŋ 'in', 7. Madhura 'Madura', 8. masʈi 'must', 9. baɖa 'there
>>
>> is', 10. langhar 'prayer-house']

> ɖaq kamma-a bhai baqna si a-zhalan, kudhu biq R+N-ati.   'Wherever you
> 1   2   3   4   5 6   7   8   9
>> walk to you must be careful.' [1. ɖaq 'to', 2. kamma 'whither',
>>
>> 3. bhai 'just', 4. baqna 'you', 5. si 'rel. particle', 6. a-zhalan
>>
>> 'to walk', 7. kudhu 'must', 8. biq 'with', 9. R+N-ati 'be careful']

When preceded by certain words with the suffix -a, the -a of this derivative
is optionally omitted.

> sumili-a ɖaq kamma bhai, pizhər a-R+runtuŋ.   'Wherever they go,
> 1   2   3   4   5   6
>> they're always together.' [1. sumili-a 'no matter, even if', 2.
>>
>> ɖaq 'to', 3. kamma 'whither', 4. bhai 'just', 5. pizhər 'always',
>>
>> 6. a-R+runtuŋ 'to be together']

R+ -n 'every---, any---'

> ɖara-na a-lətis-an R+kamma-n.   'Their blood splattered all over.'
> 1   2   3
>> [1. ɖara-na 'their blood', 2. a-lətis-an 'to splatter', 3. kamma
>> 'whither']

> kaɖla namuŋ intar ɖaq malaŋ + taq intar ɖaq R+kaq-ɖimma-n puli.   'I
> 1   2   3   4   5   6   3   4   7   8

only went to Malang; I didn't go anywhere else.' [1. kaḍla 'I',
2. namuŋ 'only', 3. intar 'to go', 4. ḍaq 'to', 5. malaŋ 'Malang',
6. taq 'not', 7. kaq-ḍimma 'where', 8. puli 'else, again']

ta-siar ḍaq R+kaq-kamma-n k-ənəŋ-an. 'were scattered everywhere'
   1   2   3   4

[1. ta-siar 'be scattered', 2. ḍaq 'to', 3. kaq-kamma 'whither',
4. k-ənəŋ-an 'place']

R+ (followed by noun) 'wherever there is a'

R+ḍimma R+k-anaq nakal 'wherever there is a naughty child' [1. ḍimma
   1   2   3

'where', 2. R+k-anaq 'child', 3. nakal 'naughty']

Interrogatives[31]

	K	T	A
'what'	apa	napi	punapa
			panapa
'who'	sapa	sira	pasira
'which'	kəma	kuq-kəma	kaq-kəma
	kamma	kuq-kamma	kaq-kamma

sapa za.ria? 'Who's that?'
apa za.ria? 'What's that?'
si kəma taŋ bukṹ? 'Which one is my book?'

kəma si sala / ukum! 'Punish the guilty one.' [1. kəma 'which',
1   2 3   4

2. si 'rel. particle', 3. sala 'wrong, guilty', 4. ukum 'punish']

R+k-anaq rua / apa-na baqna? 'What relation is that child to you?'
  1   2   3   4

[1. R+k-anaq 'child', 2. rua 'that', 3. apa-na 'what of', 4. baqna
'you']

Derivatives

apa 'what' has a number of verbal derivatives which will not be considered
here. Other derivatives follow:

-an 'plural'

apa-an si i-ghiba baqna ḍaq madhura? 'What did you take to Madura?'
  1   2   3   4   5   6

[1. apa 'what', 2. si 'rel. particle', 3. i-ghiba 'be carried',
4. baqna 'you', 5. ḍaq 'to', 6. madhura 'Madura']

si i-ka-parlu / parkakas apa-an? 'What equipment is needed?' [1. si
1   2   3   4
    'rel. particle', 2. i-ka-parlu 'be needed', 3. parkakas 'equipment',
    4. apa 'what']

sapa-an bhai si N-turuq-a? 'Just who will go along?' [1. sapa 'who',
1   2   3   4
    2. bhai 'just', 3. si 'rel. particle', 4. N-turuq-a 'will go along']

kəma-an taŋ anɟiq? 'Which ones are mine?' [1. kəma 'which', 2. taŋ
1   2   3
    'my', 3. anɟiq 'possession']

R+ -an livelier than the preceding, '--- in the world, --- do you call,
--- kind of'.

Rf+laku-n R+apa-an ria? 'What kind of work is this?' [1. Rf+laku-n
1   2   3
    'work', 2. apa 'what', 3. ria 'this']

R+ -n 'any and every, all sorts of'

R+k-anaq si a-main i ɟinnaq / N-ghiba R+apa-n + mula-na rəsəm. 'The
1   2 3   4 5   6   7   8   9
    children who play here bring all kinds of things, and so it's
    dirty.' [1. R+k-anaq 'child', 2. si 'rel. particle', 3. a-main 'to
    play', 4. i 'in', 5. ɟinnaq 'here', 6. N-ghiba 'to bring', 7. apa
    'what', 8. mula-na 'and so', 9. rəsəm 'dirty, messy']

R+ or Rt+ '---ever, every ---'

R+apa si i-ghiba-a / pa-saɟia! 'Prepare everything that will be
1   2 3   4
    taken.' [1. apa 'what', 2. si 'rel. particle', 3. i-ghiba-a
    'will be taken', 4. pa-saɟia 'prepare']

R+sapa bhai / tantu tau. 'Everyone surely knows.' [1. sapa 'who',
1   2   3   4
    2. bhai 'just', 3. tantu 'sure', 4. tau 'to know']

R+kəma R+k-anaq nakal 'whichever children are naughty' [1. kəma
1   2   3
    'which', 2. R+k-anaq 'child', 3. nakal 'naughty']

abaq-na taq N-k-ucaq R+apa ɟaq sinkuq. 'He didn't say anything to
1   2   3   4   5   6
    me.' [1. abaq-na 'he', 2. taq 'not', 3. N-k-ucaq 'to say', 4. apa
    'what', 5. ɟaq 'to', 6. sinkuq 'I']

<u>-a bhai K, -a saus A</u> 'every, any, any at all'

    hal si təlu-q macəm ingha.panika / masti baḍa i ḍaləm bhasa punapa-a
    1   2   3   4   5   6   7   8 9 10   11

    saus. 'Those three things must be in any language (each and every
    12

    language).' [1. hal 'matter', 2. si 'rel. particle', 3. təlu-q

    'three', 4. macəm 'kind', 5. ingha.panika 'that', 6. masti 'must',

    7. baḍa 'there is', 8. i 'in', 9. ḍaləm 'in', 10. bhasa 'language',

    11. punapa 'what', 12. saus 'just']

    sapa-a bhai / tantu tau. 'Anyone knows that.' [1. sapa 'who', 2.
    1   2   3   4

    bhai 'just', 3. tantu 'sure', 4. tau 'to know']

    sapa-a bhai tantu a-paŋ-rasa takuq. 'Anyone would have been afraid.'
    1   2   3   4   5

    [1. sapa 'who', 2. bhai 'just', 3. tantu 'sure', 4. a-paŋ-rasa 'to

    feel', 5. takuq 'be afraid']

    si kəma-a bhai / mun R+ñala, pukul! 'Whichever they are, when they
    1 2   3   4   5   6

    annoy you, hit them!' [1. si 'rel. particle', 2. kəma 'which',

    3. bhai 'just', 4. mun 'if', 5. R+ñala 'to annoy', 6. pukul 'hit!']

A derivative of the apa series with a prefixed sa- is always associated with
the negative taq in the meaning 'not so much, not very much': taq sa-apa K, taq
sa-napi T, taq sa-punapa A.

  <u>Other question words</u>

    <u>'why'</u>

<u>K</u>	<u>T</u>	<u>A</u>
a-r-apa	a-napi	a-punapa
r-apa		

    <u>'how'</u>

ba-ramma	kadhi napi	kadhi punapa
ḍaq-ramma		
ḍaq-ba-ramma		

<u>Derivatives</u>

  <u>'why'</u> Note the different reduplication order in the following:

    a-r-apa-a 'what for'

R+a-r-apa-a 'what for (frequently)'

taq a-r-apa 'it doesn't matter'

taq a-R+r-apa 'it doesn't matter'

Other substitutes

'thus'

K	T	A
ba-ria	ba-rintu	kadhi panika
ba-rinnaq	ḍaq-rintu	kadhi kaq-ḍintu (refers ahead)
ḍaq-ba-ria ḍaq-ria	ḍaq-ba-rintu	sa-kaq-ḍintu (refers back)

'so much, this much, that much'

sa-ba-ria	sa-ba-rintu	sa-panika
sa-za.ria		
sa-ba-rinnaq		

mun cuma sa-ba-ria, sinkuq tau N-ituŋ. 'If it's only so much, I can
1   2   3   4   5 6

    count it.' [1. mun 'if', 2. cuma 'only', 3. sa-ba-ria 'so much',
    4. sinkuq 'I', 5. tau 'to know', 6. N-ituŋ 'to count']

parlu bhadhan kaḍla N-təraŋ.aghi-a kadhi kaq-ḍintu. 'I must explain
 1   2   3   4

    it as follows.' [1. parlu 'to be needed', 2. bhadhan kaḍla 'I',
    3. N-təraŋ.aghi-a 'will explain', 4. kadhi kaq-ḍintu 'as follows']

N-dhaddhi-aghi R+N-bhidha-na cara paŋ-urip-an, sa-kaq-ḍintu zhughan
1   2   3   4   5   6

    bhasa-na. 'Caused a differentiation in their way of life as well
    7

    as their language.' [1. N-dhaddhi-aghi 'to cause', 2. R+N-bhidha-
    na 'differentiation of', 3. cara 'way', 4. paŋ-urip-an 'way of
    living', 5. sa-kaq-ḍintu 'thus', 6. zhughan 'also', 7. bhasa-na
    'their language']

Derivatives

   'thus' sa-ba-ria-an (bhai) 'just so much (and no more)'

NUMBERS

The numbers 'one' and 'ten' in Madurese have two forms: plain and proclitic.
The numbers from 'two' to 'nine' have four forms:[32] plain, -q, Rf+, and proclitic.[33]

		Plain		Proclitic
'one'		sittuŋ		sa.
'ten'		sa.pulu		sa.pulu.

	plain	-q	Rf+	
'two'	ḍua	ḍua-q	Rf+ḍua-q	ḍu.
'three'	təlu	təlu-q	Rf+təlu-q	təlu.
'four'	ənpa	ənpa-q	Rf+ənpa-q	ənpa-q.
				pa-q.
'five'[34]	lima	lima-q	Rf+lima	lima.
			Rf+lima-q	
'six'	ənəm	ənəm	Rf+ənəm	ənəm
				nəm
'seven'	pittu	pittu-q	Rf+pittu-q	pittu-ŋ
'eight'	ballu	ballu-q	Rf+ballu-q	ballu-ŋ
'nine'	saŋa	saŋa-q	Rf+saŋa-q	saŋa-ŋ

In rapid speech the Rf set has a prefixed Rf. (Rf dot juncture).

11.	sa.bəlas	19.	saŋa.bɔlas
12.	ḍu.bəlas	20.	ḍu.pulu
13.	təlu.bəlas	21.	sa.likur
14.	ənpaq.bəlas	22.	ḍu.likur
	paq.bəlas	23.	təlu.likur
	paq.bhəlas		
15.	lima.bəlas	24.	paq.likur
16.	nəm.bəlas	25.	sa.ghamiq
	nəm.bhəlas	26.	nəm.likur
17.	pittu.bəlas	27.	pittu.likur
18.	ballu.bəlas	28.	ballu.likur

29.	saŋa.likur	600.	nəm.atus
30.	təlu.pulu	700.	pittu-ŋ.atus
31-39.	təlu.pulu followed by plain and -q set.	800.	ballu-ŋ.atus
40.	paq.pulu	900.	saŋa-ŋ.atus
41-49.	paq.pulu followed by plain and -q set.	1,000.	sa.ibu
			s.ibu
50.	sa.ikət	2,000.	ḍu.ibu
	s.ikət		
60.	sa.bidhak	3,000.	təlu.ibu
70.	pittu-ŋ.pulu	4,000.	ənpaq.ibu
			paq.ibu

80.	ballu-ŋ.pulu	5,000.	lima.ibu
90.	saŋa-ŋ.pulu	6,000.	nəm.ibu
100.	sa.ratus	7,000.	pittu-ŋ.ibu
	s.atus		
200.	ɖu.ratus	8,000.	ballu-ŋ.ibu
300.	təlu.ratus	9,000.	saŋa-ŋ.ibu
400.	ənpaq.ratus	10,000.	sa.pulu.ibu
	paq.ratus		sa.laksa
500.	lima.ratus	100,000	sa.ratus-ibu
			sa.kəʈi
		1,000,000	sa.zuta

Dialect forms

West Madurese: sɪttɑ́ŋ for sittuŋ 'one'.

Several other stems have derivatives similar to those of the numbers to be discussed below. These stems are:

K	T	A
baranpa	sa-napi	sa-punapa 'how much'[35]

ibaŋ 'each'

s.uraŋ 'one person, alone'

dhibiq (West Madurese: dhiriq) 'self'

These stems have certain derivatives which they do not share with the numbers. These special derivatives are:

R+baranpa-n (K)   R+sa-napi-n (T)   R+sa-punapa-n (A) 'several'

R+ibaŋ-an 'separately, to do it separately'

R+s.ibaŋ, R+s.ibaŋ-an 'each his own, respectively'

paŋ-s.uraŋ-an 'for one person, individual(ly)'

dhibiq-an 'alone'

The shortened form of the numbers have been discussed on page 180.

Following are the environments of the different sets and their derivatives.
  1) Plain set.

The plain forms of the numbers occur as the stems of various derivatives.

ka- 'group of'

sa-əla-na R+k-anaq ka-ɖua za.ria a-tukar, 'After those two children
    1   2   3   4   5
    fought,' [1. sa-əla-na 'after', 2. R+k-anaq 'children', 3. ɖua
    'two', 4. za.ria 'those', 5. a-tukar 'to fight']

anaq-na cuma ka-ənpa. 'He only has four children.' [1. anaq-na 'his
  1   2   3
    children', 2. cuma 'only', 3. ənpa 'four']

tamuj-na cuma ka-ballu. 'There are only eight guests.' [1. tamuj-na
  1   2   3
    'the guests', 2. cuma 'only', 3. ballu 'eight']

baqna a-R+unzhaŋ ka-baranpa uriŋ? 'How many people did you invite?'
  1   2   3   4
    [1. baqna 'you', 2. a-R+unzhaŋ 'to invite', 3. baranpa 'how much',
    4. uriŋ 'person']

lazhu N-utus santri-na ka-s.uraŋ. 'Then he sent one of his pupils.'
  1   2   3   4
    [1. lazhu 'then', 2. N-utus 'to send', 3. santri-na 'his religious
    pupil', 4. s.uraŋ 'one person']

dhibiq 'self'   ka-dhibiq 'alone'

ka- -an 'group of'

si ka-unzhaŋ-an maləm-na i ɖinnaq / cuma ka-ballu-an. 'Only eight
1   2   3   4 5   6   7
    people were invited here last night.' [1. si 'rel. particle',
    2. ka-unzhaŋ-an 'to be invited', 3. maləm-na 'last night', 4. i
    'in', 5. ɖinnaq 'here', 6. cuma 'only', 7. ballu 'eight']

si a-zhalan / cuma ka-s.uraŋ-an. 'He's walking all by himself.'
1   2   3   4
    [1. si 'rel. particle', 2. a-zhalan 'to walk', 3. cuma 'only',
    4. s.uraŋ 'one person']

baranpa 'how many'   ka-baranpa-an 'a group of how many'
dhibiq 'self'   ka-dhibiq-an 'alone'

R+ -an and R+ka- -an also occur in the same meaning, 'group of'.

Verbal derivatives of the plain set are as follows:

N-pa- (intransitive) 'to be divided into'

ghəntiŋ-na / bəla N-pa-təlu. 'The tile split into three parts.'
  1   2   3
    [1. ghəntiŋ-na 'the tile', 2. bəla 'to split', 3. təlu 'three']

pau / N-pa-ɖua. 'The mango is in two pieces.' [1. pau 'mango',
1   2
    2. ɖua 'two'.

<u>N-pa-</u> (transitive) 'to divide into'

> zhukuq niŋ sa.kilố za.ria / su baqna i-pa-baranpa? 'Into how many
> 　　　1　　　2　　　3　　　4　　　　　5　6　　　7
>
> parts did you divide that 1 kg. of fish?' [1. zhukuq 'fish',
> 2. niŋ 'only', 3. sa.kilố 'one kilogram', 4. za.ria 'that', 5.
> su 'by', 6. baqna 'you', 7. baranpa 'how many']

> N-pa-ɖua pau. 'to divide the mango in two.' [1. ɖua 'two', 2.pau
> 　　　1　　　2
>
> 'mango']

<u>N-ka- -i</u> 'action is performed by so many (people)' This derivative is most
common in the passive.

> si N-ankaq miza / i-ka-lima-i. 'The table was lifted by five people.'
> 1　　2　　　3　　　4
>
> [1. si. 'rel. particle', 2. N-ankaq 'to lift', 3. miza 'table',
> 4. lima 'five']

> bənku si raza rua / i-ka-təlu-i. 'That large house is lived in by
> 1　　2　　3　　4　　　5
>
> three (families).' [1. bənku 'house', 2. si 'rel. particle',
> 3. raza 'big', 4. rua 'that', 5. təlu 'three']

> nasiq sa.piriŋ kiniq za.ria / i-ka-baranpa-i? 'That small plate of
> 1　　　2　　　3　　　4　　　　　5
>
> rice is for how many people?' [1. nasiq 'rice', 2. sa.piriŋ 'a
> plate', 3. kiniq 'small', 4. za.ria 'that', 5. baranpa 'how many']

> s.uraŋ 'one person'　　　　　i-ka-s.uraŋ-i 'done alone'

<u>N-pa-ka- -i</u> (rare) 'make 1 into ...' (transitive)

<u>sittuŋ</u> has some special derivatives:

> R+sittuŋ-na plus noun 'each and every ...'
> N-sittuŋ, N-pa-N-sittuŋ 'to concentrate, to put all one's efforts
> 　　into' (intransitive).
> N-pa-N-sittuŋ } 'to do the action in the same place' (intransitive).
> N-pa-sittuŋ }
> N-pa-sittuŋ 'to put in the same place' (transitive).
> N-pa-N-sittuŋ 'to concentrate, direct' (transitive).

2) -q set.

Used in counting and when stating the number when no noun is present.

pas N-k-kucaq + sittuŋ. basir N-baləs N-k-ucaq + ḍua-q. 'Then he said
1   2   3   4   5   2   6

'one'. Basir answered saying 'two'.' [1. pas 'then', 2. N-k-ucaq
'to say', 3. sittuŋ 'one', 4. basir 'Basir', 5. N-baləs 'to re-
spond', 6. ḍua-q 'two']

ənpa-q i-tanba təlu-q / paḍa ban pittu-q. '4 plus 3 equals 7.'
1   2   3   4   5   6

[1. ənpa-q 'four', 2. i-tanba 'be added', 3. təlu-q 'three', 4.
paḍa 'same', 5. ban 'with', 6. pittu-q 'seven']

Used preceding nouns in counting, for example:

təlu-q hal ingha.panika 'those three things'
ḍua-q carita 'two stories'

Used following certain nouns which occur in sets, for example:

kəlas sittuŋ 'class one'
kəlas ḍua-q 'class two'
pukul ḍua-q 'two o'clock'

Used after intransitive verbals, for example:

a-bagi ḍua-q 'it is divided in two'
a-cankim ḍua-q 'he has two chins'
tikəl lima-q 'five-fold'

Used before agghiq and -agghiq 'more', and before ibaŋ 'each'.

ballu-q-agghiq or ballu-q agghiq 'eight more'
ḍua-q ibaŋ 'two each'

-an

This derivative occurs following the word kari 'left over', but only for
the numbers 'two' and 'three'.

kari ḍua-q-an 'two left over'
kari təlu-q-an 'three left over'

(ghan) R+ 'at a time, in groups of'

si tuzuq nəŋ kamar / R+təlu-q. 'They were sitting in the room in
1   2   3   4   5

groups of three.' [1. si 'rel. particle', 2. tuzuq 'to sit',
3. nəŋ 'in', 4. kamar 'room', 5. təlu-q 'three']

i-bhakta-i-a ghan R+sittuŋ. 'will be carried one at a time.' [1.
1   2   3

203

i-bhakta-i-a 'will be carried', 2. ghan 'particle', 3. sittuŋ
'one']

R+ -an 'at a time'

    kunpul-an-na / cuma R+ballu-q-an. 'He gathered only eight at a time.'
     1   2   3

    [1. kunpul-an-na 'what he gathered', 2. cuma 'only', 3. ballu-q
    'eight']

kapiŋ- 'ordinal', usually preceded by si 'rel. particle'.

    si kapiŋ-ɖua-q 'the second'
    si kapiŋ-ballu-q 'the eighth'
    si kapiŋ-baranpa 'the how manieth'

kapiŋ-sittuŋ 'first' does occur, but R+aɖaq is more common in this meaning.

Verbal derivatives from -q set:

N-pa-R+ 'make into groups of' (transitive)

    N-pa-R+ɖua-q 'make into groups of two'

-a (rare) in places where -a is required. For example:

    supaza ballu-q-a 'to make it eight'

3) Rf+ set.

This set is used in counting where no counter words[36] are present.

    azam Rf+təlu-q 'three chickens'
    majjit Rf+ ɖua-q 'two corpses'
    N-pa-abiq Rf+lima 'he finished up five (of them)'
    a-baza Rf+təlu-q 'to have three grandchildren'

Verbal derivatives

N-pa-R+ 'make into groups of' (transitive)

    N-pa-R+Rf+ɖua-q 'make into groups of two'

(ghan) R+ 'by ...s'

    ghan R+Rf+lima-q 'by fives'

4) Proclitic set.

Connected to what follows by dot juncture (in very slow speech by word
juncture) the proclitic set is used before counter words. Special forms occur
before bəlas 'tens' and likur 'twenties'; see the list of numbers above on pages

        biddhaŋ saŋa-ŋ.cankir 'nine cups of hot water'

        təlu.sin 'three cents'

        dhalubaŋ təlu.lambar 'three sheets of paper'

        bənku ballu-ŋ.kurən 'nine groups of houses'

        nasiq sa.kəpəl 'a handful of rice'

        ɖu.kali 'two times'

        azam lima.migghiq 'five chickens'

Proclitic numbers are also found in certain derivatives. For example, derived from maləm 'night' are: sa-ɖu.maləm 'day after tomorrow' and ɖu.maləm-an-na, ɖu.ləm-ən-na 'day before yesterday' with proclitic ɖu. 'two'.

<u>Fractions</u> par- -n, pər- -n

Fractions are made with the -q or proclitic form of the numbers for the numerator and a derivative of the plain set (with some variation) or more rarely the -q set for the denominator.[37]

1/2	sa-təŋa	sa.pər-ɖua-q (rare)
1/3	sa.pər-təlu-n	sa.pər-təlu-q
2/3	ɖua-q pər-təlu-n	ɖua-q pər-təlu-q
	ɖu.pər-təlu-n	ɖu.pər-təlu-q
1/4	sa.pər-apat	sa.pər-ənpa-q
	sa.par-apat	
1/5	sa.pər-lima-n	sa.pər-lima-q
1/6	sa.pər-ənəm	
1/7	sa.pər-pittu-n	sa.pər-pittu-q
1/8	sa.pər-ballu-n	sa.pər-ballu-q
1/9	sa.pər-saŋa-n	sa.pər-saŋa-q
1/10	sa.pər-sa.pulu	

<u>Numeral counters</u>

The numeral counters are those counters which occur as parts of numbers (see pages 199-200): bəlas 'teen', pulu 'ten', likur 'twenty', ghamiq 'twenty five', etc.

<u>Derivatives</u>:

  <u>-an</u> 'the ...s'

tanghal likur-an 'the twenties (of the month)'

anka atus-an 'numbers in the hundreds'

R+baranpa-n kəʈi-n 'several hundred thousands'

ibu-n 'to be in the thousands'

bintaŋ ibu-n 'thousands of stars'

<u>a- -an</u> 'to be in the ...s'

a-ibu-n 'to be in the thousands'

a-kəʈi-an 'to be in the hundreds of thousands'

APPENDIX

Personal Pronouns

Numbered notes in the pronoun sets refer to comments and dialect forms given below each set.

	K	T	A	AM, AT	
1.	sinkuq[1]	bula[2]	kaɗla[3]	bhadhan kaɗla[4]	'I'
2.	baqna[5]	dhika	sanpian	panzhənəŋan[6]	'you'

Notes to table

1. Proper names or titles are also used as substitutes for first person pronouns.

   ### Dialect forms

   Kangean: aku

   West Madurese: ənkuq

   The form isun 'I' is now obsolete.

   Forms literally meaning 'this' also occur: tia, atia.

2. tuntu 'this' is also used.

3. The form kɗla also occurs.

4. Literally 'my body'. This form is often shortened to dhan kaɗla.

5. Name, title, or title plus name are also used as substitutes for second person pronouns.

   ### Dialect forms

   West Madurese: baqn, baqən; dhiriq-na 'self of'

   Central Madurese: ənbaq-na; dhiriq-na 'self of'

   Kangean: kau

   The word piaŋ 'you' (K) is now obsolete.

   The word siɗa 'you' is infrequently used and is more kasar than baqna.

6. Probably to be associated with the root zhənəŋ which occurs in such derivatives as: zh-um-ənəŋ 'to stand.'

Madurese has no third person pronoun. Nominal substitutes are used. Most commonly used are the name or title or title plus name of the referent. Other substitutes are: abaq-na 'his body (B); salira-na, salira.ipun 'his body (AT)'.

Madurese has no plural pronouns. Indonesian words are now commonly used. They are as follows:

> 1st person inclusive: kita → [kita]
> 1st person exclusive: kami → [kami]
> 3rd person: meréka → [mərɛka]

Madurese translations are sometimes used:

> 1st person inclusive: sinkuq ban baqna kabbhi 'I and you all'
> 1st person exclusive: sinkuq kabbhi 'I all'
> 3rd person: abaq-na kabbhi 'he all'

Dialect forms

> Kangean: 1st person plural: kita → [kɛta]
>   2nd person plural: kau kabbhi → [kao kabbhi]

Possessive Pronouns

For the most part the possessive pronouns are the same as the personal pronouns given above. In the following table X indicates the position of the possessed noun. Noun substitutes also occur as mentioned above. Where -na is given, .ipun also occurs.

K	T	A	AT, AM
1. taŋ X[1]	X bula[1]	X kaɗla[1]	X bhadhan kaɗla[1]
saŋ X[1]	X-na bula	X-na kaɗla	X-na bhadhan kaɗla
X sinkuq[1]			
X-na sinkuq[1]			
2. X-na baqna[2]	X dhika[3]	X sanpian[3]	X panzhənəŋan[3]
	X-na dhika	X-na sanpian	X-na panzhənəŋan
3. X-na[4]			X.ipun

<u>Notes to table</u>

1. In rapid speech, taŋ and saŋ are connected to what follows by dot juncture, e.g. taŋ.aliq 'my younger sibling'.

First person pronouns occur more commonly without preceding -na.[38]

Other AT and AM forms already mentioned also occur in this position.

> <u>Dialect forms</u>
>
> Kangean: X aku
>
>   X-ku

2. <u>Dialect forms</u>

> Kangean: X-nu
>
>   X-mu
>
>   X-na kau

3. T, A, AM, and AT forms rarely occur with preceding -na.[38]

4. .na is obsolescent. For example:

> usual   -na surat-na → sòràddhâ 'his letter'
>
> obsolescent   .na surat.na → sòràttà 'his letter'

> <u>Dialect forms</u>
>
> Pinggirpapas (East Madura): -ḍa

1. By grammatically borderline cases I mean those forms about whose existence
    informants were in doubt.

2. Immediate constituent analysis here is based on the following rules of thumb:

    a. an existing IC is selected over a non-existing IC, e.g. a-R+tañ̄a
        'to keep on asking' is composed of a-tañ̄a 'to ask' plus R+ 'repe-
        tition'. The other possibility *R+tañ̄a does not occur.

    b. correct addition of meaning resulting in the word meaning, e.g.
        R+N-pa-taq.tau 'to pretend not to know' is taken as R+N-pa-[taq.tau]
        where the meanings are taq.tau 'not know' and R+N-pa- 'to pretend
        to' rather than R+N-pa-tau 'to pretend to know' plus taq 'not
        which would produce 'not to pretend to know'.

    c. parallel derivations are analyzed in the same manner.

    d. overall simplicity of derivational histories is aimed at.

3. Proclitics will not generally be written with following dot juncture when
    quoted in isolation.

    See pages 199-200   for proclitic numbers.

4. These will not be described here.

    For further discussion of inflection, see L. Bloomfield, Language
    222-6 (New York, 1933) and C. Hockett, Course in Modern Linguistics 209-13
    (New York, 1958).

5. The elements which make up compounds, e.g. kuraŋ and azhar in kuraŋ-azhar
    'rude' are considered to be roots, not null-affix derivatives of roots.

6. Defined on pages 111-112.

7. A small number of stems we would like to call verbals for syntactic reasons
    and because of the prefixes with which they cooccur cannot cooccur with the
    suffix -a because they already have the suffix -na. These will be discussed

more fully on pages 148-150.

8. Contrary to fact clauses are also often introduced by zhaq sakiŋ-a where sakiŋ is a particle. The following verbal does not have -a. The Indonesian word tjoba 'try', pronounced cubàq in Madurese, is often used today in place of zhaq sakiŋ-a.

9. N- is here being used as a cover symbol for the entire transitive inflection: N-, i-, stem. See page 101.

10. Since there is no way of differentiating N- → a- (intransitive) from a-(intransitive), such cases have been assigned to the a- prefix.

11. When directly following a modified noun, as in aiŋ kutur-an 'dish water', such verbals cannot cooccur with -a 'future'.

12. Some speakers use -in. This is considered substandard by educated Madurese.

13. Some speakers use -aghin. This is considered substandard. For other dialect forms, e.g. Kangean -aghən, Bawean -akən, see Kiliaan 1:11.

14. Other doubtful forms which are not covered by the juncture rules of Chapter II also occur rarely. In these cases neither P-1 rules nor consonant doubling takes place. For example:

kabhar 'news'	ŋàbhàràghí 'to notify'
abas 'see'	ŋàbàsàghí 'to look at'

These are so rare and unsure that it was not considered necessary to set up an entirely different juncture to handle them.

15. For further examples see Kiliaan 2:17.

16. There is also often syntactic ambiguity. For example:

sinkuq i-N-bəli-aghi uriŋ. means 'People buy (something) for me.' or 'People are bought for me.'

17. Kiliaan 2:46 gives examples of this derivative meaning 'to have (something) done (by somebody else)'. Such derivatives apparently do not occur in the eastern dialect.

18. In subsequent formulations (N-) means that N is present is the basic derivative has N- and is absent if the basic derivative does not have N-, i.e.

they follow the basic derivative.

19. In a syntactic analysis this might be handled by one or a set of transformational rules deriving these constructions from sentences with the basic derivatives.

20. One informant gave the following as the difference between N- -aghi and N-pa- -aghi. The former is 'to do the action for someone with their permission or at their request', the latter means 'to do the action for someone with or without their permission or request'. There is not enough information to confirm this since N-pa- -aghi is fairly rare in the corpus and in unelicited speech.

21. Passive forms in i-N-pa-N-, e.g. i-N-pa-N-bəli-aghi 'to be bought for', were also elicited. In these the subject of the sentence was the person for whom the action was done. Such forms, which were never given spontaneously, are highly suspicious, and are probably due to parallelism to i-N- (see pages 130-131).

22. For a discussion of levels involved in this and the following pages see A. Stevens, Language Levels in Madurese, Language 41.294-302 (1965).

23. Nouns in pa- generally only have third person modifiers, e.g. pa-buru-na 'his running', but not *taŋ pa-buru 'my running', and rarely pa-buru-na sinkuq 'my running'. See footnote 38 below.

    There are some exceptions to deriving this from the basic derivative, e.g. bəlas 'to have pity' but pa-N-bəlas-na 'his pitying', derived from N-bəlas-i 'to have pity on'.

24. The syntax of this is not entirely clear and there are certain restrictions not taken into account by this statement.

25. Exceptions occur such as: N-inum 'to drink'; but both pa-inum-an and pa-N-inum-an 'water trough'.

26. In previous examples the shortened forms have been given without indication of S+, e.g. su 'with, by', and not S+musu 'with, by'.

27. This could have been handled in a different way. By introducing this rule only after the P-Rules, the correct vowel quality would have been generated before the consonant was lost.

> e.g. kaq-ḍintu → kȧq-ḍíntò (by P-Rules) → kȧq-íntò (by reduction rule) 'here'

28. Forms in əntu are infrequent in standard Madurese.

29. Forms in əntu and əsa are infrequent in standard Madurese. Neither əntu nor əsa occurs without preceding ḍaq. 'to'.

30. The interrogative locationals also occur preceded by ḍari 'from' in the meaning 'from where'.

31. Forms with kamma are infrequent in standard Madurese.

32. Another set consisting of ḍua, təlu, ənpa-q, lima, ənəm, pittu-q, ballu-q, and saŋa-q infrequently occurs before nouns, e.g. təlu hal ingha.panika 'those three things', ḍua carita 'two stories'.

33. Where more than one form is given, the words are in free variation.

34. The form lima-ŋ only occurs before kali 'time' in the expression lima-ŋ kali 'the five Moslem daily prayers'.

35. sa-apa K, and sa-r-apa K infrequently occur in standard Madurese in the meaning 'how much'.

36. Counter words cooccur with the proclitic set of numbers in certain syntactic constructions. See page 205.

37. Fractions are followed by -na when syntactically necessary, e.g. sa.pər-təlu-n-na 'a third of...'

38. Nominalized verbals (see pages 165-166, 169-170, 176-178 and 184-186) always have -na or .ipun before all possessive pronouns. They cannot cooccur with taŋ or saŋ 'my'. For example: baḍa-na sinkuq 'my being', but not *taŋ baḍa. This is also true of the shortened form caq (from ucaq 'word'), e.g. caq-na 'he says', caq-na sinkuq 'I say', caq.ipun kaúla 'I say'.

INDEX TO AFFIXES

215